COOKING ESSENTIALS

APPETIZERS, ENTRÉES AND DESSERTS FROM AROUND THE WORLD

This 2008 edition published by Metro Books,
by arrangement with Murdoch Books Pty Limited.

Design concept: Heather Menzies
Design layout: Heather Menzies, Craig Peterson
Photographer: Jared Fowler
Stylist: Cherise Koch

Metro Books
122 Fifth Avenue
New York, NY 10011

ISBN-13: 978-1-4351-0999-5

Printed and bound in Singapore

1 3 5 7 9 10 8 6 4 2

IMPORTANT: Those who might be at risk from the effects of salmonella poisoning (the elderly, pregnant women, young children and those suffering from immune deficiency) should consult their doctor with any concerns about eating raw eggs.

COOKING ESSENTIALS

APPETIZERS, ENTRÉES AND DESSERTS FROM AROUND THE WORLD

METRO BOOKS
NEW YORK

contents

APPETIZERS	8
ENTRÉES	130
DESSERTS	264
INDEX	396

A Global Feast

The most complex meal we're likely to whip up these days is one consisting of the three classic courses: an appetizer, an entrée, and a dessert. There's a lovely symmetry to such a meal, and a dinner or lunch modeled on this simple succession of dishes is always a winning formula. The appetizer acts as a curtain raiser, sparking appetites and holding a promise of delights to come. The entrée is the focus of the meal and is, arguably, the one that cooks invest the most energy into preparing and presenting. Then there's the dessert, which is undoubtedly the most anticipated of all the courses. After all, it's a rare person who doesn't adore a sweet ending.

Planning a three-course meal is a pleasurable adventure and there are many different approaches. A good way to begin is to consider the season. If the weather is wintry, then a warming soup, a hearty roast (or meaty braise) and an old-fashioned dessert will be just the ticket. But when the warmer months do finally come, lighter dishes such as salads, pizzas, barbecues and fruit-based desserts are appropriate. Cooking in step with the seasons allows you to showcase the best and freshest of produce and it won't cost the earth.

Another approach to planning a menu is to investigate the myriad dining possibilities afforded by world cuisines, and this is where this book really shines. Within these pages you can find the inspiration to contruct menus from around the world; Japan, for example, or Morocco or Italy. Seek out ingredients from specialist food stores and markets and enjoy the whole experience of preparing a global feast.

Whatever your preferred approach to dining is, Cooking Essentials offers you endless possibilities. It is all you'll need to create every memorable appetizer, entrée and dessert you could wish for or want!

appetizers

Red Gazpacho

❋ SERVES 4
❋ PREPARATION TIME: 40 MINUTES
❋ COOKING TIME: NIL

2 lb 4 oz vine-ripened tomatoes
2 slices day-old white Italian bread,
    crust removed, broken into pieces
1 medium red bell pepper, seeded,
    membrane removed and roughly
    chopped
2 medium garlic cloves, chopped
1 small green chili, chopped, optional
1 teaspoon sugar
2 tablespoons red wine vinegar
2 tablespoons extra virgin olive oil
8 ice cubes

GARNISH
$\frac{1}{2}$ small cucumber, seeded
    and finely diced
$\frac{1}{2}$ medium red bell pepper, seeded,
    membrane removed and finely diced
$\frac{1}{2}$ medium green pepper, seeded,
    membrane removed and finely diced
$\frac{1}{2}$ medium red onion, finely diced
$\frac{1}{2}$ medium ripe tomato, diced

Score a cross in the base of the tomatoes. Put in a heatproof bowl and cover with boiling water. Leave for 30 seconds, then transfer to cold water and peel the skin away from the cross. Cut the tomatoes in half, scoop out the seeds and roughly chop.

Soak the bread in cold water for 5 minutes, then squeeze out any excess liquid. Put the bread in a food processor with the tomato, pepper, garlic, chili, sugar and vinegar, and process until combined and smooth.

With the motor running, add the oil to make a smooth creamy mixture. Season to taste. Refrigerate for at least 2 hours. Add a little extra vinegar, if desired.

To make the garnish, mix all the ingredients in a bowl. Put two ice cubes in each bowl of soup and serve the garnish in separate bowls.

Scallops with Buckwheat Noodles and Dashi Broth

9 oz dried buckwheat noodles
1/4 cup mirin
1/4 cup light soy sauce
2 teaspoons rice vinegar
1 teaspoon dashi granules
2 medium scallions, sliced
1 teaspoon finely chopped fresh ginger
24 large scallops (without roe)
5 fresh black fungus, chopped (see Note)
1 sheet nori, shredded

Add the noodles to a large saucepan of boiling water and stir to separate. Return to a boil, adding 1 cup cold water and repeat this step three times, as it comes to a boil. Drain and rinse under cold water.

Put the mirin, soy sauce, vinegar, dashi and 3 1/2 cups water in a non-stick wok. Bring to a boil, then reduce the heat and simmer for 3–4 minutes. Add the scallions and ginger and keep at a gentle simmer.

Heat a chargrill pan or plate until very hot and sear the scallops in batches for 30 seconds each side. Remove from the pan. Divide the noodles and black fungus among four deep serving bowls. Pour 3/4 cup of the broth into each bowl and top with six scallops each. Garnish with the shredded nori and serve immediately.

NOTE: If fresh black fungus is not available, use dried and soak it in warm water for 20 minutes.

New England Clam Chowder

※ SERVES 4
※ PREPARATION TIME: 35 MINUTES
※ COOKING TIME: 45 MINUTES

3 lb 5 oz clams or pipis, in shell
2 teaspoons oil
3 medium bacon slices, chopped
1 medium onion, chopped
1 medium garlic clove, crushed
4½ cups diced potatoes
1¼ cups fish stock
2 cups whole milk
½ cup whipping cream
3 tablespoons chopped Italian parsley

Discard any clams that are broken, already open or do not close when tapped on the bench. If necessary, soak in cold water for 1–2 hours to remove any grit. Drain and put in a large heavy-based saucepan with 1 cup water. Cover and simmer over low heat for 5 minutes, or until open. Discard any clams that do not open. Strain and reserve the liquid. Remove the clam meat from the shells.

Heat the oil in a clean saucepan. Add the bacon, onion and garlic and cook, stirring, over medium heat until the onion is soft and the bacon golden. Add the potato and stir well.

Measure the reserved clam liquid and add water to make 1¼ cups. Add to the pan with the stock and milk. Bring to a boil, reduce the heat, cover and simmer for 20 minutes, or until the potato is tender. Uncover and simmer for 10 minutes, or until slightly thickened. Add the cream, clam meat and parsley and season to taste. Heat through gently before serving, but do not allow to boil or the liquid may curdle.

Tomato Bread Soup (Pappa al Pomodoro)

1 lb 10 oz vine-ripened tomatoes
1 loaf (about 1 lb) day-old crusty
    Italian bread
1 tablespoon olive oil
3 medium garlic cloves, crushed
1 tablespoon concentrated tomato purée
5 cups hot vegetable stock or water
1 tablespoon torn basil leaves
2–3 tablespoons extra virgin olive oil,
    plus extra, to serve

Score a cross in the base of the tomatoes. Put in a heatproof bowl and cover with boiling water. Leave for 30 seconds, then transfer to cold water and peel the skin away from the cross. Cut the tomatoes in half, scoop out the seeds and chop the flesh.

Discard most of the crust from the bread and tear the bread into $1^1/_4$ inch pieces.

Heat the oil in a large saucepan. Add the garlic, tomato and tomato purée, then reduce the heat and simmer, stirring occasionally, for 10–15 minutes, or until reduced. Add the stock and bring to a boil, stirring for about 3 minutes. Reduce the heat to medium, add the bread pieces and cook, stirring, for 5 minutes, or until the bread softens and absorbs most of the liquid. Add more stock or water if the soup is too thick. Remove from the heat. Stir in the basil leaves and olive oil, and leave for 5 minutes so the flavors have time to develop. Drizzle with a little olive oil before serving.

Pasta and Bean Soup

$1^1/_4$ cups cranberry beans,
    soaked in water overnight
1 ham hock
1 medium onion, chopped
pinch ground cinnamon
pinch cayenne pepper
2 teaspoons olive oil
2 cups chicken stock
$4^1/_2$ oz tagliatelle (plain or spinach),
    broken into short lengths

Drain and rinse the cranberry beans, cover with cold water in a saucepan and bring to a boil. Stir, lower the heat and simmer for 15 minutes.

Drain the beans and transfer to a large saucepan with a tight-fitting lid. Add the ham hock, onion, cinnamon, cayenne, olive oil and stock, and enough cold water to cover. Cover and simmer over low heat for 1 hour, or until the beans are cooked and have begun to thicken the stock. Remove the hock and cut off any meat. Chop the meat and return it to the pan, discarding the bone. Season to taste.

When ready to serve, bring the soup back to a boil, toss in the tagliatelle and cook until *al dente*. Remove the pan from the heat and set aside for 1–2 minutes before serving.

Tomato Bread Soup (Pappa al Pomodoro)

Lobster Bisque

❋ SERVES 4–6
❋ PREPARATION TIME: 20 MINUTES
❋ COOKING TIME: 1 HOUR

1 raw lobster tail (about 14 oz)
1/3 cup butter
1 large onion, chopped
1 large carrot, chopped
1 medium celery stalk, chopped
1/4 cup brandy
1 cup white wine
6 medium parsley sprigs
1 medium thyme sprig
2 medium bay leaves
1 tablespoon concentrated tomato purée
4 cups fish stock
2 medium tomatoes, chopped
2 tablespoons rice flour or cornstarch
1/2 cup whipping cream

Remove the meat from the lobster tail. Wash the shell and crush into large pieces with a mallet or rolling pin, then set aside. Chop the meat into small pieces, cover and chill.

Melt the butter in a large saucepan, add the onion, carrot and celery and cook over low heat for 20 minutes, stirring occasionally, until the vegetables are softened but not brown.

In a small saucepan, heat the brandy, set alight with a long match and carefully pour over the vegetables. Shake the pan until the flame dies down. Add the white wine and the lightly crushed lobster shell. Increase the heat and boil until the liquid is reduced by half. Add the parsley, thyme, bay leaves, concentrated tomato purée, fish stock and chopped tomato. Simmer, uncovered, for 25 minutes, stirring occasionally.

Strain the mixture through a fine sieve or dampened cheesecloth, pressing gently to extract all the liquid. Discard the vegetables and lobster shell. Return the liquid to a cleaned pan.

Blend the rice flour or cornstarch with the cream in a small bowl. Add to the liquid and stir over medium heat until the mixture boils and thickens. Add the lobster meat and season to taste. Cook, without boiling, for 10 minutes, or until the lobster is just cooked. Serve hot.

NOTE: If you don't dampen the cheesecloth when straining the mixture, it will soak up too much of the liquid.

Crab and Corn Eggflower Noodle Broth

* SERVES 4
* PREPARATION TIME: 15 MINUTES
* COOKING TIME: 15 MINUTES

2½ oz dried thin egg noodles
1 tablespoon peanut oil
1 teaspoon finely chopped fresh ginger
3 medium scallions, thinly sliced,
    white and green parts separated
6 cups chicken stock
⅓ cup mirin
1⅓ cups fresh baby corn, sliced on the
    diagonal into ½ inch slices
1 cup fresh crabmeat
1 tablespoon cornstarch mixed
    with 1 tablespoon water
2 eggs, lightly beaten
2 teaspoons lime juice
1 tablespoon soy sauce
3 tablespoons torn cilantro leaves

Cook the noodles in a large saucepan of boiling salted water for 3 minutes, or until just tender. Drain, then rinse under cold water. Set aside.

Heat a non-stick wok over high heat, add the peanut oil and swirl to coat the side of the wok. Add the ginger and white part of the scallions and cook over medium heat for 1–2 minutes. Add the stock, mirin and corn and bring to a boil, then simmer for 3 minutes. Stir in the noodles, crabmeat and cornstarch mixture. Return to a simmer and stir constantly until it thickens. Reduce the heat and pour in the egg in a thin stream, stirring constantly — do not boil. Gently stir in the lime juice, soy sauce and half the cilantro.

Divide the noodles among four bowls and ladle on the soup. Top with the green scallions and remaining cilantro leaves.

White Gazpacho (Ajo Blanco)

* SERVES 4–6
* PREPARATION TIME: 20 MINUTES
* COOKING TIME: 3 MINUTES

1 loaf day-old white Italian bread
1 cup blanched almonds
3–4 medium garlic cloves, chopped
½ cup extra virgin olive oil
⅓ cup sherry or white
    wine vinegar
1½ cups vegetable stock
2 tablespoons olive oil, extra
3 cups cubed day-old white Italian bread,
    extra, with crust removed
1 cup small seedless green grapes

Remove the crusts from the loaf of bread. Soak the bread in cold water for 5 minutes, then squeeze out any excess liquid. Chop the almonds and garlic in a food processor until well ground. Add the bread and process until smooth.

With the motor running, add the oil in a slow steady stream until the mixture is the consistency of thick mayonnaise. Slowly add the sherry and 1¼ cups of stock. Blend for 1 minute. Season with salt. Refrigerate for at least 2 hours. The soup thickens on refrigeration so you may need to add the remaining stock or water to thin it.

When ready to serve, heat the extra oil in a frying pan, add the bread cubes and toss over medium heat for 2–3 minutes, or until golden. Drain on paper towel. Serve the soup very cold. Garnish with bread cubes and grapes.

Crab and Corn Eggflower Noodle Broth

Garlic Fish Stew (Bourride)

❈ SERVES 8
❈ PREPARATION TIME: 25 MINUTES
❈ COOKING TIME: 1 HOUR 10 MINUTES

1 tablespoon butter
1 tablespoon olive oil
4 slices white bread, crusts removed and
    cut into ⅝ inch cubes
4 lb 8 oz assorted firm white fish
    fillets (such as bass, whiting and cod)

AÏOLI
5 egg yolks
4 medium garlic cloves, crushed
3–5 teaspoons lemon juice
1 cup olive oil

STOCK
⅓ cup olive oil
1 large onion, chopped
1 medium carrot, sliced
1 medium leek, white part only, chopped
1⅔ cups dry white wine
1 teaspoon dried fennel seeds
2 medium garlic cloves, bruised
2 bay leaves
1 large strip orange zest
2 medium thyme sprigs

To make the croutons, heat the butter and oil in a heavy-based frying pan. When the butter begins to foam, add the bread cubes and cook for 5 minutes, or until golden. Drain on crumpled paper towel. Set aside.

Fillet the fish (or ask your fishmonger to do it), reserving the heads and bones for the stock.

To make the aïoli, put 2 of the egg yolks, garlic and 3 teaspoons lemon juice in a food processor and blend until creamy. With the motor still running, slowly drizzle in the oil. Season and add the remaining lemon juice, to taste. Set aside until needed.

To make the stock, heat the olive oil in large saucepan or stockpot and add the onion, carrot and leek. Cook over low heat for 12–15 minutes, or until the vegetables are soft. Add the fish heads and bones, wine, fennel seed, garlic, bay leaves, orange zest, thyme, black pepper and ½ teaspoon salt. Cover with 8 cups water. Bring to a boil and skim off the froth. Reduce the heat and simmer for 30 minutes. Strain into a pot, crushing the bones well to release as much flavor as possible. Return to the heat.

Preheat the oven to 235°F. Cut the fish fillets into large pieces about 3½ inches long. Add to the stock and bring to a simmer, putting the heavier pieces in first and adding the more delicate pieces later. Poach for 6–8 minutes, until the flesh starts to become translucent and begins to flake easily. Transfer the fish pieces to a serving platter and moisten with a little stock. Cover with foil and keep warm in the oven.

Place 8 tablespoons of the aïoli in a large bowl and add the remaining 3 egg yolks, stirring constantly. Ladle a little stock into the aïoli mixture, blend well and return slowly to the rest of the stock. Stir continuously with a wooden spoon for 8–10 minutes over low heat, or until the soup has thickened and coats the back of a spoon. Do not boil or the mixture will curdle. To serve, scatter the croutons and fish pieces into individual bowls and ladle the stock over the top.

Risoni and Mushroom Broth

❋ SERVES 4
❋ PREPARATION TIME: 15 MINUTES
❋ COOKING TIME: 20–25 MINUTES

1/3 cup butter
2 medium garlic cloves, sliced
2 large onions, sliced
4 cups thinly sliced mushrooms
5 cups chicken stock
2/3 cup risoni
1 1/4 cups whipping cream

Melt the butter in a large saucepan over low heat. Add the garlic and onion and cook for 1 minute. Add the sliced mushrooms and cook gently, without coloring, for 5 minutes. (Set aside a few mushroom slices to use as a garnish.) Add the chicken stock and cook for 10 minutes. Allow to cool slightly before transferring to a food processor and blending until smooth.

Meanwhile, add the risoni in a large saucepan of rapidly boiling salted water and cook until *al dente*. Drain and set aside.

Return the soup to a clean pan and stir in the risoni and cream. Heat through and season to taste. Garnish with the reserved mushrooms.

Shrimp and Basil Soup

❋ SERVES 4
❋ PREPARATION TIME: 45 MINUTES
❋ COOKING TIME: 15–20 MINUTES

1 lb 2 oz raw shrimp
2 tablespoons olive oil
1 1/3 tablespoons butter
2 medium garlic cloves
1 small red onion, thinly sliced
2 medium celery stalks, cut into thin
    batons
3 small carrots, cut into thin batons
1 tablespoon finely chopped Italian parsley
1 1/2 tablespoons finely chopped basil
pinch cayenne pepper
1/2 cup dry sherry
4 cups chicken stock
1/2 cup shell pasta
1/4 cup whipping cream

Peel the shrimp and gently pull out the dark vein from the back of each shrimp, starting from the head end.

In a large saucepan, heat the oil and butter. Add the garlic cloves and the onion and cook over low heat for 2–3 minutes. Add the celery and carrot and fry until the vegetables are golden, but not brown. Add the parsley, basil and cayenne pepper. Stir briefly, add the shrimp and toss through. Remove the garlic cloves. Pour in the sherry, increase the heat and cook for 2–3 minutes. Add the chicken stock, bring back to a boil, reduce the heat and simmer for 5 minutes. Add the shell pasta and simmer until the pasta is *al dente*. Stir in the cream and season to taste.

Risoni and Mushroom Broth

Soup with Pesto (Soupe au Pistou)

2 medium ripe tomatoes
3 Italian parsley stalks
1 large rosemary sprig
1 large thyme sprig
1 large marjoram sprig
¼ cup olive oil
2 medium onions, thinly sliced
1 medium leek, white part only, thinly sliced
1 medium bay leaf
2½ cups winter squash, cut
   into small pieces
1½ cups diced potato
1 medium carrot, halved lengthways and
   thinly sliced
8 cups vegetable stock or water
⅔ cup fresh or frozen fava beans
½ cup fresh or frozen peas
2 small zucchini, finely chopped
½ cup short macaroni or shell pasta

PESTO
¾ cup basil leaves
2 large garlic cloves, crushed
⅓ cup olive oil
⅓ cup freshly grated parmesan cheese

Score a cross in the base of each tomato. Put in a heatproof bowl and cover with boiling water. Leave for 30 seconds then transfer to cold water, drain, peel away the skin from the cross and chop the flesh. Tie the parsley, rosemary, thyme and marjoram together with string.

Heat the oil in a heavy-based saucepan and add the onion and leek. Cook over low heat for 10 minutes, or until soft. Add the herb bunch, bay leaf, winter squash, potato, carrot, 1 teaspoon salt and the stock. Cover and simmer for 10 minutes, or until vegetables are almost tender.

Add the fava beans, peas, zucchini, tomatoes and pasta. Cover and cook for 15 minutes, or until the vegetables are very tender and the pasta is *al dente*. Add more water if necessary. Remove the herbs, including the bay leaf.

To make the pesto, finely chop the basil and garlic in a food processor. Pour in the oil gradually, processing until smooth. Stir in the parmesan and ½ teaspoon freshly ground black pepper and serve spooned over the soup.

NOTE: The flavor of this soup improves if refrigerated overnight then gently reheated.

Green Pea Soup

🌼 SERVES 4–6

🌼 PREPARATION TIME: 20 MINUTES

🌼 COOKING TIME: 1 HOUR 40 MINUTES

1½ cups dried green split peas
2 tablespoons oil
1 medium onion, finely chopped
1 medium celery stalk, finely sliced
1 medium carrot, finely sliced
1 tablespoon ground cumin
1 tablespoon ground coriander
2 teaspoons grated fresh ginger
5 cups vegetable stock
2 cups frozen green peas
1 tablespoon chopped mint
yogurt or sour cream, to serve

Soak the split peas in cold water for 2 hours. Drain the peas well.

Heat the oil in a large heavy-based saucepan and add the onion, celery and carrot. Cook over medium heat for 3 minutes, stirring occasionally, until soft but not browned. Stir in the cumin, coriander and ginger, then cook for 1 minute. Add the split peas and stock to pan. Bring to a boil, then reduce the heat to low. Simmer, covered, for 1½ hours, stirring occasionally. Add the frozen peas to the pan and stir to combine.

Allow to cool slightly before transferring to a food processor and blending, in batches, until smooth. Return to a clean pan and gently reheat. Season to taste and then stir in the mint. Serve in bowls with a swirl of yogurt or sour cream.

Corn Chowder

🌼 SERVES 8

🌼 PREPARATION TIME: 15 MINUTES

🌼 COOKING TIME: 30 MINUTES

⅓ cup butter
2 large onions, finely chopped
1 medium garlic clove, crushed
2 teaspoons cumin seeds
4 cups vegetable stock
2 medium potatoes, chopped
1 cup canned creamed corn
2 cups corn kernels
3 tablespoons chopped Italian parsley
1 cup grated cheddar cheese
2 tablespoons snipped chives, to garnish

Heat the butter in large heavy-based saucepan. Add the onion and cook over medium–high heat for 5 minutes, or until golden. Add the garlic and cumin seeds, cook for 1 minute, stirring constantly. Add the vegetable stock and bring to a boil. Add the potatoes and reduce the heat. Simmer, uncovered, for 10 minutes.

Add the creamed corn, corn kernels and parsley. Bring to a boil, then reduce the heat and simmer for 10 minutes. Stir through the cheese and season to taste. Heat gently until the cheese melts.

Serve immediately, sprinkled with the chives.

Green Pea Soup

Pie~Crust Mushroom Soup

* SERVES 4
* PREPARATION TIME: 25 MINUTES
* COOKING TIME: 35 MINUTES

14 oz large mushrooms
$\frac{1}{4}$ cup butter
1 medium onion, finely chopped
1 medium garlic clove, crushed
$\frac{1}{4}$ cup all-purpose flour
3 cups chicken stock
2 tablespoons thyme leaves
2 tablespoons sherry
1 cup whipping cream
2 sheets frozen puff pastry, thawed
1 egg, lightly beaten

Preheat the oven to 400°F. Peel and roughly chop the mushrooms, including the stems.

Melt the butter in a large saucepan, add the onion and cook over medium heat for 3 minutes, or until soft. Add the garlic and cook for 1 minute. Add the mushrooms and cook until soft. Sprinkle with the flour and stir for 1 minute. Stir in the stock and thyme and bring to a boil. Reduce the heat and simmer, covered, for 10 minutes. Allow to cool slightly before transferring to a food processor and blending, in batches.

Return the soup to the pan, stir in the sherry and cream then pour into four ovenproof bowls (use small, deep bowls rather than wide shallow ones, or the pastry may sag into the soup).

Cut rounds of pastry slightly larger than the bowl tops and cover each bowl with pastry. Seal the pastry edges and brush lightly with the egg. Place the bowls on a baking sheet and bake for 15 minutes, or until golden and puffed.

Tofu Miso Soup

❋ SERVES 4
❋ PREPARATION TIME: 10 MINUTES
❋ COOKING TIME: 15 MINUTES

½ cup dashi granules
⅓ cup miso paste
1 tablespoon mirin
1⅓ cups cubed firm tofu
1 medium scallion, sliced, to serve

Using a wooden spoon, combine 4 cups water and the dashi granules in a small saucepan and bring to a boil.

Combine the miso paste and mirin in a small bowl, then add to the pan. Stir the miso over medium heat, taking care not to let the mixture boil once the miso has dissolved, or it will lose flavor. Add the tofu cubes to the hot stock and heat, without boiling, over medium heat for 5 minutes. Serve in individual bowls, garnished with the scallion.

Chinese Chicken and Corn Soup

❋ SERVES 4
❋ PREPARATION TIME: 10 MINUTES
❋ COOKING TIME: 15 MINUTES

3 cups chicken stock
2 x 7 oz boneless, skinless chicken breasts
3–4 corn cobs
1 tablespoon vegetable oil
4 medium scallions, thinly sliced,
    white and green parts separated
1 medium garlic clove, crushed
2 teaspoons grated fresh ginger
1¼ cups canned creamed corn
2 tablespoons light soy sauce
1 tablespoon Chinese rice wine
1 tablespoon cornstarch
2 teaspoons sesame oil

Bring the stock to simmering point in a small saucepan. Add the chicken and remove the pan from the heat. Cover the pan and leave the chicken to cool in the liquid. Remove the chicken with a slotted spoon, then finely shred the meat using your fingers. Cut the corn kernels from the cobs — you should get about 2 cups of kernels.

Heat a wok over medium–high heat, add the oil and swirl to coat the side of the wok. Add the white part of the scallions, garlic and ginger and stir-fry for 30 seconds. Add the stock, corn kernels, creamed corn, soy sauce, rice wine and 1 cup water. Stir until the soup comes to a boil, then reduce the heat and simmer for 10 minutes. Add the chicken meat.

Meanwhile, stir the cornstarch, sesame oil and 1 tablespoon water together in a small bowl until smooth. Add a little of the hot stock, stir together, then pour this mixture into the soup. Bring to simmering point, stirring constantly for 3–4 minutes, or until slightly thickened. Season to taste. Garnish with the scallion greens.

Tofu Miso Soup

Stuffed Artichokes

❀ SERVES 6
❀ PREPARATION TIME: 1 HOUR 30 MINUTES
❀ COOKING TIME: 1 HOUR 25 MINUTES

1/2 cup lemon juice
12 medium globe artichokes
2 cups ground lamb
1/2 cup fresh breadcrumbs
1 egg, lightly beaten
1 tablespoon chopped thyme
olive oil, for deep-frying
1/2 cup extra virgin olive oil
1/2 teaspoon ground turmeric
1 medium bay leaf
1 1/2 cups chicken stock
2 2/3 tablespoons butter
2 tablespoons all-purpose flour

Fill a large bowl with water and add 1/4 cup of the lemon juice. Peel the outer leaves from the artichokes, trimming the bases and stems to reveal the bases. Cut the tops off to reveal the chokes and remove the chokes. Put the artichokes in the bowl of acidulated water.

Put the lamb, breadcrumbs, egg and thyme in a bowl, season and mix well. Pat the artichokes dry with paper towels and fill each with 2 tablespoons of the lamb mixture.

Fill a deep-fryer or large heavy-based saucepan one-third full of olive oil and heat to 350°F, or until a cube of bread dropped into the oil browns in 15 seconds. Cook the artichokes in batches for 5 minutes, or until golden brown. Drain well.

Put the extra virgin olive oil, turmeric, bay leaf, remaining lemon juice and 1 cup of the stock in a 5-cup flameproof casserole dish. Season, then bring to the boil. Add the artichokes, reduce the heat, cover and simmer for 1 hour, or until tender, adding more stock if necessary. Turn the artichokes twice during cooking. Remove the artichokes and keep them warm. Reserve the cooking liquid.

Melt the butter in a saucepan, add the flour and stir for 1 minute, or until pale and foamy. Remove from the heat and gradually stir in the reserved cooking liquid. Return to the heat and stir until the sauce boils and thickens, then reduce the heat and simmer for 2 minutes. Serve immediately with the artichokes.

Tomato and Small Mozzarella Cheese Balls Salad

✻ SERVES 4
✻ PREPARATION TIME: 10 MINUTES
✻ COOKING TIME: NIL

3 large vine-ripened tomatoes
1 2/3 cups fresh small mozzarella cheese
   balls
12 basil leaves
1/4 cup extra virgin olive oil

Slice the tomato into 12 $1/2$ inch slices. Slice the mozzarella cheese into 24 slices the same thickness as the tomato.

Arrange the tomato slices on a plate, alternating them with two slices of mozzarella cheese and placing a basil leaf between the cheese slices.

Drizzle with the olive oil and season well.

Shrimp and Cucumber Salad

✻ SERVES 4
✻ PREPARATION TIME: 20 MINUTES
✻ COOKING TIME: NIL

1 short cucumber, peeled
13 oz raw shrimp
1/4 cup rice vinegar
1 tablespoon sugar
1 tablespoon Japanese soy sauce
1 teaspoon finely grated fresh ginger
1 tablespoon white sesame seeds, toasted

Halve the cucumber lengthways and remove the seeds. Cut into thin slices, sprinkle thoroughly with salt and set aside for 5 minutes. Rinse to remove the salt and pat dry with paper towels. Put the shrimp in a saucepan of lightly salted boiling water and simmer for 2 minutes, or until just cooked. Drain, then plunge them into cold water. When the shrimp are cool, peel them, leaving the tails intact. Gently pull out the dark vein from the back of each shrimp, starting at the head end.

Put the vinegar, sugar, soy sauce and ginger in a large bowl and stir until the sugar dissolves. Add the shrimp and cucumber, cover and marinate in the refrigerator for 1 hour.

Drain the shrimp and cucumber from the marinade. Arrange on serving plates, sprinkle with the sesame seeds and serve.

Tomato and Small Mozzarella Cheese Balls Salad

Asparagus with Citrus Hollandaise

* SERVES 4
* PREPARATION TIME: 15 MINUTES
* COOKING TIME: 8 MINUTES

24 medium asparagus spears,
   woody ends trimmed
¾ cup butter
4 egg yolks
1–2 tablespoons lemon, lime or
   orange juice
shavings of parmesan or pecorino
   cheese (optional)

Put the asparagus in a saucepan of boiling water. Simmer for 2–4 minutes, or until just tender. Drain well.

Melt the butter in a small saucepan. Skim any froth from the top and discard. Allow the butter to cool.

Combine the egg yolks and 2 tablespoons water in a small saucepan and whisk for 30 seconds, or until pale and creamy. Place the pan over very low heat and continue whisking for 3 minutes, or until the mixture thickens.

Remove from the heat. Add the cooled butter gradually, whisking constantly (leave the whey in the bottom of the pan). Stir in the lemon, lime or orange juice and season to taste. Drizzle the sauce over the asparagus and garnish with cheese shavings (if desired).

Thai Beef Salad

❀ SERVES 6
❀ PREPARATION TIME: 20 MINUTES
❀ COOKING TIME: 5 MINUTES

1 lb 2 oz lean beef fillet
2 tablespoons peanut oil
2 medium garlic cloves, crushed
1 tablespoon grated jaggery
    or unpacked brown sugar
3 tablespoons finely chopped cilantro
    roots and stems
1/3 cup lime juice
2 tablespoons fish sauce
1/4 teaspoon ground white pepper
2 small red chilies, seeded and
    thinly sliced
2 medium red Asian shallots, thinly sliced
2 long cucumbers, sliced into
    thin ribbons
2 large handfuls mint
1 cup trimmed bean sprouts
1/4 cup chopped toasted peanuts

Thinly slice the beef across the grain. Heat a wok over high heat, then add 1 tablespoon of the oil and swirl to coat the side of the wok. Add half the beef and cook for 1–2 minutes, or until medium–rare. Remove from the wok and put on a plate. Repeat with the remaining oil and beef.

Put the garlic, jaggery, cilantro, lime juice, fish sauce, pepper and 1/4 teaspoon salt in a bowl, and stir until all the sugar has dissolved. Add the chili and shallots and mix well.

Pour the sauce over the hot beef, mix together well, then allow the beef to cool to room temperature.

In a separate bowl, toss together the cucumber and mint, and refrigerate until required.

Pile up a bed of the cucumber and mint on a serving platter, then top with the beef, bean sprouts and peanuts.

Prosciutto, Camembert and Fig Salad

❀ SERVES 4
❀ PREPARATION TIME: 10 MINUTES
❀ COOKING TIME: 5 MINUTES

1/3 cup thinly sliced prosciutto
1 medium curly oak leaf lettuce
4 medium fresh figs, quartered
1/3 cup thinly sliced camembert cheese
1 medium garlic clove, crushed
1 tablespoon mustard
2 tablespoons white wine vinegar
1/3 cup olive oil

Cook the prosciutto under a hot broiler until crisp.

Arrange the lettuce leaves on a large plate and top with the figs, camembert and prosciutto.

Whisk together the garlic, mustard, vinegar and olive oil and drizzle over the salad.

Thai Beef Salad

Caesar Salad

❋ SERVES 6

❋ PREPARATION TIME: 25 MINUTES

❋ COOKING TIME: 20 MINUTES

1 small baguette
2 tablespoons olive oil
2 medium garlic cloves, halved
4 medium bacon slices, trimmed of fat
2 medium romaine lettuces
10 anchovy fillets, halved lengthways
1 cup shaved parmesan cheese
parmesan cheese shavings, extra,
    to serve

DRESSING
1 egg yolk
2 medium garlic cloves, crushed
2 teaspoons dijon mustard
2 anchovy fillets
2 tablespoons white wine vinegar
1 tablespoon worcestershire sauce
¾ cup olive oil

Preheat the oven to 350°F. To make the croutons, cut the baguette into 15 thin slices and brush both sides of each slice with oil. Spread them on a baking sheet and bake for 10–15 minutes, or until golden brown. Leave to cool slightly, then rub each side of each slice with the cut edge of a garlic clove. The baked bread can then be broken roughly into pieces or cut into small cubes.

Cook the bacon under a hot broiler until crisp. Drain on paper towels until cooled, then break into chunky pieces.

Tear the lettuce into pieces and put in a large serving bowl with the bacon, anchovies, croutons and parmesan.

To make the dressing, place the egg yolk, garlic, mustard, anchovies, vinegar and worcestershire sauce in a food processor or blender. Season and process for 20 seconds, or until smooth. With the motor running, add enough oil in a thin stream to make the dressing thick and creamy.

Drizzle the dressing over the salad and toss very gently until well distributed. Sprinkle the parmesan shavings over the top.

Frisée and Garlic Crouton Salad

❋ SERVES 4–6
❋ PREPARATION TIME: 20 MINUTES
❋ COOKING TIME: 10 MINUTES

1 tablespoon olive oil
1²/₃ cup speck, rind removed, cut into
   ¹/₄ x ³/₄ inch pieces
¹/₂ baguette, sliced
4 medium garlic cloves
1 baby curly frisée
1 cup walnuts, toasted

VINAIGRETTE
1 medium French shallot, finely chopped
1 tablespoon dijon mustard
¹/₄ cup tarragon vinegar
²/₃ cup extra virgin olive oil

To make the vinaigrette, whisk together the shallot, mustard and vinegar in a small bowl. Slowly add the oil, whisking constantly until thickened. Set aside.

Heat the oil in a large frying pan. Add the speck, bread and garlic and cook over medium–high heat for 5–8 minutes, or until the bread and speck are both crisp. Remove the garlic from the pan.

Put the frisée, baguette, speck, walnuts and vinaigrette in a large bowl. Toss together well and serve.

Fresh Beet and Goat's Cheese Salad

❋ SERVES 4
❋ PREPARATION TIME: 20 MINUTES
❋ COOKING TIME: 30 MINUTES

4 medium fresh beets, with leaves
1²/₃ cup trimmed green beans
1 tablespoon red wine vinegar
2 tablespoons extra virgin olive oil
1 medium garlic clove, crushed
1 tablespoon capers, rinsed and squeezed
   dry, roughly chopped
³/₄ cup goat's cheese

Trim the leaves from the beets, scrub the bulbs and rinse. Put in a large saucepan of salted water, bring to a boil, reduce the heat, cover and simmer for 30 minutes.

Meanwhile, bring a saucepan of water to a boil, add the beans and cook for 3 minutes. Remove, plunge into cold water, and drain well. Add the beet leaves to the boiling water and cook for 3–5 minutes. Drain, plunge into a bowl of cold water, then drain well. Drain and cool the beets, peel the skins off and cut into thin wedges.

To make the dressing, mix the vinegar, oil, garlic, capers and ¹/₂ teaspoon each of salt and pepper. Divide the beans, beet leaves and bulbs among four serving plates. Crumble the goat's cheese over the top of each and drizzle with dressing. Delicious served with fresh crusty bread.

Frisée and Garlic Crouton Salad

Crab and Mango Salad

2 x 1½ inch squares fresh coconut
1 teaspoon olive oil
2 cups trimmed watercress
1 cup snow pea sprouts
1 cup small cooked shrimp
2⅓ cups cooked fresh or canned
    crabmeat, drained if canned
1 firm medium mango, cut into thin strips
cilantro leaves, to garnish
1 medium lime, cut into slices, to garnish

DRESSING
⅓ cup light olive oil
¼ cup lime juice
1 teaspoon fish sauce
½ small green chili, finely chopped
1 tablespoon finely chopped cilantro leaves
2 teaspoons grated fresh ginger

To make the dressing, combine all the ingredients and season. Set aside to allow the flavors to infuse.

Peel the coconut into wafer-thin slices with a vegetable peeler. Heat the olive oil in a frying pan and gently fry the coconut, stirring, until golden. Drain on crumpled paper towels.

Combine the watercress and snow pea sprouts and arrange on a platter.

Peel the shrimp, leaving the tails intact. Gently pull out the dark vein from the back of each shrimp, starting at the head end. Lightly toss the crabmeat, shrimp, mango and three-quarters of the toasted coconut and dressing together. Pile in the center of the watercress and snow pea sprout mixture, scatter the remaining coconut over the top and garnish with the cilantro leaves and lime slices.

NOTE: If you can't get fresh coconut, use ½ cup flaked coconut and toast it.

Salmon and Fennel Salad

PREPARATION TIME: 15 MINUTES
COOKING TIME: NIL

2 medium fennel bulbs
2 teaspoons dijon mustard
1 teaspoon sugar
1/2 cup olive oil
2 tablespoons lemon juice
7 oz smoked salmon, cut into strips
2 tablespoons snipped chives
1 tablespoon chopped dill, optional
arugula, to serve

Trim the fronds from the fennel. Slice the fennel bulbs and chop the fronds.

To make the dressing, whisk together the mustard, sugar, olive oil and lemon juice in a large bowl.

Add the sliced fennel bulb, salmon, chives and 1 tablespoon fennel fronds or dill to the bowl. Season and toss gently. Serve with the arugula and maybe some toast.

Stuffed Mushrooms

SERVES 4–6
PREPARATION TIME: 25 MINUTES
COOKING TIME: 15–20 MINUTES

8 large cap mushrooms
1/3 cup olive oil
1/4 cup finely chopped prosciutto
1 medium garlic clove, crushed
2 tablespoons soft fresh breadcrumbs
1/3 cup freshly grated parmesan cheese
2 tablespoons chopped Italian parsley

Preheat the oven to 375°F. Lightly grease an ovenproof dish. Remove the mushroom stalks and finely chop them.

Heat 1 tablespoon of the oil in a frying pan, add the prosciutto, garlic and mushroom stalks and cook for 5 minutes. Mix in a bowl with the breadcrumbs, parmesan and parsley.

Brush the mushroom caps with 1 tablespoon of the olive oil and place them, gill side up, on the ovenproof dish. Divide the stuffing among the caps and bake for 20 minutes. Drizzle with the remaining oil and serve hot or warm.

Salmon and Fennel Salad

Salad Niçoise

❋ SERVES 4
❋ PREPARATION TIME: 30 MINUTES
❋ COOKING TIME: 15 MINUTES

3 eggs
2 medium vine-ripened tomatoes
1 1/2 cups trimmed baby green beans
1/2 cup olive oil
2 tablespoons white wine vinegar
1 large garlic clove, halved
1 1/2 oz iceberg lettuce heart
1 small red bell pepper
1 short cucumber
1 medium celery stalk
1/4 large red onion, thinly sliced
1 1/2 cups canned tuna, drained and broken
  into chunks
12 medium Kalamata olives
1 1/2 oz tinned anchovy fillets, drained
2 teaspoons baby capers, rinsed and
  squeezed dry
12 small basil leaves

Put the eggs in a saucepan of cold water. Bring to a boil, then reduce the heat and simmer for 10 minutes. Stir during the first few minutes to center the yolks. Cool under cold water, then peel and cut into quarters. Meanwhile, score a cross in the base of each tomato. Put in a heatproof bowl and cover with boiling water. Leave for 30 seconds, then transfer to cold water and peel the skin away from the cross. Cut each tomato into eight pieces.

Cook the beans in a saucepan of boiling water for 2 minutes, rinse under cold water, then drain.

Meanwhile, to make the dressing, whisk together the oil and vinegar.

Rub the garlic over the base and sides of a platter. Cut the lettuce into eight wedges and arrange over the base. Remove the seeds and membrane from the red pepper and thinly slice. Cut the cucumber and celery into thin 2 inch lengths. Layer the egg, tomato, beans, pepper, cucumber and celery over the lettuce. Scatter the onion and tuna over them, then the olives, anchovies, capers and basil. Drizzle with dressing and serve.

Clams in White Wine

❋ SERVES 4
❋ PREPARATION TIME: 10 MINUTES
❋ COOKING TIME: 20 MINUTES

2 lb 4 oz clams (see Note)
2 large tomatoes
2 tablespoons olive oil
1 small onion, finely chopped
2 medium garlic cloves, crushed
1 tablespoon chopped Italian parsley
pinch freshly grated nutmeg
1/3 cup dry white wine
Italian parsley, to garnish

Soak the clams in salted water for 1 hour to release any grit. Rinse under running water and discard any open clams. Score a cross in the base of each tomato. Put in a heatproof bowl and cover with boiling water. Leave for 30 seconds, then transfer to cold water and peel the skin away from the cross. Cut the tomatoes in half, scoop out the seeds and finely chop.

Heat the oil in a large flameproof casserole dish and cook the onion over low heat for 5 minutes, or until softened. Add the garlic and tomato and cook for 5 minutes. Stir in the parsley and nutmeg and season. Add 1/3 cup water.

Add the clams and cook over low heat until they open. Discard any clams that don't open. Add the wine and cook over low heat for 3–4 minutes, or until the sauce thickens, gently moving the dish back and forth a few times, rather than stirring the clams, so that the clams stay in the shells. Serve at once, with bread.

NOTE: You can use mussels instead of clams in this recipe.

San Choy Bau with Noodles

1 lb 2 oz raw shrimp
vegetable oil, for deep-frying
1 cup dried rice vermicelli (see Notes)
1/4 cup chicken stock
2 tablespoons Chinese rice wine
2 tablespoons soy sauce
2 tablespoons hoisin sauce
1 tablespoon brown bean sauce
1/2 teaspoon sugar
1/4 cup peanut oil
1 medium garlic clove, crushed
1 tablespoon finely chopped fresh ginger
3 medium scallions, thinly sliced
    and green ends reserved, to garnish
2/3 cup ground pork (see Notes)
12 iceberg lettuce leaves, trimmed into
    neat cups

Peel the shrimp and gently pull out the dark vein from the back of each shrimp, starting at the head end. Roughly chop.

Fill a deep heavy-based saucepan or deep-fryer one-third full of oil and heat to 325°F, or until a cube of bread dropped into the oil browns in 20 seconds. Add the dried rice vermicelli to the oil in batches and deep-fry until puffed up but not browned — this will only take a few seconds, so watch it carefully. Remove with a slotted spoon and drain well on crumpled paper towels.

To make the stir-fry sauce, put the chicken stock, Chinese rice wine, soy sauce, hoisin sauce, brown bean sauce, sugar and 1/2 teaspoon salt in a small bowl and stir together until well combined.

Heat the peanut oil in a wok over high heat and swirl to coat. Add the garlic, ginger and scallions and stir-fry for 1 minute, being careful not to burn the garlic.

Add the pork to the wok, breaking up the lumps with the back of a wooden spoon, then cook for 4 minutes. Add the shrimp meat and stir-fry for 2 minutes, or until it begins to change color.

Add the stir-fry sauce and stir until combined. Cook over high heat for 2 minutes, or until the mixture thickens slightly.

Divide the noodles among the lettuce cups, spoon the pork and shrimp mixture over the noodles and garnish with the reserved scallions. Serve at once.

NOTES: Make sure the ground pork is not too lean or the mixture will be dry. When deep-frying the vermicelli, take care not to allow the oil to become too hot or the noodles will expand and brown very quickly. Have everything you need ready before you start deep-frying — a slotted spoon for removing the noodles and a tray lined with crumpled paper towels. Remember to deep-fry the noodles in small batches as they will dramatically increase in volume when cooked.

Shrimp Cocktail

¼ cup whole-egg mayonnaise
2 teaspoons ketchup
dash of Tabasco sauce
¼ teaspoon worcestershire sauce
2 teaspoons heavy cream
¼ teaspoon lemon juice
24 cooked large shrimp
4 lettuce leaves, shredded
lemon wedges, for serving

Mix the mayonnaise, ketchup, Tabasco sauce, cream and juice together in a small bowl.

Peel the shrimp, leaving the tails intact on eight of them. Gently pull out the dark vein from the back of each shrimp, starting at the head end.

Divide the lettuce among four glasses. Arrange the shrimp without the tails in the glasses and drizzle with the sauce. Hang two of the remaining shrimp over the edge of each glass and serve with lemon wedges.

Salt Cod Purée (Brandade de Morue)

½ salt cod
1¼ cups diced roasting potatoes
¾ cup olive oil
1 cup whole milk
4 medium garlic cloves, crushed
2 tablespoons lemon juice
olive oil, extra, to drizzle

Put the salt cod in a large bowl, cover with cold water and soak for 24 hours, changing the water frequently. Drain the cod and place in a large saucepan of clean water. Bring to a boil over medium heat, reduce the heat and simmer for 30 minutes. Drain, then cool for 15 minutes.

Meanwhile, cook the potatoes in a saucepan of boiling salted water for 12–15 minutes, or until tender. Drain and keep warm.

Remove the skin from the fish and break the flesh into large flaky pieces, discarding any bones. Put the flesh in a food processor. Using two separate pans, gently warm the oil in one, and the milk and garlic in another.

Start the food processor and, with the motor running, alternately add small amounts of the milk and oil until you have a thick, paste-like mixture. Add the potato and process this in short bursts until combined, being careful not to overwork the mixture once the potato has been added. Transfer to a bowl and gradually add the lemon juice, to taste, and plenty of freshly ground black pepper. Gently lighten the mixture by fluffing it up with a fork. Drizzle with the oil before serving. Serve warm or cold with fried bread.

Shrimp Cocktail

Chilled Buckwheat Noodles

❋ SERVES 4
❋ PREPARATION TIME: 25 MINUTES
❋ COOKING TIME: 15 MINUTES

9 oz dried buckwheat noodles
1½ inch piece ginger
1 medium carrot
4 medium scallions, outside layer
   removed
1 sheet nori, to garnish
pickled ginger, to garnish
thinly sliced pickled daikon, to garnish

DIPPING SAUCE
3 tablespoons dashi granules
½ cup Japanese soy sauce
⅓ cup mirin

Put the noodles in a large saucepan of boiling water. When the water returns to a boil, pour in 1 cup cold water. Bring the water back to a boil and cook the noodles for 2–3 minutes, or until just tender — take care not to overcook them. Drain the noodles in a colander and then cool under cold running water. Drain thoroughly and set aside.

Cut the ginger and carrot into fine matchsticks about 1½ inches long. Slice the scallions very finely. Bring a small saucepan of water to a boil, add the ginger, carrot and scallions and blanch for about 30 seconds. Drain and place in a bowl of iced water to cool. Drain again when the vegetables are cool.

To make the dipping sauce, combine 1½ cups water, the dashi granules, soy sauce, mirin and a good pinch each of salt and pepper in a small saucepan. Bring the sauce to a boil, then cool completely. When ready to serve, pour the sauce into four small dipping bowls.

Gently toss the cooled noodles and vegetables to combine. Arrange in four individual serving bowls.

Toast the nori by holding it with tongs over low heat and moving it back and forward for about 15 seconds. Cut it into thin strips with scissors, and scatter the strips over the noodles. Place a little pickled ginger and daikon on the side of each plate. Serve the noodles with the dipping sauce. The noodles should be dipped into the sauce before being eaten.

Oysters with Bloody Mary Sauce

✳ SERVES 6
✳ PREPARATION TIME: 20 MINUTES
✳ COOKING TIME: NIL

24 oysters
¼ cup tomato juice
2 teaspoons vodka
1 teaspoon lemon juice
½ teaspoon worcestershire sauce
1–2 drops Tabasco sauce
1 medium celery stalk
1–2 teaspoons snipped chives

Remove the oysters from their shells. Clean and dry the shells. Combine the tomato juice, vodka, lemon juice, worcestershire sauce and Tabasco sauce in a small bowl.

Cut the celery stalk into very thin batons and place in the bases of the oyster shells. Top with an oyster and drizzle with tomato mixture. Sprinkle with the snipped chives.

Gravlax with Mustard Sauce

✳ SERVES 12
✳ PREPARATION TIME: 10 MINUTES
✳ COOKING TIME: NIL

¼ cup sugar
2 tablespoons sea salt
1 teaspoon crushed black peppercorns
5 lb 8 oz salmon, filleted, skin on
1 tablespoon vodka or brandy
4 tablespoons very finely chopped dill

MUSTARD SAUCE
1½ tablespoons cider vinegar
1 teaspoon sugar
½ cup olive oil
2 teaspoons chopped dill
2 tablespoons dijon mustard

Combine the sugar, salt and peppercorns in a small dish. Remove any bones from the salmon with tweezers. Pat dry with paper towels and lay a fillet, skin side down, in a shallow tray or ovenproof dish. Sprinkle the fillet with half the vodka, rub half the sugar mixture into the flesh, then sprinkle with half the dill. Sprinkle the remaining vodka over the second salmon fillet and rub the remaining sugar mixture into the flesh. Lay it, flesh side down, on top of the other fillet. Cover with plastic wrap, place a heavy board on top and then weigh the board down with three heavy cans or a foil-covered brick. Refrigerate for 24 hours, turning it over after 12 hours.

To make the mustard sauce, whisk all the ingredients together, then cover until needed.

Uncover the salmon and lay the fillets on a wooden board. Brush off the dill and seasoning with a stiff pastry brush. Sprinkle with the remaining dill, pressing it onto the salmon flesh, shaking off any excess. Serve whole on the serving board, or thinly sliced on an angle towards the tail, with the sauce.

NOTE: Gravlax can be refrigerated, covered, for up to a week.

Oysters with Bloody Mary Sauce

Crab Cakes with Avocado Salsa

* SERVES 4
* PREPARATION TIME: 15 MINUTES
* COOKING TIME: 6 MINUTES

2 eggs, lightly beaten
2 cups canned crabmeat, drained
1 medium scallion, finely chopped
1 tablespoon mayonnaise
2 teaspoons sweet chili sauce
1¼ cups fresh white breadcrumbs
oil, for pan-frying
lime wedges, to serve
cilantro leaves, to garnish

AVOCADO SALSA
2 medium plum tomatoes, chopped
1 small red onion, finely chopped
1 large avocado, diced
¼ cup lime juice
2 tablespoons chervil
1 teaspoon sugar

Combine the eggs, crabmeat, scallion, mayonnaise, sweet chili sauce and breadcrumbs in a bowl. Stir well and season. Using wet hands, form the crab mixture into eight small flat patties. Cover and refrigerate for 30 minutes.

To make the avocado salsa, put the tomato, onion, avocado, lime juice, chervil and sugar in a bowl. Season and toss gently to combine.

Heat the oil in a large heavy-based frying pan to 350°F, or until a cube of bread dropped into the oil browns in 15 seconds. Cook the crab cakes over medium heat for 6 minutes, or until golden brown on both sides. Drain well on crumpled paper towels. Serve the crab cakes with the bowl of avocado salsa and some lime wedges. Garnish with the cilantro leaves.

Garlic Shrimp

※ SERVES 4
※ PREPARATION TIME: 20 MINUTES
※ COOKING TIME: 15 MINUTES

2 lb 12 oz raw shrimp
1/3 cup melted butter
3/4 cup olive oil
8 medium garlic cloves, crushed
2 medium scallions, thinly sliced

Preheat the oven to 500°F. Peel the shrimp, leaving the tails intact. Gently pull out the vein from the back of each shrimp, starting at the head end. Cut a slit down the back of each shrimp.

Combine the butter and oil and divide among four 2-cup ovenproof pots. Divide half the crushed garlic among the pots.

Place the pots on a baking sheet and heat in the oven for 10 minutes, or until the mixture is bubbling. Divide the shrimp and remaining garlic among the pots. Return to the oven for 5 minutes, or until the shrimp are cooked. Stir in the scallions. Season to taste. Serve with bread to mop up the juices.

NOTE: Garlic shrimp can also be made in a cast-iron frying pan in the oven or on the stovetop.

Baked Shrimp with Feta

※ SERVES 4
※ PREPARATION TIME: 20 MINUTES
※ COOKING TIME: 30 MINUTES

10 1/2 oz raw large shrimp
2 tablespoons olive oil
2 small red onions, finely chopped
1 large garlic clove, crushed
1 3/4 cups diced tomatoes
2 tablespoons lemon juice
2 tablespoons fresh oregano or
    1 teaspoon dried
1 1/3 cups feta cheese
extra virgin olive oil, for drizzling
chopped Italian parsley, to garnish

Peel the shrimp, leaving the tails intact. Gently pull out the dark vein from the back of each shrimp, starting at the head end.

Preheat the oven to 350°F. Heat the oil in a saucepan over medium heat, add the onion and cook, stirring, for 3 minutes. Add the garlic and cook for a few seconds, then add the tomato and cook for 10 minutes, or until the mixture has reduced and thickened. Add the lemon juice and oregano. Season to taste.

Pour half the sauce into a 3-cup ovenproof dish, about 6 inches square. Place the shrimp on top, spoon on the sauce and crumble feta over the top. Drizzle with the olive oil and sprinkle with freshly cracked black pepper.

Bake for 15 minutes, or until the shrimp are just cooked. Garnish with the parsley. Serve immediately.

Garlic Shrimp

Scallops Provençale

❋ SERVES 4

❋ PREPARATION TIME: 20 MINUTES

❋ COOKING TIME: 30 MINUTES

20 scallops, on the shell
3 cups medium tomatoes
¼ cup olive oil
1 medium onion, finely chopped
4 medium French shallots, finely chopped
¼ cup dry white wine
¼ cup butter
4 medium garlic cloves, crushed
2 tablespoons finely chopped Italian
    parsley
½ teaspoon thyme
2 tablespoons fresh breadcrumbs

Take the scallops off their shells. Rinse and reserve the shells. If the scallops need to be cut off, use a small, sharp knife to slice them free, being careful to leave as little meat on the shell as possible. Slice or pull off any vein, membrane or hard white muscle, leaving any roe attached.

Score a cross in the base of each tomato. Put the tomatoes in a heatproof bowl and cover with boiling water. Leave for 30 seconds, then transfer to cold water and peel the skin away from the cross. Cut each tomato in half, scoop out the seeds and finely dice the flesh.

Heat 2 tablespoons of the oil in a frying pan over medium heat until hot, add the onion and shallots, then reduce the heat to low and cook slowly for 5 minutes, or until soft. Add the wine and simmer for several minutes until reduced slightly, then add the tomato. Season and cook, stirring occasionally, for 20 minutes, or until thick and pulpy. Preheat the oven to 350°F.

Heat the butter and remaining oil in a frying pan over high heat until foamy. Cook half the scallops for 1–2 minutes each side, or until lightly golden. Remove and repeat with the remaining scallops. Set aside.

Add the garlic to the hot scallop pan and stir for 1 minute. Remove from the heat and stir in the parsley, thyme and breadcrumbs.

To serve, warm the shells on a baking sheet in the oven. Put a small amount of tomato mixture on each shell, top with a scallop and sprinkle with the breadcrumb and parsley mixture.

California Rolls

❋ SERVES 12
❋ PREPARATION TIME: 25 MINUTES
+ 1 HOUR DRAINING + COOLING
❋ COOKING TIME: 25 MINUTES

1 cup Japanese short-grain rice
1 tablespoon rice vinegar
2 generous pinches of sugar
1 large egg
1 teaspoon sake
1 teaspoon oil
2 sheets roasted nori, 8 x 7 inches
2 x 1¼ oz crabsticks, cut into strips
¼ cup pickled daikon, cut into very
   thin batons
¼ cup carrot, cut into very thin batons
¼ cup cucumber, cut into very thin batons
Japanese soy sauce, to serve
wasabi paste, to serve
pickled ginger, to serve

Wash the rice under cold running water until the water runs clear, then drain thoroughly. Drain for an hour. Put the rice into a saucepan and cover with cold water. Cover the pan and bring the water to a boil. Reduce the heat and simmer for 10 minutes. When the rice is cooked, remove the pan from the heat and leave, covered, for 10 minutes.

To make the sushi dressing, mix together the vinegar, a pinch of the sugar and a pinch of salt.

Spread the rice over the base of a non-metallic dish or bowl, pour the sushi dressing over the top and use a rice paddle or spatula to mix the dressing through the rice, separating the grains as you do so. Fan the rice until it cools to room temperature. Cover the pan with a damp dish towel and set aside — do not refrigerate.

To make the omelet, gently combine the egg, sake, a pinch of sugar and a pinch of salt. Heat the oil in a small frying pan. Add the egg mixture and cook until firm around the edges but still slightly soft in the middle. Roll the omelet, then tip it out of the pan. Cool, then slice into strips.

Put a nori sheet on a sushi mat, shiny side down. Add half of the rice, leaving a ¾ inch gap at the edge furthest away from you. Lay half of the fillings on the rice in the following order: omelet, crabstick, daikon, carrot, cucumber. Starting with the end nearest to you, tightly roll the mat and the nori. Repeat this process with the remaining ingredients.

Using a sharp knife, cut each roll into six slices. After cutting each slice, rinse the knife under cold running water to prevent sticking. Serve with Japanese soy sauce, wasabi and pickled ginger.

Crispy Fried Crab

※ SERVES 4
※ PREPARATION TIME: 30 MINUTES
※ COOKING TIME: 15 MINUTES

2 lb 4 oz fresh crab
1 egg, lightly beaten
1 medium red chili, finely chopped
1/2 teaspoon crushed garlic
1/4 teaspoon ground white pepper
oil, for deep-frying
lemon wedges, to serve

SEASONING MIX
1/3 cup all-purpose flour
1/3 cup rice flour
3 teaspoons sugar
1 teaspoon ground white pepper

Freeze the crab for about 1 hour until immobilized. Scrub the crab clean. Pull back the apron and remove the top shell (it should come off easily and in one piece). Remove the intestines and the gray feathery gills. Twist off the legs and claws. Using a sharp, heavy knife, chop the body into four pieces. Crack the claws with a good hit with the back of a knife.

Beat the egg with the chili, garlic, pepper and 1/2 teaspoon salt in a large bowl. Put the crab pieces in the mixture, cover and refrigerate for 1 hour.

Sift the seasoning ingredients together onto a large plate. Dip all the crab segments in the seasoning and dust off any excess.

Fill a deep-fryer or heavy-based saucepan one-third full of oil and heat to 350°F, or until a cube of bread dropped into the oil browns in 15 seconds. Carefully cook the claws in batches for 7–8 minutes, the body portions for 3–4 minutes, and the legs for 2 minutes. Drain on crumpled paper towels before serving with lemon wedges.

NOTE: Serve the crab as soon as it's cooked. You will need a crab cracker to crack the claws so you can remove the flesh.

Barbecued Octopus

❀ SERVES 6
❀ PREPARATION TIME: 15 MINUTES
❀ COOKING TIME: 5 MINUTES

²/₃ cup olive oil
¹/₃ cup chopped oregano
3 tablespoons chopped Italian parsley
1 tablespoon lemon juice
3 small red chilies, seeded and finely
   chopped
3 medium garlic cloves, crushed
2 lb 4 oz baby octopus
lime wedges, to serve

To make the marinade, combine the oil, herbs, lemon juice, chili and garlic in a large bowl and mix well.

Use a small, sharp knife to remove the octopus heads. Grasp the bodies and push the beaks out from the center with your index finger, then remove and discard. Slit the heads and remove the gut. If the octopus are too large, cut them into smaller portions.

Mix the octopus with the herb marinade. Cover and refrigerate for several hours, or overnight. Drain and reserve the marinade. Cook on a very hot, lightly oiled barbecue or in a very hot frying pan for 3–5 minutes, or until the flesh turns white. Turn frequently and brush generously with the marinade during cooking.

Grilled Squid with Salsa Verde

❀ SERVES 6
❀ PREPARATION TIME: 10 MINUTES
❀ COOKING TIME: 10 MINUTES

2 lb 4 oz squid
1 cup olive oil
2 tablespoons lemon juice
2 medium garlic cloves, crushed
2 tablespoons chopped oregano
2 tablespoons chopped Italian parsley, to serve
6 lemon wedges, to serve

SALSA VERDE
4 anchovy fillets, drained
1 tablespoon capers
1 medium garlic clove, crushed
3 tablespoons chopped Italian parsley
1 small handful basil
1 small handful mint
2 teaspoons red wine vinegar
¹/₄ cup extra virgin olive oil
1 teaspoon dijon mustard

To clean the squid, pull the tentacles away from the tube (the intestines should come away at the same time). Remove the intestines from the tentacles by cutting under the eyes, then remove the beak if it remains in the center of the tentacles by using your fingers to push up the center. Pull away the quill (the transparent cartilage) from inside the body and remove. Remove and discard any white membrane. Under cold running water pull away the skin from the hood. Cut into ¹/₂ inch rings and add to the tentacles. Add the oil, lemon juice, garlic and oregano to the bowl, and toss to coat the squid. Marinate for 30 minutes.

To make the salsa verde, chop the anchovies, capers, garlic, parsley, basil and mint in a food processor in short bursts until roughly blended. Transfer to a bowl and stir in the vinegar. Mix in the oil, then the mustard.

Heat a barbecue or chargrill pan until hot. Drain the squid rings and cook them in batches for 1–2 minutes each side. Season the squid rings and sprinkle with the parsley. Serve with the salsa verde and lemon wedges.

Barbecued Octopus

Mussels with Black Beans and Cilantro

❄ SERVES 4
❄ PREPARATION TIME: 20 MINUTES
❄ COOKING TIME: 10 MINUTES

3 lb 5 oz black mussels
1 tablespoon peanut oil
2 tablespoons black beans, rinsed and
   mashed
2 medium garlic cloves, finely chopped
1 teaspoon finely chopped fresh ginger
2 long red chilies, seeded and finely
   chopped
2 teaspoons finely chopped cilantro leaves
1 tablespoon finely chopped cilantro stem
1/4 cup Chinese rice wine
2 tablespoons lime juice
2 teaspoons sugar
steamed rice, to serve

Scrub the mussels with a stiff brush and pull out the hairy beards. Discard any broken mussels, or open ones that don't close when tapped on the bench. Rinse well.

Heat a wok until very hot, add the oil and swirl to coat the base and side. Add the black beans, garlic, ginger, chili, 1 teaspoon cilantro leaves and the cilantro stem, and cook over low heat for 2–3 minutes, or until fragrant. Pour in the rice wine and increase the heat to high. Add half the mussels in a single layer and cover with a tight-fitting lid. Cook for 2–3 minutes, or until the mussels have just opened. Discard any mussels that do not open. Remove from the wok, and repeat with the remaining mussels until all are cooked.

Transfer the mussels to a serving dish, leaving the cooking liquid in the wok. Add the lime juice, sugar and remaining cilantro leaves to the wok and cook for 30 seconds. Pour the sauce over the mussels and serve with steamed rice.

Asian Oysters

🌸 SERVES 4
🌸 PREPARATION TIME: 15 MINUTES
🌸 COOKING TIME: 5 MINUTES

12 oysters, on the shell
2 medium garlic cloves, finely chopped
³/₄ x ³/₄ inch piece ginger, cut into thin
   batons
2 medium scallions, thinly sliced,
   diagonally
¹/₄ cup Japanese soy sauce
¹/₄ cup peanut oil
cilantro leaves, to garnish

Line a large bamboo steamer with baking paper.
Arrange the oysters in a single layer on top.

Put the garlic, ginger and scallions in a bowl, mix
together well, then sprinkle over the oysters. Spoon
1 teaspoon of soy sauce over each oyster. Cover and
steam over a wok of simmering water for 2 minutes.

Heat the peanut oil in a small saucepan until smoking
and carefully drizzle a little over each oyster. Garnish
with the cilantro leaves and serve immediately.

Scallop Ceviche

🌸 SERVES 2–4
🌸 PREPARATION TIME: 20 MINUTES
🌸 COOKING TIME: NIL

16 scallops, on the shell
1 teaspoon finely grated lime zest
2 medium garlic cloves, chopped
2 medium red chilies, seeded and chopped
¹/₄ cup lime juice
1 tablespoon chopped Italian parsley
1 tablespoon olive oil

Take the scallops off their shells. Rinse and reserve
the shells. If the scallops need to be cut off, use a
small, sharp knife to slice them free, being careful to
leave as little meat on the shell as possible. Slice or
pull off any vein, membrane or hard white muscle,
leaving any roe attached.

In a non-metallic bowl, mix together the lime zest,
garlic, chili, lime juice, parsley and olive oil, and
season. Put the scallops in the dressing and stir to coat.
Cover with plastic wrap and refrigerate for 2 hours to
"cook" the scallop meat.

To serve, slide each scallop back onto a half shell and
spoon the dressing over. Serve cold.

NOTE: The scallops will keep for 2 days in the dressing.

Asian Oysters

Creamy Baked Scallops

❋ SERVES 4
❋ PREPARATION TIME: 20 MINUTES
❋ COOKING TIME: 10 MINUTES

24 scallops, on the shell
1 cup fish stock
1 cup dry white wine
¼ cup butter
4 medium scallions, chopped
1 medium bacon slice, finely chopped
1 cup thinly sliced button mushrooms
¼ cup all-purpose flour
¾ cup whipping cream
1 teaspoon lemon juice
1 cup fresh breadcrumbs
2 tablespoons melted butter, extra

Take the scallops off their shells. Rinse and reserve the shells. If the scallops need to be cut off, use a small, sharp knife to slice them free, being careful to leave as little meat on the shell as possible. Slice or pull off any vein, membrane or hard white muscle, leaving any roe attached. Cut the scallops in half.

Heat the fish stock and white wine in a saucepan and add the scallops. Cover and simmer over medium heat for 2–3 minutes, or until the scallops are opaque and tender. Remove the scallops with a slotted spoon, cover and set aside. Bring the liquid in the pan to a boil and reduce until 1½ cups remain.

Melt the butter in a saucepan and add the scallions, bacon and mushrooms. Cook over medium heat for 3 minutes, stirring occasionally, until the scallions are soft but not brown.

Stir in the flour and cook for 2 minutes. Remove from the heat and gradually stir in the reduced stock. Return to the heat and stir until the mixture boils and thickens. Reduce the heat and simmer for 2 minutes. Stir in the cream, lemon juice and season to taste. Cover, set aside and keep warm.

Combine the breadcrumbs and extra butter in a small bowl. Preheat the broiler to high.

Divide the scallops among the shells. Spoon the warm sauce over the scallops and sprinkle with the breadcrumb mixture. Place under the broiler until the breadcrumbs are golden brown. Serve immediately.

Carpaccio

❋ SERVES 8
❋ PREPARATION TIME: 15 MINUTES
❋ COOKING TIME: NIL

14 oz beef tenderloin
1 tablespoon extra virgin olive oil
arugula leaves, torn, to serve
²/₃ cup shaved parmesan cheese, to serve
medium black olives, cut into slivers,
    to serve

Remove all the visible fat and sinew from the beef, then freeze for 1–2 hours, until firm but not solid. This makes the meat easier to slice thinly.

Cut paper-thin slices of beef with a large, sharp knife. Arrange on a serving platter and allow to return to room temperature.

Just before serving, drizzle with oil, then scatter with arugula, parmesan and olives.

NOTE: The beef can be cut into slices a few hours in advance, covered and refrigerated. Drizzle with oil and garnish with the other ingredients just before serving.

Snails with Garlic and Herb Butter

❋ SERVES 6
❋ PREPARATION TIME: 15 MINUTES
❋ COOKING TIME: 5 MINUTES

1³/₄ cups canned snails
¹/₂ cup softened butter
4 medium garlic cloves, crushed
2 tablespoons chopped Italian parsley
2 teaspoons snipped chives
36 snail shells (available from specialty
    food stores), or use ovenproof
    ramekins
¹/₄ cup fresh white breadcrumbs

Preheat the oven to 400°F. Rinse the snails under cold water. Drain well and set aside. In a small bowl, combine the butter, garlic, parsley and chives until smooth. Season. Put a small amount of the butter and a snail in each shell. Seal the shells with the remaining butter and sprinkle with the breadcrumbs.

Place the snails on a baking sheet with the open end of the snail facing up so that the butter will not run out of the shell. Bake for 5–6 minutes, or until the butter is bubbling and the breadcrumbs are lightly browned. Serve with crusty baguettes.

Carpaccio

Stuffed Shrimp Omelets

❋ SERVES 8
❋ PREPARATION TIME: 25 MINUTES
❋ COOKING TIME: 15 MINUTES

1 lb 2 oz raw shrimp
1½ tablespoons oil
4 eggs, lightly beaten
2 tablespoons fish sauce
8 medium scallions, chopped
6 medium cilantro roots, chopped
2 medium garlic cloves, chopped
1 small red chili, seeded and chopped
2 teaspoons lime juice
2 teaspoons grated jaggery
    or unpacked brown sugar
3 tablespoons chopped cilantro leaves
1 small red chili, extra, chopped
    to garnish
cilantro sprigs, to garnish
sweet chili sauce, to serve

Peel the shrimp. Gently pull out the dark vein from the back of each shrimp, starting from the head end, then chop the shrimp meat.

Heat a wok over high heat, add 2 teaspoons of the oil and swirl to coat. Combine the egg with half of the fish sauce. Add 2 tablespoons of the mixture to the wok and swirl to a 6¼ inch round. Cook for 1 minute, then gently lift out. Repeat with the remaining egg mixture to make eight omelets.

Heat the remaining oil in the wok. Add the shrimp, scallions, cilantro root, garlic and chili. Stir-fry for 3–4 minutes, or until the shrimp are cooked. Stir in the lime juice, jaggery, cilantro leaves and the remaining fish sauce.

Divide the shrimp mixture among the omelets and fold each into a small firm parcel. Cut a slit in the top and garnish with the chili and cilantro sprigs. Serve with sweet chili sauce.

Quail in Grape Leaves

❋ SERVES 4
❋ PREPARATION TIME: 15 MINUTES
❋ COOKING TIME: 25 MINUTES

12 medium black grapes, halved
1 tablespoon olive oil
1 medium garlic clove, crushed
4 large quail
8 fresh or preserved vine leaves
4 medium prosciutto slices
black grapes, extra, halved, to garnish

Preheat the oven to 350°F. Toss the grapes with the oil and crushed garlic. Put six grape halves in the cavity of each quail.

If you are using fresh vine leaves, blanch them for 1 minute in boiling water, then remove the central stem. If using preserved vine leaves, wash them under running water to remove any excess preserving liquid.

Wrap each quail in a piece of prosciutto and place each quail on top of a vine leaf. Place another vine leaf on top of each quail and wrap into parcels, tying with string to secure. Bake on a baking sheet for 20–25 minutes, or until juices run clear when tested with a skewer. Serve garnished with the extra grapes.

Sweet and Sour Liver (Fegato Garbo e Dolce)

❋ SERVES 4
❋ PREPARATION TIME: 10 MINUTES
❋ COOKING TIME: 10 MINUTES

2²/₃ tablespoons butter
¹/₃ cup olive oil
1 lb 5 oz calves' livers, cut into
    long thin slices
1 cup fresh white breadcrumbs
1 tablespoon sugar
2 medium garlic cloves, crushed
¹/₄ cup red wine vinegar
1 tablespoon chopped Italian parsley

Heat the butter and half the oil in a heavy-based frying pan over medium heat. Coat the liver in breadcrumbs, pressing them on firmly with your hands. Shake off the excess and place in the pan when the butter begins to foam. Cook on each side for 1 minute, or until the crust is brown and crisp. Remove from the pan and keep warm.

Add the remaining oil to the frying pan and cook the sugar and garlic over low heat until golden. Add the vinegar and cook for 30 seconds, or until almost evaporated. Add the parsley and pour over the liver. Serve hot or at room temperature.

Quail in Vine Leaves

Savory Egg Custard

* PREPARATION TIME: 20 MINUTES
* COOKING TIME: 20 MINUTES

3/4 cup chopped chicken breast fillets
2 teaspoons sake
2 teaspoons Japanese soy sauce
2 medium leeks, sliced
1 small carrot, sliced
5 cups chopped spinach

CUSTARD
4 cups boiling water
1/2 cup dashi granules
2 tablespoons Japanese soy sauce
6 eggs

Place the chicken pieces into six heatproof bowls. Combine the sake and soy sauce, and pour the mixture over the chicken.

Divide the vegetables between the six bowls.

To make the custard, combine the water and dashi granules in a heatproof bowl and stir to dissolve; cool completely. Combine the dashi, soy sauce and eggs, and strain equal amounts into the six bowls.

Cover the bowls with foil, place them in a steamer, and cook on high for 20–30 minutes. Test the custard by inserting a fine skewer into the center; it is cooked when the skewer comes out with no moisture clinging to it. Serve immediately.

Rice and Peas (Risi e Bisi)

❋ SERVES 4
❋ PREPARATION TIME: 15 MINUTES
❋ COOKING TIME: 25 MINUTES

6 cups chicken or vegetable stock
2 teaspoons olive oil
2²⁄₃ tablespoons butter
1 small onion, finely chopped
½ cup cubed pancetta
2 tablespoons chopped Italian parsley
2½ cups young peas
1 cup risotto rice
½ cup freshly grated parmesan cheese

Pour the stock into a saucepan and bring to a boil. Reduce the heat, cover with a lid and keep at a low simmer.

Heat the oil and half the butter in a large wide heavy-based saucepan and cook the onion and pancetta over low heat for 5 minutes until softened. Stir in the parsley and peas and add two ladlefuls of the stock. Simmer for 6–8 minutes.

Add the rice and the remaining stock. Simmer until the rice is *al dente* and most of the stock has been absorbed. Stir in the remaining butter and the parmesan, season and serve.

Garlic Bucatini

❋ SERVES 4
❋ PREPARATION TIME: 10 MINUTES
❋ COOKING TIME: 20 MINUTES

5½ cups bucatini or penne
⅓ cup olive oil
8 medium garlic cloves, crushed
2 tablespoons chopped Italian parsley
freshly grated parmesan cheese, to serve

Cook the bucatini in a large saucepan of rapidly boiling water until *al dente*. Drain and return to the pan.

Heat the olive oil over low heat in a frying pan and add the garlic. Cook for 1 minute before removing from the heat. Add the garlic oil and the parsley to the pasta and toss to distribute thoroughly. Serve with parmesan cheese.

Rice and Peas (Risi e Bisi)

Duck Breast with Wild Rice

※ SERVES 4
※ PREPARATION TIME: 15 MINUTES
※ COOKING TIME: 1 HOUR

$\frac{1}{2}$ cup wild rice
2 teaspoons oil
$\frac{1}{2}$ cup roughly chopped pecans
$\frac{1}{2}$ teaspoon ground cinnamon
$\frac{1}{3}$ cup long-grain white rice
2 tablespoons finely chopped Italian
    parsley
4 medium scallions, thinly sliced
2 medium duck breasts
zest of 1 orange

DRESSING
$\frac{1}{3}$ cup olive oil
1 teaspoon grated orange zest
2 tablespoons orange juice
2 teaspoons walnut oil
1 tablespoon chopped preserved ginger

To make the dressing, thoroughly mix the ingredients together and season. Set aside.

Put the wild rice in a saucepan with $1\frac{1}{4}$ cups water. Bring to a boil and cook, covered, for 30 minutes, or until tender. Drain away any excess water.

Meanwhile, heat the oil in a large frying pan. Add the pecans and cook, stirring, until golden. Add the cinnamon and a pinch of salt, and cook for 1 minute.

Bring a large saucepan of water to a boil. Add the white rice and cook, stirring occasionally, for 12 minutes, or until tender. Drain and mix with the wild rice and pecans in a large, shallow bowl. Add the parsley and scallions. Add half the dressing and toss well.

Put the duck, skin side down, in a cold frying pan, then heat the pan over high heat. Cook for 5 minutes, or until crisp, then turn over and cook for another 5 minutes. Tip out any excess fat and add the remaining dressing and the orange zest, and cook until bubbling. Transfer the duck to a serving dish and slice, diagonally. Serve with the rice, drizzled with any juices.

Spaghettini with Garlic and Chili

※ SERVES 4–6
※ PREPARATION TIME: 10 MINUTES
※ COOKING TIME: 20 MINUTES

1 lb 2 oz spaghettini
1/2 cup extra virgin olive oil
2–3 medium garlic cloves, finely chopped
1–2 medium red chilies, seeded and finely
   chopped
3 tablespoons chopped Italian parsley
freshly grated parmesan cheese, to serve

Cook the spaghettini in a large saucepan of rapidly boiling salted water until *al dente*. Drain and return to the pan.

Meanwhile, heat the extra virgin olive oil in a large frying pan. Add the garlic and chili, and cook over very low heat for 2–3 minutes, or until the garlic is golden. Take care not to burn the garlic or chili as this will make the sauce bitter.

Toss the parsley and the oil, garlic and chili mixture through the pasta. Season. Serve with the parmesan.

Cheese Tortellini with Nutty Herb Sauce

※ SERVES 4–6
※ PREPARATION TIME: 15 MINUTES
※ COOKING TIME: 15 MINUTES

4 1/2 cups ricotta-filled fresh or
   dried tortellini or ravioli
1/4 cup butter
3/4 cup finely chopped walnuts
2/3 cup pine nuts
2 tablespoons chopped Italian parsley
2 teaspoons thyme
1/4 cup ricotta cheese
1/4 cup whipping cream

Add the pasta to a large saucepan of rapidly boiling water and cook until *al dente*. Drain and return to the pan.

To make the sauce, heat the butter in a heavy-based frying pan over medium heat until foaming. Add the walnuts and pine nuts and stir for 5 minutes, or until golden brown. Add the parsley, thyme and season.

Beat the ricotta with the cream. Add the sauce to the pasta and toss well to combine. Top with a dollop of ricotta cream. Serve immediately.

Spaghettini with Garlic and Chili

Fennel Risotto Balls with Cheesy Filling

❈ SERVES 4–6
❈ PREPARATION TIME: 30 MINUTES
❈ COOKING TIME: 50 MINUTES

6 cups vegetable stock
1 tablespoon oil
2 tablespoons butter
2 medium garlic cloves, crushed
1 medium onion, finely chopped
2 medium fennel bulbs, thinly sliced
1 tablespoon balsamic vinegar
$1/2$ cup dry white wine
3 cups risotto rice
$1/2$ cup freshly grated parmesan cheese
$1/2$ cup snipped chives
1 egg, lightly beaten
1 cup chopped sun-dried tomatoes
$2/3$ cup cubed mozzarella cheese
$1/2$ cup frozen peas, thawed
$1/2$ cup all-purpose flour, seasoned
3 eggs, extra
2 cups dry breadcrumbs
oil, for deep-frying

Pour the stock into a saucepan and bring to a boil. Reduce the heat, cover with a lid and keep at a low simmer.

Heat the oil and butter in a large saucepan and cook the garlic and onion over medium heat for 3 minutes, or until softened but not browned. Add the fennel and cook for 10 minutes, or until it starts to caramelize. Add the vinegar and wine, increase the heat and boil until the liquid evaporates. Stir in the rice until well coated.

Add $1/2$ cup hot stock, stirring constantly over medium heat until the liquid is absorbed. Continue adding more stock, $1/2$ cup at a time, stirring, for 20–25 minutes, or until all the stock is absorbed and the rice is tender and creamy.

Remove from the heat and stir in the parmesan, chives, egg and tomato. Transfer to a bowl, cover and cool. Put the mozzarella and peas in a bowl and mash together. Season.

Put the flour in one bowl, the extra eggs in another and the breadcrumbs in a third. Lightly beat the eggs. With wet hands, shape the risotto into 14 even balls. Flatten each ball out, slightly indenting the center. Put a heaped teaspoon of the pea mash into the indentation, then shape the rice around the filling to form a ball. Roll each ball in seasoned flour, then dip in the extra egg and roll in breadcrumbs. Place on a foil-covered tray and refrigerate for 30 minutes.

Fill a deep-fryer or large saucepan one-third full of oil and heat to 350°F, or until a cube of bread dropped into the oil browns in 15 seconds. Cook the risotto balls in batches for 5 minutes, or until golden and crisp and the cheese has melted inside. Drain on crumpled paper towels and season with salt. If the cheese has not melted by the end of the cooking time, cook the balls on a tray in a 350°F oven for 5 minutes. Serve with a salad.

Penne alla Napolitana

🌸 SERVES 4–6
🌸 PREPARATION TIME: 20 MINUTES
🌸 COOKING TIME: 25 MINUTES

2 tablespoons olive oil
1 medium onion, finely chopped
2–3 medium garlic cloves, finely chopped
1 small carrot, finely diced
1 medium celery stalk, finely diced
3¼ cups canned chopped tomatoes
    or 5 cups ripe peeled, chopped
    tomatoes
1 tablespoon concentrated tomato purée
3 tablespoons shredded basil
5½ cups penne
freshly grated parmesan cheese, to serve,
    optional

Heat the oil in a large frying pan. Add the onion and garlic and cook for 2 minutes, or until golden. Add the carrot and celery and cook for a further 2 minutes.

Add the tomato and concentrated tomato purée. Simmer for 20 minutes, or until the sauce thickens, stirring occasionally. Stir in the shredded basil and season to taste.

While the sauce is cooking, cook the pasta in a large saucepan of rapidly boiling salted water until *al dente*. Drain well and return to the pan.

Add the sauce to the pasta and mix well. Serve with freshly grated parmesan cheese, if desired.

Spaghetti Puttanesca

🌸 SERVES 6
🌸 PREPARATION TIME: 15 MINUTES
🌸 COOKING TIME: 20 MINUTES

⅓ cup olive oil
2 medium onions, finely chopped
3 medium garlic cloves, finely chopped
½ teaspoon chili flakes
6 large ripe tomatoes, diced
4 tablespoons capers, rinsed and
    squeezed dry
8 anchovy fillets in oil, drained and
    chopped
¾ cup medium Kalamata olives
3 tablespoons chopped Italian parsley
13 oz spaghetti

Heat the olive oil in a saucepan, add the onion and cook over medium heat for 5 minutes. Add the garlic and chili flakes to the saucepan and cook for 30 seconds. Add the tomato, capers and anchovies. Simmer over low heat for 10–15 minutes, or until the sauce is thick and pulpy. Stir the olives and parsley through the sauce.

While the sauce is cooking, cook the spaghetti in a large saucepan of rapidly boiling salted water until *al dente*. Drain and return to the pan.

Add the sauce to the pasta and stir it through. Season to taste and serve immediately.

Penne alla Napolitana

Herb-Filled Ravioli with Sage Butter

❋ SERVES 4
❋ PREPARATION TIME: 1 HOUR
❋ COOKING TIME: 10 MINUTES

PASTA
2½ cups all-purpose flour
3 eggs, beaten
¼ cup olive oil

FILLING
1 cup ricotta cheese
2 tablespoons freshly grated parmesan
    cheese, plus extra, shaved, to garnish
2 teaspoons snipped chives
1 tablespoon chopped Italian parsley
2 teaspoons chopped basil
1 teaspoon chopped thyme

SAGE BUTTER
¾ cup butter
12 sage leaves

Sift the flour into a bowl and make a well in the center. Gradually mix in the eggs and oil. Turn out onto a lightly floured surface and knead for 6 minutes, or until smooth. Cover with plastic wrap and leave for 30 minutes.

Mix together the ricotta, parmesan and herbs. Season.

Divide the dough into four even portions. Lightly flour a large work surface and using a floured long rolling pin, roll out one portion from the center to the edge. Continue, always rolling from in front of you outwards. Rotate the dough often. Fold the dough in half and roll it out again. Continue this process seven times to make a smooth circle of pasta about ¼ inch thick. Roll this sheet out quickly and smoothly to a thickness of ⅛ inch. Make four sheets of pasta, two slightly larger than the others. Cover with a dish towel.

Spread one of the smaller sheets out on a work surface and place heaped teaspoons of filling at 2 inch intervals. Brush a little water between the filling along the cutting lines. Place a larger sheet on top and firmly press the sheets together along the cutting lines. Cut the ravioli with a pastry wheel or knife and transfer to a lightly floured baking sheet. Repeat with the remaining dough and filling.

To make the sage butter, melt the butter over low heat in a small heavy-based saucepan, without stirring or shaking. Pour the clear butter into another container and discard any white sediment. Return the clarified butter to a clean pan and heat gently over medium heat. Add the sage leaves and cook until crisp but not brown. Remove, drain on paper towels and reserve the butter.

Cook the ravioli in batches in a large saucepan of salted simmering water for 5–6 minutes, or until tender. Top with warm sage butter and leaves and garnish with shaved parmesan.

NOTE: Don't cook the ravioli in rapidly boiling water or the squares will split and lose the filling.

Spaghetti Carbonara

※ SERVES 6
※ PREPARATION TIME: 10 MINUTES
※ COOKING TIME: 20 MINUTES

1 lb 2 oz spaghetti
8 medium bacon slices
4 eggs
1/2 cup freshly grated parmesan cheese
1 1/4 cups whipping cream
snipped chives, to garnish

Cook the spaghetti in a large saucepan of rapidly boiling salted water until *al dente*. Drain and return to the pan.

While the pasta is cooking, discard the bacon rind and cut the bacon into thin strips. Cook in a heavy-based frying pan over medium heat until crisp. Remove and drain on paper towels.

Beat the eggs, parmesan and cream in a bowl until well combined. Add the bacon and pour the sauce over the warm pasta. Toss gently until pasta is well coated.

Return the pan to the heat and cook over low heat for 1 minute, or until slightly thickened. Season with freshly ground black pepper and serve garnished with snipped chives.

Fettucine Alfredo

※ SERVES 6
※ PREPARATION TIME: 10 MINUTES
※ COOKING TIME: 15 MINUTES

1 lb 2 oz fettucine or tagliatelle
1/3 cup butter
1 1/2 cups freshly grated
   parmesan cheese
1 1/4 cups whipping cream
3 tablespoons chopped Italian parsley

Cook the pasta in a large saucepan of rapidly boiling salted water until *al dente*. Drain and return to the pan.

Meanwhile, heat the butter in a saucepan over low heat. Add the parmesan and cream and bring to a boil, stirring constantly. Reduce the heat and simmer for 10 minutes, or until the sauce has thickened slightly. Add the parsley, season to taste and stir well to combine. Add the sauce to the warm pasta and toss well to combine.

Spaghetti Carbonara

Lemony Herb and Fish Risotto

※ SERVES 4
※ PREPARATION TIME: 20 MINUTES
※ COOKING TIME: 30 MINUTES

1/4 cup butter
14 oz skinless white fish fillets, cut into
    1 1/4 inch cubes
5 cups fish stock
1 medium onion, finely chopped
1 medium garlic clove, crushed
1 teaspoon ground turmeric
1 1/2 cups risotto rice
2 tablespoons lemon juice
1 tablespoon chopped Italian parsley
1 tablespoon chopped chives
1 tablespoon chopped dill

Melt half the butter in a frying pan. Add the fish in batches and fry over medium–high heat for 3 minutes, or until the fish is just cooked through. Remove from the pan and set aside.

Pour the fish stock into another pan, bring to a boil, cover and keep at simmering point.

To the first pan, add the remaining butter, onion and garlic and cook over medium heat for 3 minutes, or until the onion is tender. Add the turmeric and stir for 1 minute. Add the rice and stir to coat, then add 1/2 cup of the fish stock and cook, stirring constantly, over low heat until all the stock has been absorbed. Continue adding 1/2 cup of stock at a time until all the stock has been added and the rice is translucent, tender and creamy.

Stir in the lemon juice, parsley, chives and dill. Add the fish and stir gently. Serve, maybe garnished with slices of lemon or lime and fresh herb sprigs.

NOTE: The rice must absorb the stock between each addition — the whole process will take about 20 minutes. If you don't have time to make your own stock, you can buy fresh or frozen fish stock from delicatessens, some seafood outlets and most supermarkets.

Fettucine with Zucchini and Crisp Fried Basil

🌸 SERVES 6
🌸 PREPARATION TIME: 15 MINUTES
🌸 COOKING TIME: 15 MINUTES

1 cup olive oil
handful basil leaves
1 lb 2 oz fettucine or tagliatelle
3½ cups medium zucchini
¼ cup butter
2 medium garlic cloves, crushed
¾ cup freshly grated parmesan cheese

To crisp-fry the basil leaves, heat the oil in a small frying pan, add two leaves at a time and cook for 1 minute, or until crisp. Remove with a slotted spoon and drain on paper towel. Repeat with the remaining basil leaves.

Cook the fettucine in a large saucepan of rapidly boiling salted water until *al dente*. Drain and return to the pan.

While the pasta is cooking, grate the zucchini. Heat the butter in a deep heavy-based saucepan over low heat until the butter is foaming. Add the garlic and cook for 1 minute. Add the zucchini and cook, stirring occasionally, for 1–2 minutes or until softened. Add to the hot pasta. Add the parmesan and toss well. Serve the pasta garnished with the crisp basil leaves.

NOTE: The basil leaves can be fried up to 2 hours in advance. Store in an airtight container after cooling.

Blue Cheese Tagliatelle

🌸 SERVES 6
🌸 PREPARATION TIME: 15 MINUTES
🌸 COOKING TIME: 20 MINUTES

2 medium zucchini
2 tablespoons butter
1 medium garlic clove, crushed
3½ fl oz white wine
¾ cup crumbled blue cheese
¼ cup whipping cream
1 lb 2 oz white or green tagliatelle
2–3 tablespoons freshly grated parmesan cheese
chopped Italian parsley, to garnish

Slice the zucchini. Melt the butter in a frying pan. Add the zucchini and garlic and cook until the zucchini is tender. Stir in the wine, cheese, cream and a pinch of black pepper. Simmer for 10 minutes.

Meanwhile, cook the tagliatelle in a large saucepan of rapidly boiling salted water until *al dente*. Drain, rinse under warm water and drain again.

Return the pasta to the pan. Add the sauce and toss through the pasta for a few minutes over low heat. Serve sprinkled with the parmesan and parsley.

Fettucine with Zucchini and Crisp Fried Basil

Tagliatelle with Chicken Livers and Cream

* SERVES 4
* PREPARATION TIME: 12 MINUTES
* COOKING TIME: 15 MINUTES

13 oz tagliatelle
10½ oz chicken livers
2 tablespoons olive oil
1 medium onion, finely chopped
1 medium garlic clove, crushed
1 cup whipping cream
1 tablespoon snipped chives
1 teaspoon wholegrain mustard
2 eggs, beaten
freshly grated parmesan cheese, to serve
snipped chives, to serve

Cook the tagliatelle in a large saucepan of rapidly boiling salted water until *al dente*. Drain and return to the pan.

While the pasta is cooking, trim any green or discolored parts from the chicken livers, then slice them. Heat the olive oil in a large frying pan. Add the onion and garlic and stir over low heat until the onion is tender.

Add the chicken liver to the pan and cook gently for 2–3 minutes. Remove from the heat and stir in the cream, chives and mustard and season to taste. Return to the heat and bring to a boil. Add the beaten eggs and stir quickly to combine. Remove from the heat.

Add the sauce to the hot pasta and toss well to combine. Serve sprinkled with parmesan and snipped chives.

Linguine Pesto

❋ SERVES 4–6
❋ PREPARATION TIME: 15 MINUTES
❋ COOKING TIME: 15 MINUTES

2 cups firmly packed basil
2 medium garlic cloves, crushed
¼ cup pine nuts, toasted
¾ cup olive oil
½ cup freshly grated parmesan cheese,
    plus extra, to serve
1 lb 2 oz linguine

Process the basil, garlic and pine nuts together in a food processor. With the motor running, add the oil in a steady stream until mixed to a smooth paste. Transfer to a bowl, stir in the parmesan and season to taste.

Cook the pasta in a large saucepan of rapidly boiling salted water until *al dente*. Drain and return to the pan. Toss enough of the pesto through the pasta to coat it well. Serve sprinkled with parmesan.

NOTE: Refrigerate any leftover pesto in an airtight jar for up to a week. Cover the surface with a layer of oil. Freeze for up to a month.

Spaghetti Vongole

❋ SERVES 4
❋ PREPARATION TIME: 25 MINUTES
❋ COOKING TIME: 35 MINUTES

5 cups small clams in shell or
    canned clams in brine
1 tablespoon lemon juice
⅓ cup olive oil
3 medium garlic cloves, crushed
3½ cups canned crushed
    tomatoes
9 oz spaghetti
4 tablespoons chopped Italian parsley

If using fresh clams, clean thoroughly. Place in a large saucepan with the lemon juice. Cover the pan and shake over medium heat for 7–8 minutes until the shells open, discarding any clams that don't open. Remove the clam flesh from the shell of the opened clams and set aside; discard the empty shells. If using canned clams, drain, rinse well and set aside.

Heat the oil in a large saucepan. Add the garlic and cook over low heat for 5 minutes. Add the tomato and stir to combine. Bring to a boil and simmer, covered, for 20 minutes. Add freshly ground black pepper, to taste, and the clams, and stir until heated through.

While the sauce is cooking, cook the spaghetti in a large saucepan of rapidly boiling salted water until *al dente*. Drain and return to the pan. Gently stir in the sauce and the chopped parsley until combined.

Linguine Pesto

Vol~au~vents

* SERVES 4
* PREPARATION TIME: 20 MINUTES
* COOKING TIME: 30 MINUTES

2 sheets frozen puff pastry,
   thawed
1 egg, lightly beaten

SAUCE AND FILLING
$2^2/_3$ tablespoons butter
2 medium scallions, finely chopped
2 tablespoons all-purpose flour
$1^1/_2$ cups whole milk
your choice of filling (see Note)

Preheat the oven to 425°F. Line a baking sheet with baking paper. Roll out the pastry to an 8 inch square. Cut four circles of pastry with a 4 inch cutter. Place the rounds onto the tray and cut $2^1/_2$ inch circles into the center of the rounds with a cutter, taking care not to cut right through the pastry. Place the baking sheet in the refrigerator for 15 minutes.

Using a floured knife blade, "knock up" the sides of each pastry round by making even indentations about $^1/_2$ inch apart around the circumference. This should allow even rising of the pastry as it cooks. The dough can be made ahead of time up to this stage and frozen until needed.

Carefully brush the pastry with the egg, avoiding the "knocked up" edge as any glaze spilt on the sides will stop the pastry from rising. Bake for 15–20 minutes, or until the pastry has risen and is golden brown and crisp. Cool on a wire rack. Remove the center from each pastry circle and pull out and discard any partially cooked pastry from the center. The pastry can be returned to the oven for 2 minutes to dry out if the center is undercooked. The pastry cases are now ready to be filled with a hot filling before serving.

To make the sauce, melt the butter in a saucepan, add the scallions and stir over low heat for 2 minutes, or until soft. Add the flour and stir for 2 minutes, or until lightly golden. Gradually add the milk, stirring until smooth. Stir constantly over medium heat for 4 minutes, or until the mixture boils and thickens. Season well. Remove and stir in your choice of filling (see Note).

NOTE: Add 2 cups of any of the following to your white sauce: sliced, cooked mushrooms; peeled, deveined and cooked shrimp; chopped, cooked chicken breast; poached, flaked salmon; cooked and dressed crabmeat; oysters; steamed asparagus spears.

Spinach and Ricotta Gnocchi

🌼 SERVES 4–6

🌼 PREPARATION TIME: 45 MINUTES

🌼 COOKING TIME: 30 MINUTES

4 slices white bread
1/2 cup whole milk
10 cups frozen spinach, thawed
1 cup ricotta cheese
2 eggs
1/2 cup freshly grated parmesan cheese
1/4 cup all-purpose flour
parmesan cheese shavings, to serve

Remove the crust from the bread and soak the bread in the milk, in a shallow dish, for 10 minutes. Squeeze out all the excess liquid. Squeeze the excess liquid from the spinach.

Combine the bread in a bowl with the spinach, ricotta, eggs and parmesan, then season. Use a fork to mix thoroughly. Cover and refrigerate for 1 hour.

Lightly dust your hands in flour. Roll heaped teaspoonfuls of the mixture into dumplings. Lower batches of the gnocchi into a large saucepan of boiling salted water. Cook for about 2 minutes, or until the gnocchi rise to the surface. Transfer to serving plates. Drizzle with foaming butter, if you wish, and serve with the parmesan shavings.

Pasta and Spinach Timbales

🌼 SERVES 6

🌼 PREPARATION TIME: 25 MINUTES

🌼 COOKING TIME: 45 MINUTES

2 tablespoons butter
1 tablespoon olive oil
1 medium onion, chopped
2 1/2 cups spinach, steamed and well
   drained
8 eggs, lightly beaten
1 cup whipping cream
3 1/2 oz spaghetti or taglioni, cooked
1/2 cup grated cheddar cheese
1/2 cup freshly grated parmesan cheese

Preheat the oven to 350°F. Brush six 1-cup ramekins with some melted butter or oil. Line the bases with baking paper. Heat the butter and oil together in a frying pan. Add the onion and stir over low heat until the onion is tender. Add the well-drained spinach and cook for 1 minute. Remove from the heat and leave to cool. Whisk in the eggs and cream. Stir in the spaghetti and grated cheeses then season to taste. Stir well and spoon into the prepared ramekins.

Place the ramekins in an ovenproof dish. Pour boiling water into the dish to come halfway up the sides of the ramekins. Bake for 30–35 minutes, or until set. Halfway through cooking you may need to cover the top with foil to prevent excess browning. Near the end of cooking time, test the timbales with the point of a knife. When cooked, the knife should come out clean.

Allow the timbales to rest for 15 minutes before turning them out. Run the point of a knife around the edge of each ramekin. Invert onto serving plates.

Spinach and Ricotta Gnocchi

Moroccan Chicken Pie

※ SERVES 6–8
※ PREPARATION TIME: 30 MINUTES
※ COOKING TIME: 1 HOUR 20 MINUTES

3/4 cup butter
3 lb 5 oz chicken, cut into 4 portions
1 large onion, finely chopped
3 teaspoons ground cinnamon
1 teaspoon ground ginger
2 teaspoons ground cumin
1/4 teaspoon cayenne pepper
1/2 teaspoon ground turmeric
1/2 teaspoon saffron threads soaked in
    2 tablespoons warm water
1/2 cup chicken stock
4 eggs, lightly beaten
1/2 cup chopped cilantro
3 tablespoons chopped Italian parsley
1/3 cup chopped almonds
1/4 cup confectioners' sugar
16 sheets filo pastry
confectioners' sugar, extra, to dust

Preheat the oven to 350°F. Grease a 12 inch pizza tray.

Melt 2²/₃ tablespoons butter of the butter in a large frying pan. Add the chicken, onion, 2 teaspoons of the cinnamon, all the other spices and the stock. Season, cover and simmer for 30 minutes, or until the chicken is cooked through.

Remove the chicken from the sauce. When cool enough to handle, remove the meat from the bones, discard the skin and bones and shred the meat into thin strips.

Bring the liquid in the pan to a simmer and add the eggs. Cook the mixture, stirring constantly, until the eggs are cooked and the mixture is quite dry. Add the chicken, chopped cilantro and parsley, season well and mix. Remove from the heat.

Bake the almonds on a baking sheet until golden brown. Cool slightly, then blend in a food processor or spice grinder with the icing sugar and remaining cinnamon until they resemble coarse crumbs.

Melt the remaining butter. Place a sheet of filo on the pizza tray and brush with melted butter. Place another sheet on top in a pinwheel effect and brush with butter. Continue brushing and layering until you have used eight sheets. Put the chicken mixture on top and sprinkle with the almond mixture.

Fold the overlapping filo over the top of the filling. Place a sheet of filo over the top and brush with butter. Continue to layer buttered filo over the top in the same pinwheel effect until you have used eight sheets. Tuck the overhanging edges over the pie to form a neat round parcel. Brush well with the remaining butter. Bake the pie for 40–45 minutes, or until cooked through and golden. Dust with icing sugar before serving.

Cheese and Mushroom Pies

❋ SERVES 6
❋ PREPARATION TIME: 40 MINUTES
❋ COOKING TIME: 30 MINUTES

$2^{2}/_{3}$ tablespoons butter

2 medium garlic cloves, crushed

$5^{1}/_{2}$ cups sliced button mushrooms

1 small red bell pepper, seeded,
    membrane removed and finely chopped

$^{2}/_{3}$ cup sour cream

3 teaspoons wholegrain mustard

$^{1}/_{2}$ cup finely grated gruyère
    or cheddar cheese

6 sheets frozen puff pastry, thawed

$^{1}/_{2}$ cup finely grated gruyère
    or cheddar cheese, extra

1 egg, lightly beaten, to glaze

Preheat the oven to 375°F. Lightly grease two baking sheets with melted butter or oil. Heat the butter in a large frying pan. Add the garlic and mushrooms and cook over medium heat, stirring occasionally, until the mushrooms are tender and the liquid has evaporated. Remove from the heat and cool. Stir in the red pepper.

Combine the sour cream, mustard and cheese. Cut 12 circles with a $5^{1}/_{2}$ inch diameter from the pastry. Spread the cream mixture over six of the circles, leaving a $^{1}/_{2}$ inch border. Top each with mushroom mixture. Sprinkle each with 2 teaspoons of the extra cheese. Brush the outer edges with beaten egg then place the reserved pastry rounds on top of the filling, sealing the edges with a fork. Brush the tops of the pastry with egg. Sprinkle the remaining cheese over the pastry. Place the pies on baking sheets and bake for 20 minutes, or until lightly browned and puffed.

Pissaladière

❋ SERVES 8
❋ PREPARATION TIME: 50 MINUTES
❋ COOKING TIME: 2 HOURS

2 teaspoons dried yeast
1 teaspoon sugar
2½ cups white bread flour
2 tablespoons milk powder
1 tablespoon vegetable oil

TOMATO AND ONION TOPPING
⅓ cup olive oil
3–4 medium garlic cloves, finely chopped
6 medium onions, cut into thin rings
1¾ cup canned chopped tomatoes
1 tablespoon concentrated tomato purée
½ cup chopped Italian parsley
1 tablespoon chopped thyme
½ cup canned anchovy fillets,
   drained and halved lengthways
36 small black olives

Lightly grease two 12 inch pizza trays. Put the yeast, sugar and 1 cup warm water in a small bowl and stir well. Leave in a warm, draught-free place for 10 minutes, or until bubbles appear on the surface. The mixture should be frothy and slightly increased in volume. If your yeast doesn't foam, it is dead, so you will have to discard it and start again.

Sift 2 cups of the flour, the milk powder and ½ teaspoon salt into a large bowl and make a well in the center. Add the oil and yeast mixture and mix thoroughly. Turn out onto a lightly floured surface and knead for 10 minutes, gradually adding small amounts of the remaining flour, until the dough is smooth and elastic.

Place in an oiled bowl and brush the surface with oil. Cover with plastic wrap and leave in a warm place for 30 minutes, or until doubled in size.

To make the topping, heat the oil in a saucepan. Add the garlic and onion and cook, covered, over low heat for about 40 minutes, stirring frequently. The onion should be softened but not browned. Uncover and cook, stirring frequently, for another 30 minutes, or until lightly golden. Take care not to burn. Allow to cool.

Put the tomatoes in a saucepan and cook over medium heat, stirring frequently, for 20 minutes, or until thick and reduced to about 1 cup. Remove from the heat and stir in the concentrated tomato purée and herbs. Season to taste. Cool, then stir into the onion mixture.

Preheat the oven to 425°F. Punch down the dough, then turn out onto a floured surface and knead for 2 minutes. Divide in half. Return one half to the bowl and cover. Roll the other out to a 12 inch circle and press into the tray. Brush with olive oil. Spread half the onion and tomato mixture evenly over the dough, leaving a small border. Arrange half the anchovy fillets over the top in a lattice pattern and place an olive in each square. Repeat with the rest of the dough and topping. Bake for 15–20 minutes, or until the dough is cooked through and lightly browned.

Gnocchi Romana

❋ SERVES 4
❋ PREPARATION TIME: 20 MINUTES
❋ COOKING TIME: 40 MINUTES

3 cups whole milk
½ teaspoon freshly grated nutmeg
⅔ cup semolina
1 egg, beaten
1½ cups freshly grated parmesan cheese
¼ cup melted butter
½ cup whipping cream
½ cup freshly grated mozzarella cheese

Line a deep jelly roll tin with baking paper. Combine the milk and half the nutmeg in a saucepan and season to taste. Bring to a boil, reduce the heat and gradually stir in the semolina. Cook, stirring occasionally, for 5–10 minutes, or until the semolina is very stiff.

Remove the pan from the heat, add the egg and 1 cup of the parmesan. Stir to combine and then spread the mixture in the prepared tin. Refrigerate for 1 hour, or until the mixture is firm.

Preheat the oven to 350°F. Lightly grease a shallow casserole dish. Cut the semolina into rounds using a floured 1½ inch cutter and arrange in the dish.

Pour the melted butter over the top, followed by the cream. Combine the remaining grated parmesan with the mozzarella and sprinkle them on the rounds. Sprinkle with the remaining nutmeg. Bake for 20–25 minutes, or until the mixture is golden.

Potato and Onion Pizza

※ SERVES 4
※ PREPARATION TIME: 40 MINUTES
※ COOKING TIME: 45 MINUTES

2 teaspoons dried yeast
1/2 teaspoon sugar
1 1/2 cups white bread flour
1 cup whole-wheat all-purpose flour
1 tablespoon olive oil

TOPPING
1 large red bell pepper
1 medium potato
1 large onion, sliced
1 cup soft goat's cheese, crumbled
  into small pieces
1/4 cup capers
1 tablespoon dried oregano
1 teaspoon olive oil

Mix the yeast, sugar, a pinch of salt and 1 cup warm water in a bowl. Leave in a warm, draught-free place for 10 minutes, or until bubbles appear on the surface. The mixture should be frothy and slightly increased in volume. If your yeast doesn't foam, it is dead, so you will have to discard it and start again.

Sift both flours into a bowl. Make a well in the center, add the yeast mixture and mix to a firm dough. Knead on a lightly floured surface for 5 minutes, or until smooth. Place in a lightly oiled bowl, cover with plastic wrap or a damp dish towel and leave in a warm, draught-free place for 1–1 1/2 hours, or until doubled in size.

Preheat the oven to 400°F. Brush a 12 inch pizza tray with oil. Punch down the dough and knead for 2 minutes. Roll out to a 14 inch round. Put the dough on the tray and tuck the edge over to form a rim.

To make the topping, cut the red pepper into large flattish pieces and remove the membrane and seeds. Place, skin side up, under a hot broiler until blackened. Cool in a plastic bag, then peel away the skin and cut the flesh into narrow strips.

Cut the potato into paper-thin slices and arrange over the base with the red pepper, onion and half the cheese. Sprinkle with the capers, oregano and 1 teaspoon cracked pepper and drizzle with oil. Brush the crust edge with oil and bake for 20 minutes. Add the remaining cheese and bake for 15–20 minutes, or until the crust has browned. Serve in wedges.

Sweet Potato, Feta and Pine Nut Strudel

❋ SERVES 6
❋ PREPARATION TIME: 25 MINUTES
❋ COOKING TIME: 65 MINUTES

3 cups sweet potato, cut into ³/₄ inch cubes
1 tablespoon olive oil
¹/₂ cup pine nuts, toasted (see Note)
1²/₃ cups crumbled feta cheese
2 tablespoons chopped basil
4 medium scallions, chopped
2²/₃ tablespoons melted butter
2 tablespoons olive oil, extra, for brushing
7 sheets filo pastry
2–3 teaspoons sesame seeds

Preheat the oven to 350°F. Brush the sweet potato with oil and bake for 20 minutes, or until softened and slightly colored. Transfer to a bowl and cool slightly.

Add the pine nuts, feta, basil and scallions to the bowl, mix gently and season to taste.

Mix the butter and extra oil. Remove one sheet of filo and cover the rest with a damp dish towel to prevent them from drying out. Brush each sheet of filo with the butter mixture and layer them into a pile.

Spread the prepared filling in the center of the filo, covering an area about 4 x 12 inches. Fold the sides of the pastry into the center, then tuck in the ends. Carefully turn the strudel over and place on a baking sheet, seam side down. Lightly brush the top with the butter mixture and sprinkle with sesame seeds. Bake for 35 minutes, or until the pastry is crisp and golden. Serve warm.

NOTE: To toast pine nuts, dry-fry them in a frying pan, stirring and watching them constantly so they don't burn.

Fish Wellington

🌼 SERVES 6

🌼 PREPARATION TIME: 30 MINUTES

🌼 COOKING TIME: 1 HOUR 15 MINUTES

2²/₃ tablespoons butter

3 medium onions, thinly sliced

2 x 10½ oz skinless firm white fish
   fillets (each 12 inches long)

½ teaspoon sweet paprika

2 medium red bell peppers, quartered,
   seeded and membrane removed

1 large eggplant, cut into ½ inch thick
   slices

2 sheets frozen puff pastry, thawed

⅓ cup dry breadcrumbs

1 egg, lightly beaten

1 cup plain yogurt

1–2 tablespoons chopped dill

Melt the butter in a saucepan, add the sliced onion and stir to coat. Cover and cook over low heat, stirring occasionally, for 15 minutes. Uncover and cook, stirring, for 15 minutes, or until the onion is very soft and lightly browned. Cool, then season to taste.

Rub one side of each fish fillet with paprika. Place one on top of the other, with the paprika on the outside. If the fillets have a thin and a thick end, sandwich together so the thickness is even along the length (thin ends on top of thick ends).

Cook the red pepper quarters, skin side up, under a hot broiler until the skin blackens and blisters. Cool in a plastic bag, then peel. Place the eggplant on a greased baking sheet and brush with oil. Sprinkle with salt and pepper. Broil until golden, then turn to brown the other side.

Preheat the oven to 425°F. Roll the pastry out on a lightly floured surface until large enough to enclose the fish, about 10 x 14 inches. The pastry size and shape will be determined by the fish. Sprinkle the breadcrumbs lengthways along the center of the pastry and place the fish over the breadcrumbs. Top with the onion, then a layer of red pepper, followed by a layer of eggplant.

Brush the pastry edges with beaten egg. Fold the pastry over, pinching firmly together to seal. Use any trimmings to decorate. Brush with egg, then bake for 30 minutes. Cover loosely with foil if the pastry is overbrowning. Slice to serve.

Mix the yogurt and dill with a little salt and pepper in a bowl. Serve with the Wellington.

Goat's Cheese Galette

❋ SERVES 6

❋ PREPARATION TIME: 20 MINUTES

❋ COOKING TIME: 1 HOUR 15 MINUTES

PASTRY
1 cup plain all-purpose flour
¼ cup olive oil

FILLING
1 tablespoon olive oil
2 medium onions, thinly sliced
1 teaspoon thyme
½ cup ricotta cheese
¼ cup goat's cheese
2 tablespoons pitted niçoise olives
1 egg, beaten
¼ cup whipping cream

To make the pastry, sift the flour and a pinch of salt into a bowl and make a well in the center. Add the olive oil and mix with a flat-bladed knife until crumbly. Gradually add $^1/_4 - ^1/_3$ cup water until the mixture comes together. Remove and pat together to form a disc. Refrigerate for 30 minutes.

Meanwhile, to make the filling, heat the oil in a frying pan. Add the onion, cover and cook for 30 minutes. Season and stir in half the thyme. Cool.

Preheat the oven to 350°F. Lightly flour the workbench and roll out the pastry to a 12 inch circle. Then put on a heated baking tray. Evenly spread the onion over the pastry, leaving a $^3/_4$ inch border. Sprinkle the ricotta and goat's cheese evenly over the onion. Put the olives over the cheeses, then sprinkle with the remaining thyme. Fold the pastry border in to the edge of the filling, pleating as you go.

Combine the egg and cream, then pour over the filling. Bake in the lower half of the oven for 45 minutes, or until the pastry is golden.

entrées

Seafood Paella

2 medium tomatoes
4 cups raw shrimp
3 cups black mussels
1¼ cups squid rings
¼ cup olive oil
1 large onion, diced
3 medium garlic cloves, finely chopped
1 small red bell pepper, seeded
   and membrane removed, thinly sliced
1 small red chili, seeded and chopped,
   optional
2 teaspoons paprika
1 teaspoon ground turmeric
1 tablespoon concentrated tomato purée
2 cups paella rice or risotto rice
½ cup dry white wine
¼ teaspoon saffron threads, soaked in
   ¼ cup hot water
5 cups fish stock
1½ cups diced skinless firm white fish
   fillets
3 tablespoons chopped Italian parsley,
   to serve
lemon wedges, to serve

Score a cross in the base of each tomato. Put the tomatoes in a heatproof bowl and cover with boiling water. Leave for 30 seconds, then transfer to cold water and peel the skin away from the cross. Cut each tomato in half, scoop out the seeds and finely chop the flesh.

Peel the shrimp, leaving the tails intact. Gently pull out the dark vein from the back of each shrimp, starting at the head end. Scrub the mussels with a stiff brush and pull out the hairy beards. Discard any broken mussels or open ones that don't close when tapped on the bench. Rinse well. Refrigerate the seafood (including the squid), covered, until ready to use.

Heat the oil in a paella pan or large, deep frying pan with a lid. Add the onion, garlic, pepper and chili to the pan and cook over medium heat for 2 minutes, or until the onion and pepper are soft. Add the paprika, turmeric and 1 teaspoon salt and stir-fry for 1–2 minutes, or until fragrant. Add the chopped tomato and cook for 5 minutes, or until softened. Add the concentrated tomato purée. Stir in the rice until it's well coated.

Pour in the wine and simmer until almost absorbed. Add the saffron and its soaking liquid and all the fish stock and bring to a boil. Reduce the heat and simmer for 20 minutes, or until almost all the liquid is absorbed into the rice. There is no need to stir the rice, but you may occasionally wish to fluff it up with a fork to separate the grains.

Add the mussels to the pan, poking the shells into the rice, cover and cook for 1–2 minutes over low heat. Add the shrimp and cook for 2–3 minutes. Add the fish, cover and cook for 3 minutes. Finally, add the squid rings and cook for 1–2 minutes. By this time, the mussels should have opened; discard any unopened ones. Cook for another 2–3 minutes if the seafood is not quite cooked, but avoid overcooking or it will toughen and dry out. Remove the pan from the heat, cover loosely with foil and leave to rest for 5–10 minutes. Serve with the parsley and lemon wedges.

Seafood Stew (Zarzuela)

❋ SERVES 4
❋ PREPARATION TIME: 40 MINUTES
❋ COOKING TIME: 1 HOUR 10 MINUTES

1 x 14 oz raw lobster tail
12–15 black mussels
3 1/2 cups diced skinless firm white fish
    fillets
all-purpose flour, seasoned
2–3 tablespoons olive oil
3/4 cup squid rings
12 large raw shrimp
1/2 cup white wine
1/2 cup brandy
3 tablespoons chopped parsley,
    to garnish

SOFRITO SAUCE
2 large tomatoes
1 tablespoon olive oil
2 medium onions, finely chopped
1 tablespoon concentrated tomato purée

PICADA SAUCE
3 slices white bread, crusts removed
1 tablespoon toasted almonds
3 medium garlic cloves
1 tablespoon olive oil

To make the sofrito sauce, score a cross in the base of each tomato. Put in a heatproof bowl and cover with boiling water. Leave for 30 seconds, transfer to cold water and peel the skin away from the cross. Cut the tomatoes in half, scoop out the seeds and chop the flesh.

Heat the oil in a saucepan over medium heat. Add the onion and stir for 5 minutes without browning. Add the tomato, tomato purée and 1/2 cup water and stir over medium heat for 10 minutes. Stir in another 1/2 cup water, season and set aside.

To make the picada sauce, finely chop the bread, almonds and garlic in a food processor. With the motor running, gradually add the oil to form a paste, adding another 1/2 tablespoon of oil if necessary.

Preheat the oven to 350°F. Cut the lobster tail into rounds through the membrane that separates the shell segments and set aside. Scrub the mussels with a stiff brush and pull out the hairy beards. Discard any broken mussels, or open ones that don't close when tapped on the bench. Rinse well.

Lightly coat the fish in flour. Heat the oil in a large frying pan and fry the fish in batches over medium heat for 2–3 minutes, or until cooked and golden brown all over. Transfer to a large casserole dish. Add a little oil to the pan if necessary, add the squid and cook, stirring, for 1–2 minutes. Remove and add to the fish. Cook the lobster rounds and shrimp for 2–3 minutes, or until the shrimp turn pink, then add to the soup.

Add the wine to the pan and bring to a boil. Reduce the heat, add the mussels, cover and steam for 4–5 minutes. Add to the soup, discarding any unopened mussels. Pour the brandy into one side of the pan and, when it has warmed, carefully ignite the brandy. Gently shake the pan until the flames die down. Pour over the seafood in the casserole dish. Pour the sofrito sauce over the top. Cover and bake for 20 minutes. Stir in the picada sauce and cook for a further 10 minutes, or until warmed through. Sprinkle with parsley and serve.

Indonesian Sambal Squid

❋ SERVES 6
❋ PREPARATION TIME: 20 MINUTES
❋ COOKING TIME: 15 MINUTES

2 lb 4 oz cleaned squid rings
1 tablespoon white vinegar
1 tablespoon tamarind pulp
$1/3$ cup boiling water
4 medium red Asian shallots, finely
   chopped
8 small red chilies, half of them seeded,
   chopped
6 medium garlic cloves
1 medium lemongrass stem, white part
   only, chopped
2 teaspoons grated fresh ginger
$1/2$ teaspoon shrimp paste
$2^{1}/2$ tablespoons peanut oil
$1/2$ teaspoon ground cumin
$1^{1}/2$ tablespoons unpacked brown sugar
steamed rice, to serve

Cut each squid ring in half lengthways and open out flat, with the inside uppermost. Score a shallow diamond pattern all over the squid rings, taking care not to cut all the way through. Cut the rings into 2 inch squares. Put the pieces in a bowl with the vinegar and 4 cups water and soak for 10 minutes, then rinse and drain the squid and set aside.

Put the tamarind in a bowl and pour in the boiling water. Allow to steep for 5 minutes, breaking up the pulp as it softens. Strain into a bowl and discard the solids.

Put the shallots, chili, garlic, lemongrass, ginger, shrimp paste and 1 teaspoon of the oil in a small food processor or mortar and pestle and blend or pound until a smooth paste is formed. Stir in the cumin.

Heat a non-stick wok over high heat, add 1 tablespoon of the oil and swirl to coat the base and side. Add the paste and cook for 5 minutes, or until it is fragrant, glossy and the liquid has evaporated. Remove from the wok.

Reheat the wok to very hot, add the remaining oil and swirl to coat. Add the squid pieces in small batches and stir-fry for 1–2 minutes, or until cooked through. Remove from the wok.

Reduce the heat to medium, then add the paste, strained tamarind water and sugar. Stir-fry for 2 minutes, or until the sauce ingredients are well combined. Return the squid to the wok and stir-fry for 1 minute, or until the squid is well coated with the sauce and heated through. Serve with steamed rice.

Steamed Fish Cutlets with Ginger and Chili

❋ SERVES 4
❋ PREPARATION TIME: 15 MINUTES
❋ COOKING TIME: 10 MINUTES

4 x 7 oz skinless firm white fish cutlets
2 inch piece ginger, cut into fine shreds
2 medium garlic cloves, chopped
2 teaspoons chopped red chili
2 tablespoons finely chopped cilantro
    stems
3 medium scallions, cut into fine shreds
    1½ inches long
2 tablespoons lime juice
lime wedges, to serve

Line a bamboo steaming basket with banana leaves or baking paper (this is so the fish will not stick or taste of bamboo).

Arrange the fish cutlets in the basket and top with the ginger, garlic, chili and cilantro. Cover and steam over a wok or large saucepan of boiling water for 5–6 minutes.

Remove the lid and sprinkle the scallions and lime juice over the fish. Cover and steam for 30 seconds, or until the fish is cooked. Serve immediately with wedges of lime and steamed rice.

Grilled Fish with Fennel and Lemon

❋ SERVES 4
❋ PREPARATION TIME: 10 MINUTES
❋ COOKING TIME: 10 MINUTES

4 whole red mullet or bream, cleaned,
    scaled and gutted
1 medium lemon, thinly sliced
1 baby fennel bulb, thinly sliced
1½ tablespoons fennel seeds
¼ cup lemon juice
⅓ cup olive oil

Cut three diagonal slashes on both sides of each fish. Put two or three slices of lemon and some slices of fennel bulb in the cavity of each fish. Bruise the fennel seeds roughly, using a mortar and pestle. Sprinkle both sides of each fish with the cracked fennel seeds and some salt and rub well into the flesh.

Mix the lemon juice and olive oil in a bowl. Heat a chargrill pan or plate and when very hot, add the fish. Drizzle a little of the juice and oil over each fish. After 5 minutes, turn carefully with tongs, ensuring the filling doesn't fall out, and drizzle with the oil mix. Gently flake a piece of flesh with a fork to test whether it is cooked through, then serve with salad.

Steamed Fish Cutlets with Ginger and Chili

Seafood Lasagne

❈ SERVES 4–6
❈ PREPARATION TIME: 15 MINUTES
❈ COOKING TIME: 45 MINUTES

9 oz instant lasagne sheets
1/2 cup scallops
4 cups raw shrimp
1 lb 2 oz skinless firm white fish
    fillets
1/2 cup butter
1 leek, thinly sliced
2/3 cup all-purpose flour
2 cups whole milk
2 cups dry white wine
1 cup grated cheddar cheese
1/2 cup whipping cream
2/3 cup grated parmesan cheese
2 tablespoons chopped Italian parsley

Preheat the oven to 350°F. Line a greased shallow ovenproof dish (about 12 inches square) with lasagne sheets, gently breaking them to fill any gaps. Set aside.

Slice or pull off any vein, membrane or hard white muscle from the scallops, leaving any roe attached.

Peel the shrimp and gently pull out the dark vein from the back of each shrimp, starting from the head end. Chop the seafood into even-sized pieces.

Melt the butter in a large saucepan over low heat, add the leek and cook, stirring, over medium heat for 1 minute, or until starting to soften. Stir in the flour and cook for 1 minute, or until pale and foaming. Remove from the heat and gradually stir in the combined milk and wine. Return to the heat and stir constantly over medium heat until the sauce boils and thickens. Reduce the heat and simmer for 2 minutes. Add the seafood and simmer for 1 minute. Remove from the heat, stir in the cheese, then season.

Spoon half the seafood mixture over the lasagne sheets in the dish, then top with another layer of lasagne sheets. Spoon the remaining seafood mixture over the lasagne sheets, then cover with another layer of lasagne sheets.

Pour the cream over the top, then sprinkle with the combined parmesan and parsley. Bake, uncovered, for 30 minutes, or until bubbling and golden brown.

Salmon Stew (Ishikari Nabe)

✻ SERVES 3–4
✻ PREPARATION TIME: 20 MINUTES
✻ COOKING TIME: 40 MINUTES

12 dried shiitake mushrooms
1 1/3 cups firm tofu
1/2 Chinese cabbage
4 salmon cutlets
2 inch pieces canned bamboo
    shoots
8 cups dashi
1/3 cup Japanese soy sauce
1/4 cup mirin or sake

SESAME SEED SAUCE
2/3 cup white sesame seeds
2 teaspoons oil
1/2 cup Japanese soy sauce
2 tablespoons mirin
3 teaspoons sugar
1/2 teaspoon instant dashi granules

Soak the mushrooms in warm water for 15 minutes, then drain. Cut the tofu into 12 squares. Coarsely shred the cabbage into 2 inch wide pieces.

Place the mushrooms, tofu, cabbage, salmon, bamboo shoots, dashi, Japanese soy sauce, mirin and a pinch of salt in a large saucepan and bring to a boil. Reduce the heat, cover and simmer over medium heat for 15 minutes. Turn the salmon cutlets over and simmer for a further 15 minutes, or until tender.

To make the sesame seed sauce, toast the sesame seeds in a frying pan over medium heat for 3–4 minutes, shaking the pan gently, until the seeds are golden brown. Remove from the pan at once to prevent burning. Grind the seeds using a mortar and pestle until a paste is formed. Add the oil, if necessary, to assist in forming a paste. Mix the paste with the Japanese soy sauce, mirin, sugar, dashi granules and 1/2 cup warm water.

Pour the salmon stew into warmed serving bowls and serve with the sesame seed sauce.

Shrimp Laksa

❋ SERVES 4–6
❋ PREPARATION TIME: 30 MINUTES
❋ COOKING TIME: 35 MINUTES

6 cups raw shrimp
1 1/2 tablespoons coriander seeds
1 tablespoon cumin seeds
1 teaspoon ground turmeric
1 medium onion, roughly chopped
2 teaspoons roughly chopped fresh ginger
3 medium garlic cloves
3 medium lemongrass stems, white part
   only, sliced
6 candlenuts or macadamia nuts,
   roughly chopped
4–6 small red chilies, roughly chopped
2–3 teaspoons shrimp paste
4 cups chicken stock
1/4 cup vegetable oil
3 cups coconut milk
4 fresh kaffir lime leaves
2 1/2 tablespoons lime juice
2 tablespoons fish sauce
2 tablespoons grated jaggery
   or unpacked brown sugar
2 1/2 cups dried rice vermicelli
1 cup trimmed bean sprouts
4 fried tofu puffs, cut into thin strips
3 tablespoons chopped Vietnamese mint
1 small handful cilantro leaves
lime wedges, to serve

Peel the shrimp, leaving the tails intact. Gently pull out the dark vein from the back of each shrimp, starting from the head end.

Dry-fry the coriander seeds in a small frying pan over medium heat for 1–2 minutes, or until fragrant, tossing constantly. Grind finely using a mortar and pestle or spice grinder. Repeat the process with the cumin seeds.

Put the ground coriander and cumin, turmeric, onion, ginger, garlic, lemongrass, candlenuts, chili and shrimp paste in a food processor or blender. Add about 1/2 cup of the stock and blend to a fine paste.

Heat a wok over low heat, add the oil and swirl to coat the base and side. Cook the paste for 3–5 minutes, stirring constantly. Pour in the remaining stock and bring to a boil, then reduce the heat and simmer for 15 minutes, or until reduced slightly. Add the coconut milk, kaffir lime leaves, lime juice, fish sauce and sugar and simmer for 5 minutes. Add the shrimp and simmer for 2 minutes, or until pink and cooked. Do not boil or cover.

Meanwhile, soak the vermicelli in boiling water for 6–7 minutes, or until soft. Drain and divide among serving bowls along with most of the sprouts. Ladle on the hot soup then top with the tofu, mint, cilantro and the remaining sprouts. Serve with lime wedges.

Baked Fish with Tomato and Onion

❋ SERVES 4
❋ PREPARATION TIME: 20 MINUTES
❋ COOKING TIME: 45 MINUTES

¼ cup olive oil
2 medium onions, finely chopped
1 small celery stalk, finely chopped
1 small carrot, finely chopped
2 medium garlic cloves, chopped
1⅔ cups canned chopped tomatoes
2 tablespoons puréed tomatoes
¼ teaspoon dried oregano
½ teaspoon sugar
1¾ oz white bread, preferably one-day old
1 lb 2 oz skinless firm white fish fillets
3 tablespoons chopped Italian parsley
1 tablespoon lemon juice

Preheat the oven to 350°F. Heat 2 tablespoons of the oil in a heavy-based frying pan. Add the onion, celery and carrot and cook over low heat for 10 minutes, or until soft. Add the garlic, cook for 2 minutes, then add the chopped tomato, puréed tomato, oregano and sugar. Simmer for about 10 minutes, stirring occasionally, until reduced and thickened. Season.

To make the breadcrumbs, chop the bread in a food processor for a few minutes, until fine crumbs form.

Arrange the fish in a single layer in an ovenproof dish. Stir the chopped parsley and the lemon juice into the sauce. Season to taste, and pour over the fish. Scatter the breadcrumbs all over the top and drizzle with the remaining oil. Bake for 20 minutes, or until the fish is just cooked.

Fish Fillets with Harissa and Olives

❋ SERVES 4
❋ PREPARATION TIME: 15 MINUTES
❋ COOKING TIME: 25 MINUTES

⅓ cup olive oil
4 skinless firm white fish fillets
seasoned flour, for dusting
1 medium onion, chopped
2 medium garlic cloves, crushed
1⅔ cups canned chopped tomatoes
2 teaspoons harissa
2 bay leaves
1 cinnamon stick
1 cup medium Kalamata olives
1 tablespoon lemon juice
2 tablespoons chopped Italian parsley

Heat half the olive oil in a heavy-based frying pan. Dust the fish fillets with flour and cook over medium heat for 2 minutes each side, or until golden. Transfer to a plate.

Add the remaining olive oil to the pan and cook the onion and garlic for 3–4 minutes, or until softened. Add the chopped tomato, harissa, bay leaves and cinnamon. Cook for 10 minutes, or until the sauce has thickened. Season to taste.

Return the fish to the pan, add the olives and cover the fish with the sauce. Remove the bay leaves and cinnamon stick and continue cooking for 2 minutes, or until the fish is tender. Add the lemon juice and parsley and serve.

Baked Fish with Tomato and Onion

Balinese Seafood Curry

3 1/4 cups raw shrimp

1 tablespoon lime juice

9 oz swordfish, cut into 1 1/4 inch cubes

9 oz squid tubes, cut into 1/2 inch rings

1/4 cup vegetable oil

2 medium red onions, chopped

2 small red chilies, seeded and sliced

1/2 cup fish stock

shredded Thai basil, to garnish

CURRY PASTE

2 medium tomatoes

5 small red chilies, seeded and chopped

5 medium garlic cloves, chopped

2 medium lemongrass stems,
   white part only, sliced

1 tablespoon coriander seeds,
   dry-roasted and ground

1 teaspoon shrimp powder,
   dry-roasted (see Notes)

1 tablespoon ground almonds

1/4 teaspoon ground nutmeg

1 teaspoon ground turmeric

3 tablespoons tamarind purée

To make the curry paste, score a cross in the base of each tomato. Put in a heatproof bowl and cover with boiling water. Leave for 30 seconds, then transfer to cold water, drain and peel away the skin from the cross. Cut the tomatoes in half, scoop out the seeds and chop the flesh. Put in a food processor with the remaining paste ingredients and blend until a thick paste forms.

Peel the shrimp and gently pull out the dark vein from the back of each shrimp, starting at the head end.

Pour the lime juice into a bowl and season. Add the seafood, coat well and allow to marinate for 20 minutes.

Heat a non-stick wok over high heat, add the oil and swirl to coat the base and side. Add the onion, chili and curry paste, and cook, stirring occasionally, over low heat for 10 minutes, or until fragrant. Add the swordfish and shrimp, and stir to coat in the curry paste mixture. Cook for 3 minutes, or until the shrimp just turn pink, then add the squid and cook for a further 1 minute. Add the stock and bring to a boil, then reduce the heat and simmer for 2 minutes, or until the seafood is cooked and tender. Season to taste and garnish with the shredded fresh basil.

NOTES: If you can't find shrimp powder, put some dried shrimp in a mortar and pestle or small food processor and grind or process into a fine powder. Use a non-stick or stainless-steel wok to cook this recipe as the tamarind will react with the metal in a regular wok and badly taint the dish.

Seared Scallops with Chili Bean Paste

❄ SERVES 4
❄ PREPARATION TIME: 20 MINUTES
❄ COOKING TIME: 15 MINUTES

1 lb 2 oz egg noodles
¼ cup peanut oil
20 medium scallops, roe removed
1 large onion, cut into thin wedges
3 medium garlic cloves, crushed
1 tablespoon grated fresh ginger
1 tablespoon chili bean paste
5½ oz choy sum, cut into 2 inch lengths
¼ cup chicken stock
2 tablespoons light soy sauce
2 tablespoons kecap manis (see Note)
1 handful cilantro leaves
1 cup bean sprouts, washed
1 large red chili, seeded and thinly sliced
1 teaspoon sesame oil
1 tablespoon Chinese rice wine

Put the noodles in a heatproof bowl, cover with boiling water and soak for 1 minute to separate. Drain, rinse, then drain again. Set aside.

Heat a wok over high heat, add 2 tablespoons peanut oil and swirl to coat the base and side. Add the scallops in batches and sear for 20 seconds on each side, or until sealed. Remove from the wok and set aside.

Add the remaining peanut oil to the wok and swirl to coat. Stir-fry the onion for 1–2 minutes, or until softened. Add the garlic and ginger and cook for 30 seconds. Stir in the chili bean paste and cook for 1 minute, or until fragrant. Add the choy sum, noodles, stock, soy sauce and kecap manis. Stir-fry for 4 minutes, or until the choy sum has wilted and the noodles have absorbed most of the liquid. Return the scallops to the wok, add the cilantro, bean sprouts, chili, sesame oil and rice wine, tossing gently until combined. Serve immediately.

NOTE: Kecap manis is an Indonesian sweet soy sauce. If you are unable to find it, use soy sauce sweetened with a little unpacked brown sugar.

Sri Lankan Fish Fillets in Tomato Curry

❉ SERVES 6
❉ PREPARATION TIME: 20 MINUTES
❉ COOKING TIME: 20 MINUTES

2 lb 4 oz skinless, boneless firm
    white fish fillets
1/4 cup vegetable oil
1 large onion, finely chopped
3 large garlic cloves, crushed
2 tablespoons grated fresh ginger
1 teaspoon black mustard seeds
5 cups canned chopped tomatoes
3 tablespoons finely chopped cilantro
2 small green chilies, seeded and finely
    chopped
2 tablespoons grated jaggery or unpacked
    brown sugar
steamed rice, to serve

MARINADE
1/4 cup lemon juice
1/4 cup coconut vinegar (see Note)
2 teaspoons cumin seeds
1 teaspoon ground turmeric
1 teaspoon cayenne pepper

To make the marinade, put the lemon juice, coconut vinegar, cumin seeds, ground turmeric, cayenne pepper and 1 teaspoon salt in a shallow, non-metallic container and mix together thoroughly.

Carefully remove any remaining bones from the fish with tweezers and cut the flesh into 1 x 4 inch pieces. Add the fish pieces to the marinade and gently toss until they are well coated. Cover with plastic wrap and refrigerate for 30 minutes.

Heat a non-stick wok over high heat, add the oil and swirl to coat the base and side. Reduce the heat to low, add the onion, garlic, ginger and mustard seeds and cook, stirring frequently, for 5 minutes. Add the fish and marinade, diced tomato, cilantro, chili and jaggery to the wok and cover. Simmer gently, stirring occasionally, for 10–15 minutes, or until the fish is cooked and just flakes when tested with a fork. Serve with steamed rice.

NOTE: Coconut vinegar is made from the sap of various palm trees.

Bream with Tomato Cheese Crust

* SERVES 4
* PREPARATION TIME: 40 MINUTES
* COOKING TIME: 15 MINUTES

2 ripe medium tomatoes
1 small onion, finely chopped
1 tablespoon concentrated tomato purée
½ teaspoon ground cumin
½ teaspoon ground coriander
Tabasco sauce, to taste
¼ teaspoon freshly ground black pepper
1 tablespoon lemon juice
1⅓ tablespoons melted butter
4 skinless bream fillets
¾ cup grated cheddar cheese
½ cup fresh breadcrumbs
lemon wedges, to serve

Score a cross in the base of each tomato. Put in a heatproof bowl and cover with boiling water. Leave for 30 seconds, then transfer to cold water and peel the skin away from the cross. Cut each tomato in half, scoop out the seeds and finely chop the flesh.

Preheat the oven to 350°F. Lightly grease a baking sheet. Put the tomato in a small bowl and mix with the onion, concentrated tomato purée, cumin, ground coriander and Tabasco.

Combine the ground pepper, lemon juice and butter in a small bowl. Put the bream fillets on the prepared tray. Brush each fillet with the pepper mixture and top with the tomato mixture. Sprinkle with the combined cheddar and breadcrumbs and bake for 15 minutes, or until the fish is tender and flakes easily when tested with a fork. Serve with lemon wedges.

Shrimp and Okra Gumbo

✳ SERVES 8
✳ PREPARATION TIME: 35 MINUTES
✳ COOKING TIME: 3 HOURS

2 tablespoons olive oil
1 lb 2 oz thickly sliced okra
7 oz sliced chorizo
1²⁄₃ cups diced smoked ham
¼ cup olive oil, extra
¼ cup all-purpose flour
2 medium onions, chopped
2 medium celery stalks, diced
1 medium red pepper, diced
6 medium garlic cloves, finely chopped
½ teaspoon cayenne pepper
2 teaspoons sweet paprika
2 teaspoons mustard powder
large pinch ground allspice
1²⁄₃ cups puréed tomatoes
1 tablespoon concentrated tomato purée
2 teaspoons finely chopped thyme
2 teaspoons finely chopped oregano
2 bay leaves
2½ tablespoons worcestershire sauce
2 cups scallops without roe
12 oysters
chopped Italian parsley, to serve
cooked long-grain rice, to serve

SHRIMP STOCK
8 cups raw shrimp
1 tablespoon olive oil
1 medium onion, chopped
1 medium carrot, chopped
1 medium celery stalk, chopped
1 medium bay leaf
2 whole cloves
3 medium garlic cloves, bruised
3 parsley stalks
1 medium thyme sprig
½ teaspoon black peppercorns

To make the stock, peel the shrimp, reserving the shells. Gently pull out the dark vein from the back of each shrimp, starting at the head end. Cover the shrimp meat and refrigerate until ready to use. Heat the oil in a large saucepan, add the shrimp shells and cook over high heat for 8 minutes, or until bright orange. Add 2.5 quarts cold water and the remaining stock ingredients and bring to a boil. Reduce the heat to low and simmer for 30 minutes, skimming occasionally, then strain well and set aside — you should have about 8 cups stock.

Meanwhile, heat the olive oil in a frying pan and sauté the okra over medium heat for 10 minutes, or until slightly softened. Remove from the pan and set aside. Add the chorizo to the pan and cook for 5 minutes, or until well browned, then set aside. Add the ham and cook for a few minutes, or until lightly browned.

Heat the extra olive oil in a large saucepan, add the flour and stir to combine. Cook, stirring regularly over medium heat for 30 seconds, or until the roux turns a color somewhere between milk and dark chocolate, but do not allow to burn. Add the onion, celery, pepper and garlic to the roux and cook for about 10 minutes, or until softened. Add the cayenne, paprika, mustard and allspice and stir for 1 minute. Add the puréed tomato, concentrated tomato purée, shrimp stock, thyme, oregano, bay leaves, worcestershire sauce, chorizo and ham and bring to a boil. Reduce the heat to low and simmer for 1 hour then add the okra and continue cooking for a further 1 hour or until the gumbo is thick and glossy.

Add the shrimp, scallops and oysters and cook for about 5–8 minutes, or until all the seafood is cooked through. Stir in the parsley and season to taste. Ladle the soup over the hot rice in individual bowls and serve with lemon wedges, if you like.

Tandoori Chicken with Cardamom Rice

❋ SERVES 4

❋ PREPARATION TIME: 15 MINUTES

❋ COOKING TIME: 45 MINUTES

1 cup Greek-style yogurt

¼ cup tandoori paste (see Note)

2 tablespoons lemon juice

4 cups cubed boneless, skinless chicken breasts

1 tablespoon oil

1 medium onion, finely diced

1½ cups long-grain rice

2 cardamom pods, bruised

3 cups hot chicken stock

9 cups baby spinach leaves

Greek-style yogurt, extra, to serve

Soak eight bamboo skewers in water for 30 minutes to prevent them burning during cooking.

Meanwhile, combine the yogurt, tandoori paste and lemon juice in a non-metallic dish. Add the chicken and coat well, then cover with plastic wrap and marinate for at least 10 minutes.

Heat the oil in a saucepan, add the onion and cook for 3 minutes, then add the rice and cardamom pods. Cook, stirring often, for 3–5 minutes, or until the rice is slightly opaque. Add the hot stock and bring to a boil. Reduce the heat to low, then cover and cook the rice, without removing the lid, for 15 minutes.

Meanwhile, wash the spinach and put it in a large saucepan with just the water clinging to the leaves. Cook, covered, over medium heat for 1–2 minutes, or until the spinach has wilted. Set aside and keep warm.

Preheat a barbecue plate or broiler to very hot. Thread the chicken cubes onto the soaked bamboo skewers, leaving the bottom quarter of the skewers empty. Cook the skewers on each side for 4–5 minutes, or until the chicken is cooked through.

Uncover the rice, fluff up with a fork and serve with the spinach, chicken and a dollop of extra yogurt.

NOTE: Tandoori paste is usually made up of a mixture of cumin, ground coriander, cinnamon, cloves, chili, ginger, garlic, turmeric, mace, salt, coloring and yogurt, though recipes do vary. There are many commercial varieties of paste available in jars from Indian grocery stores and large supermarkets.

Roast Turkey with Rice and Chestnut Stuffing

❋ SERVES 6–8
❋ PREPARATION TIME: 30 MINUTES
❋ COOKING TIME: 3 HOURS 30 MINUTES

6 lb 12 oz turkey, neck and giblets
   removed
1 large red onion, cut into 4–5 slices
2 tablespoons softened butter
$1^{1}/_{2}$ cups dry white wine
1 medium carrot, quartered
1 medium celery stalk, quartered
1 large rosemary sprig
2 teaspoons finely chopped thyme
1 cup chicken stock
2 tablespoons all-purpose flour

STUFFING
12 prunes, pitted
1 cups whole fresh chestnuts
$2^{2}/_{3}$ tablespoons butter
1 medium red onion, finely chopped
2 medium garlic cloves, crushed
$^{1}/_{3}$ cup finely chopped pancetta
   (including any fat)
$^{1}/_{2}$ cup wild rice blend
$^{1}/_{4}$ cup chicken stock
3 dried juniper berries, lightly crushed
2 teaspoons finely chopped rosemary
3 teaspoons finely chopped thyme

Preheat the oven to 325°F. Soak the prunes in hot water for 20 minutes. Meanwhile, to prepare the chestnuts, make a small cut in the skin on the flat side, put under a hot broiler and cook on both sides until well browned. Put the hot chestnuts in a bowl lined with a damp dish towel and cover with the towel. Leave until cool enough to handle, then peel. Do not allow the chestnuts to cool completely before peeling. Roughly chop the prunes and chestnuts and set aside.

To make the stuffing, melt the butter in a large saucepan and add the onion, garlic and pancetta. Cook over low heat for 5–6 minutes, or until the onion is softened but not brown. Add the rice, stock, juniper berries, prunes and chestnuts, stir well, then pour in $1^{1}/_{2}$ cups water. Bring to a boil and cook, covered, stirring once or twice, for 20–25 minutes, or until the rice is tender and all liquid has been absorbed. Remove from the heat, stir in the rosemary and thyme, and season.

Wash and pat the turkey dry. Fill the cavity with the stuffing. Cross the turkey legs and tie them together, then tuck the wings underneath the body. Arrange the onion slices in the center of a large roasting tin, then sit the turkey on top, breast side up. Season and dot with butter. Pour 1 cup of the wine into the tin, then scatter the carrot, celery, rosemary and 1 teaspoon of thyme.

Roast for $2–2^{1}/_{2}$ hours, or until cooked through and the juices run clear, basting every 30 minutes. After 1 hour, pour half the chicken stock into the tin. Once the skin becomes golden brown, cover with buttered foil.

When cooked, transfer the turkey to a carving plate, cover with foil and leave to rest in a warm spot. Meanwhile, pour the juices into a small saucepan and reduce for 8–10 minutes. Stir in the flour, then add the stock, a little at a time, stirring to form a paste. Slowly add the rest of the stock and wine, stirring so that no lumps form. Stir in the remaining thyme. Bring to a boil and continue to simmer for 6–8 minutes, or until reduced by one-third. Season. Transfer to a gravy boat. Carve the turkey and serve with the stuffing and gravy.

Seafood Pie

❋ PREPARATION TIME: 20 MINUTES
❋ COOKING TIME: 1 HOUR 20 MINUTES

2 tablespoons olive oil
3 large onions, thinly sliced
1 fennel bulb, thinly sliced
2½ cups fish stock
3 cups whipping cream
1 tablespoon brandy
3½ cups skinless snapper fillets,
    cut into large pieces
1 cup scallops
4 cups raw shrimp, peeled and deveined
2 tablespoons chopped Italian parsley
2 sheets frozen puff pastry, thawed
1 egg, lightly beaten

Preheat the oven to 425°F. Heat the oil in a deep frying pan, add the onion and fennel and cook over medium heat for 20 minutes or until caramelized.

Add the stock to the pan and bring to a boil. Cook until the liquid is almost evaporated. Stir in the cream and brandy, bring to a boil, then reduce the heat and simmer for 10 minutes, or until reduced by half. Add the seafood and parsley and toss for 3 minutes.

Lightly grease a 2.5 quart pie dish and add the seafood mixture. Arrange the pastry over the top to cover, trim the excess and press down around the edges. Decorate with any trimmings. Make a steam hole in the top and brush the pastry with egg. Bake for 30 minutes, or until cooked through and the pastry is crisp and golden.

Salmon and Lemon Cannelloni

❋ SERVES 4–6
❋ PREPARATION TIME: 25 MINUTES
❋ COOKING TIME: 40 MINUTES

16 cannelloni tubes

FILLING
1½ cups canned pink salmon
1 cup ricotta cheese
1 tablespoon lemon juice
1 egg yolk, lightly beaten
2 tablespoons finely chopped onion

SAUCE
½ cup butter
⅔ cup all-purpose flour
2¾ cups whole milk
1 teaspoon finely grated lemon zest
¼ teaspoon freshly grated nutmeg

To make the filling, drain the salmon and reserve the liquid for the sauce. Remove and discard the skin and bones. Flake the salmon flesh and mix with the ricotta, lemon juice, egg yolk and onion in a bowl. Season to taste.

To make the sauce, melt the butter in a saucepan over low heat. Stir in the flour and cook for 1 minute, or until pale and foaming. Remove from the heat and gradually stir in the milk. Return to the heat and stir constantly until the sauce boils and thickens. Reduce the heat and simmer for 2 minutes. Add the reserved salmon liquid, lemon zest and nutmeg, and season to taste. Set aside to cool.

Preheat the oven to 350°F. Fill the cannelloni tubes with filling, using a spoon or piping bag. Spread one-third of the sauce over the bottom of a shallow ovenproof dish, then sit the cannelloni tubes in the dish side-by-side. Pour the remaining sauce over the top, covering all the exposed pasta. Bake for about 30 minutes, until bubbly.

Seafood Pie

Chicken Pie with Feta

✳ SERVES 6
✳ PREPARATION TIME: 30 MINUTES
✳ COOKING TIME: 1 HOUR 10 MINUTES

2 lb 4 oz boneless, skinless chicken
   breast
2 cups chicken stock
¼ cup butter
2 medium scallions, finely chopped
½ cup all-purpose flour
½ cup whole milk
8 sheets filo pastry (12 x 16 inches)
¼ cup melted butter, extra
1⅓ cups crumbled feta
1 tablespoon chopped dill
1 tablespoon snipped chives
¼ teaspoon freshly grated nutmeg
1 egg, lightly beaten

Cut the chicken into bite-sized pieces. Pour the stock into a saucepan and bring to a boil over high heat. Reduce the heat to low, add the chicken and poach gently for 10–15 minutes, or until the chicken is cooked through. Drain, reserving the stock. Add enough water to the stock in order to bring the quantity up to 2 cups. Preheat the oven to 350°F.

Melt the butter in a saucepan over low heat, add the scallions and cook, stirring, for 5 minutes. Add the flour and stir for 30 seconds. Remove the pan from the heat and gradually add the chicken stock and milk, stirring after each addition. Return to the heat and gently bring to a boil, stirring. Simmer for a few minutes, or until the sauce thickens. Remove from the heat.

Line an ovenproof dish measuring 1½ x 7 x 10 inches with four sheets of filo pastry, brushing one side of each sheet with melted butter as you go. Place the buttered side down. The filo will overlap the edges of the dish. Cover the unused filo with a damp dish towel to prevent it drying out.

Stir the chicken, feta, dill, chives, nutmeg and egg into the sauce. Season to taste. Pile the mixture on top of the filo pastry in the dish. Fold the overlapping filo over the filling and cover the top of the pie with the remaining four sheets of filo, brushing each sheet with melted butter as you go. Scrunch the edges of the filo so they fit in the dish. Brush the top with butter. Bake for 45–50 minutes, or until the pastry is golden brown and crisp.

NOTE: If you prefer, you can use puff pastry instead of filo pastry. If you do so, bake in a 425°F oven for 15 minutes, then reduce the temperature to 350°F and cook for another 30 minutes, or until the pastry is golden.

Chicken Mulligatawny

2 medium tomatoes, peeled
1 1/3 tablespoons ghee
1 large onion, finely chopped
3 medium garlic cloves, crushed
8 curry leaves
1/4 cup Madras curry paste
1 cup red lentils, washed and drained
1/3 cup short-grain rice
1 cup coconut cream
2 tablespoons chopped cilantro leaves
mango chutney, to serve

STOCK
3 lb 5 oz chicken
1 medium carrot, chopped
2 medium celery stalks, chopped
4 medium scallions, chopped
3/4 inch piece ginger, sliced

To make the stock, put all the ingredients and 4 quarts cold water in a large stockpot or saucepan. Bring to a boil, removing any scum that rises to the surface. Reduce the heat to low and simmer, partly covered, for 3 hours. Continue to remove any scum from the surface. Carefully remove the chicken and cool. Strain the stock into a bowl and cool. Cover and refrigerate overnight. Discard the skin and bones from the chicken and shred the flesh into small pieces. Cover and refrigerate overnight.

Score a cross in the base of the tomatoes. Put in a heatproof bowl and cover with boiling water. Leave for 30 seconds then transfer to a bowl of cold water and peel the skin away from the cross. Cut the tomatoes in half, scoop out the seeds and chop the flesh.

Melt the ghee in a large saucepan over medium heat. Cook the onion for 5 minutes, or until softened but not browned. Add the garlic and curry leaves and cook for 1 minute. Add the curry paste, cook for 1 minute, then stir in the lentils. Pour in the stock and bring to a boil over high heat, removing any scum from the surface. Reduce the heat, add the tomato and simmer for 30 minutes, or until the lentils are soft.

Meanwhile, bring a large saucepan of water to a boil. Add the rice and cook for 12 minutes, stirring once or twice. Drain. Stir the rice into the soup with the chicken and coconut cream until warmed through — don't allow it to boil or it will curdle. Season. Sprinkle with the cilantro and serve with mango chutney.

Chicken Caccitore

❋ SERVES 4
❋ PREPARATION TIME: 15 MINUTES
❋ COOKING TIME: 1 HOUR

¼ cup olive oil

1 large onion, finely chopped

3 medium garlic cloves, crushed

5½ oz finely chopped pancetta

1⅓ cups thickly sliced button mushrooms

1 large chicken (at least 3 lb 8 oz),
    cut into 8 pieces

⅓ cup dry vermouth or dry white wine

3¼ cups canned chopped tomatoes

¼ teaspoon unpacked brown sugar

¼ teaspoon cayenne pepper

1 medium oregano sprig

1 medium thyme sprig

1 medium bay leaf

Heat half the olive oil in a large flameproof casserole dish. Add the onion and garlic and cook for 6–8 minutes over low heat, stirring, until the onion is golden. Add the pancetta and mushrooms, increase the heat and cook, stirring, for 4–5 minutes. Transfer to a bowl.

Add the remaining oil to the casserole dish and brown the chicken pieces, a few at a time, over medium heat. Season as they brown. Spoon off the excess fat and return all the chicken to the casserole dish. Increase the heat, add the vermouth to the dish and cook until the liquid has almost evaporated.

Add the chopped tomato, brown sugar, cayenne pepper, oregano, thyme and bay leaf, and stir in ⅓ cup water. Bring to a boil, then stir in the reserved onion mixture. Reduce the heat, cover and simmer for 25 minutes, or until the chicken is tender but not falling off the bone.

If the liquid is too thin, remove the chicken from the casserole dish, increase the heat and boil until the liquid has thickened. Discard the sprigs of herbs and adjust the seasoning.

Thai Duck and Pineapple Curry

* SERVES 4–6
* PREPARATION TIME: 10 MINUTES
* COOKING TIME: 15 MINUTES

1 tablespoon peanut oil
8 medium scallions, sliced
   diagonally into 1¼ inch lengths
2 medium garlic cloves, crushed
2–4 tablespoons Thai red curry paste
4 cups chopped Chinese roast duck
1½ cups coconut milk
1¾ cups canned pineapple pieces in
   syrup, drained
3 kaffir lime leaves
3 tablespoons chopped cilantro leaves
2 tablespoons chopped mint

Heat a wok until very hot, add the oil and swirl to coat. Add the scallions, garlic and red curry paste, and stir-fry for 1 minute, or until fragrant.

Add the duck, coconut milk, pineapple pieces, kaffir lime leaves and half the cilantro and mint. Bring to a boil, then reduce the heat and simmer for 10 minutes, or until the duck is heated through and the sauce has thickened slightly. Stir in the remaining cilantro and mint, and serve with jasmine rice.

Duck Breast with Walnut and Pomegranate Sauce

* SERVES 4
* PREPARATION TIME: 15 MINUTES
* COOKING TIME: 25 MINUTES

4 large duck breasts
1 medium onion, finely chopped
1 cup fresh pomegranate juice
2 tablespoons lemon juice
2 tablespoons unpacked brown sugar
1 teaspoon ground cinnamon
1½ cups chopped walnuts
pomegranate seeds, to garnish, optional

Preheat the oven to 350°F. Score each duck breast two or three times on the skin side. Cook in a non-stick frying pan over high heat, skin side down, for 6 minutes, or until crisp and most of the fat has been rendered. Put in an ovenproof dish.

Remove all but 1 tablespoon of fat from the pan. Add the onion to the pan and cook over medium heat for 2–3 minutes, or until golden. Add the pomegranate juice, lemon juice, sugar, cinnamon and 1 cup of the walnuts and cook for 1 minute. Pour over the duck and bake for 15 minutes. Rest the duck for 5 minutes. Skim any excess fat from the sauce.

Slice the duck and serve with the sauce. Garnish with the pomegranate seeds and remaining walnuts.

Thai Duck and Pineapple Curry

Chicken Laksa

❋ SERVES 4–6
❋ PREPARATION TIME: 30 MINUTES
❋ COOKING TIME: 35 MINUTES

1 1/2 tablespoons coriander seeds
1 tablespoon cumin seeds
1 teaspoon ground turmeric
1 medium onion, roughly chopped
1 tablespoon roughly chopped fresh ginger
3 medium garlic cloves
3 medium lemongrass stems, white part
   only, sliced
6 macadamia nuts
4–6 small red chilies
3 teaspoons shrimp paste, roasted
   (see Note)
4 cups chicken stock
1/4 cup oil
1 3/4 cups chicken thigh fillets, cut into
   3/4 inch pieces
3 cups coconut milk
4 kaffir lime leaves
2 1/2 tablespoons lime juice
2 tablespoons fish sauce
2 tablespoons grated jaggery
   or unpacked brown sugar
2 1/2 cups dried rice vermicelli
1 cup trimmed bean sprouts
4 fried tofu puffs, cut into thin batons
3 tablespoons chopped Vietnamese mint
1 handful cilantro leaves
lime wedges, to serve

Toast the coriander and cumin seeds in a frying pan over medium heat for 1–2 minutes, or until fragrant, tossing the pan constantly to prevent the seeds from burning. Grind finely using a mortar and pestle or a spice grinder.

Put all the spices, onion, ginger, garlic, lemongrass, macadamia nuts, chilies and shrimp paste in a food processor or blender. Add 1/2 cup of the stock and blend to a paste.

Heat the oil in a wok or large saucepan over low heat and gently cook the paste for 3–5 minutes, stirring constantly to prevent it burning or sticking to the bottom of the pan. Add the remaining stock and bring to a boil over high heat. Reduce the heat to medium and simmer for 15 minutes, or until reduced slightly. Add the chicken and simmer for 4–5 minutes. Add the coconut milk, lime leaves, lime juice, fish sauce and jaggery and simmer for 5 minutes over medium–low heat. Do not bring to a boil or cover with a lid, as the coconut milk will split.

Meanwhile, put the vermicelli in a heatproof bowl, cover with boiling water and soak for 6–7 minutes, or until softened. Drain and divide among large serving bowls with the bean sprouts. Ladle the hot soup over the top and garnish with some tofu strips, mint and cilantro leaves. Serve with a wedge of lime.

NOTE: To roast the shrimp paste, wrap the paste in foil and put under a hot broiler for 1 minute.

Kung Pao Chicken

※ SERVES 4
※ PREPARATION TIME: 15 MINUTES
※ COOKING TIME: 15 MINUTES

1 egg white
2 teaspoons cornstarch
1/2 teaspoon sesame oil
2 teaspoons Chinese rice wine
1 1/2 tablespoons soy sauce
2 1/2 cups cubed boneless, skinless chicken
   thighs
1/4 cup chicken stock
2 teaspoons Chinese black vinegar
1 teaspoon unpacked brown sugar
2 tablespoons vegetable oil
3 long dried red chilies, cut in half
   lengthways
3 medium garlic cloves, finely chopped
2 teaspoons finely grated fresh ginger
2 medium scallions, thinly sliced
1/3 cup roughly crushed unsalted raw
   peanuts

Lightly whisk together the egg white, cornstarch, sesame oil, rice wine and 2 teaspoons of the soy sauce in a large non-metallic bowl. Add the chicken and toss to coat in the marinade. Cover with plastic wrap and marinate in the refrigerator for 30 minutes.

To make the stir-fry sauce, combine the stock, vinegar, sugar and the remaining soy sauce in a small bowl.

Heat a wok over high heat, add 1 tablespoon of the vegetable oil and swirl to coat the base and side. Stir-fry the chicken in batches for about 3 minutes, or until browned. Remove from the wok.

Heat the remaining oil in the wok, then add the chili and cook for 15 seconds, or until it starts to change color. Add the garlic, ginger, scallions and peanuts and stir-fry for 1 minute. Return the chicken to the wok along with the stir-fry sauce and stir-fry for 3 minutes, or until heated through and the sauce has thickened slightly. Serve immediately.

NOTE: This dish is said to have been created for an important court official called Kung Pao (or Gong Bao), who was stationed in the Sichuan province of China. It is characterized by the flavors of the long, dried red chilies, popular in Sichuan cuisine, and the crunchiness of peanuts. It can also be made with meat or shrimp.

Clay Pot Chicken and Vegetables

❋ SERVES 4

❋ PREPARATION TIME: 20 MINUTES

❋ COOKING TIME: 25 MINUTES

1 lb 2 oz boneless, skinless
   chicken thighs
1 tablespoon soy sauce
1 tablespoon dry sherry
6 dried Chinese mushrooms
2 tablespoons peanut oil
2 small leeks, white part only, sliced
2 inch piece ginger, grated
$\frac{1}{2}$ cup chicken stock
1 teaspoon sesame oil
$1\frac{2}{3}$ cups sliced sweet potato
3 teaspoons cornstarch
steamed rice, to serve

Wash the chicken under cold water and pat it dry with paper towel. Cut the chicken into small pieces. Put it in a dish with the soy sauce and sherry, cover and marinate for 30 minutes in the refrigerator.

Cover the mushrooms with hot water and soak for 20 minutes. Drain and squeeze to remove any excess liquid. Remove the stems and chop the caps into shreds.

Drain the chicken, reserving the marinade. Heat half the oil in a wok, swirling gently to coat the base and side. Add half the chicken pieces and stir-fry briefly until seared on all sides. Transfer the chicken to a flameproof clay pot or casserole dish. Stir-fry the remaining chicken and add it to the clay pot.

Heat the remaining oil in the wok. Add the leek and ginger and stir-fry for 1 minute. Add the mushrooms, remaining marinade, stock and sesame oil and cook for 2 minutes. Transfer to the clay pot with the sweet potato and cook, covered, on the top of the stove over very low heat for about 20 minutes.

Dissolve the cornstarch in a little water and add it to the pot. Cook, stirring over high heat, until the mixture boils and thickens. Serve the chicken and vegetables at once with steamed rice.

NOTE: Like all stews, this is best cooked 1–2 days ahead and stored, covered, in the refrigerator to allow the flavors to mature. It can also be frozen, but omit the sweet potato. Steam or boil the potato separately when the dish is reheating and stir it through.

Chicken with 40 Cloves of Garlic

❋ SERVES 4
❋ PREPARATION TIME: 20 MINUTES
❋ COOKING TIME: 1 HOUR 45 MINUTES

$2/3$ tablespoon butter
1 tablespoon olive oil
1 large chicken
40 medium garlic cloves, unpeeled
2 tablespoons chopped rosemary
2 medium thyme sprigs
$9^1/2$ fl oz dry white wine
$2/3$ cup chicken stock
$1^3/4$ cups all-purpose flour

Preheat the oven to 350°F. Melt the butter and oil in a 4.5 quart flameproof casserole dish, then brown the chicken over medium heat until golden all over. Remove the chicken and add the garlic, rosemary and thyme and cook together for 1 minute. Return the chicken to the dish and add the wine and chicken stock. Bring to a simmer, basting the chicken with the sauce.

Put the flour in a bowl and add up to $2/3$ cup water to form a pliable paste. Divide into four and roll into cylinder shapes. Place around the rim of the casserole. Put the lid on the dish, pressing down to form a seal. Bake for $1^1/4$ hours. Remove the lid by cracking the paste. Return the chicken to the oven to brown for 15 minutes, then transfer to a plate. Reduce the juices to 1 cup over medium heat. Carve the chicken, pierce the garlic skins and squeeze the flesh onto the chicken. Serve with the sauce.

Chicken with Peppers and Olives

❋ SERVES 4
❋ PREPARATION TIME: 30 MINUTES
❋ COOKING TIME: 1 HOUR 10 MINUTES

6 medium tomatoes
3 lb 5 oz chicken, cut into 8 portions
$1/4$ cup olive oil
2 large red onions, sliced into $1/4$ inch slices
2 medium garlic cloves, crushed
3 medium red bell peppers, seeded and membrane removed, cut into $1/2$ inch strips
$1/3$ cup thickly sliced prosciutto, finely chopped
1 tablespoon chopped thyme
2 teaspoons sweet paprika
8 pitted medium black olives
8 pitted medium green olives

Score a cross in the base of each tomato. Put in a heatproof bowl and cover with boiling water. Leave for 30 seconds, then transfer to cold water and peel the skin away from the cross. Cut each tomato in half, scoop out the seeds and finely chop the flesh.

Pat the chicken dry with paper towels and season. Heat the oil in a heavy-based frying pan and cook the chicken a few pieces at a time, skin side down, for 4–5 minutes, until golden. Turn the chicken over and cook for another 2–3 minutes. Transfer to a plate.

Add the onion, garlic, peppers, prosciutto and thyme to the pan. Cook over medium heat, stirring frequently for 8–10 minutes. Add the tomato and paprika, increase the heat and cook for 10–12 minutes, until sauce is thick. Return the chicken to the pan and coat with the sauce. Cover the pan, reduce the heat and simmer the chicken for 25–30 minutes. Add the olives.

Chicken with 40 Cloves of Garlic

Barbecued Chicken with Thai Sticky Rice

* SERVES 4–6
* PREPARATION TIME: 30 MINUTES
* COOKING TIME: 1 HOUR

4 lb 8 oz chicken, cut into 8–10 pieces
8 medium garlic cloves, chopped
6 cilantro roots, chopped
1 large handful cilantro leaves, chopped
1 tablespoon finely chopped fresh ginger
1 teaspoon ground white pepper
¼ cup fish sauce
¼ cup lime juice
¼ cup whiskey, optional
3 cups long-grain glutinous rice
cucumber slices, to serve

SAUCE
6 cilantro roots, chopped
4 medium garlic cloves, chopped
2 medium bird's eye chilies, seeded and
    chopped
¾ cup vinegar
4 tablespoons grated jaggery or unpacked
    brown sugar

Put the chicken pieces in a non-metallic bowl. Combine the garlic, cilantro root and leaves, ginger, white pepper and a pinch of salt and pound to a paste using a mortar and pestle. Mix in the fish sauce, lime juice and whiskey (if desired), then pour over the chicken and mix well. Marinate for at least 6 hours in the refrigerator. At the same time, soak the rice for at least 3 hours in cold water.

To make the sauce, pound the cilantro root, garlic, chili and a pinch of salt to a paste using a mortar and pestle. Combine the vinegar, jaggery and ¾ cup water in a saucepan and stir until the jaggery has dissolved. Bring to a boil, then add the paste and cook for 8–10 minutes, or until reduced by half. Set aside until ready to serve.

Drain the rice well, then line a bamboo steamer with muslin or banana leaves, spread the rice over and cover with a tight-fitting lid. Steam over a wok or large saucepan of boiling water for 40 minutes, or until the rice is translucent, sticky and tender. If steam is escaping, wrap some foil over the top of the steamer. Keep covered until ready to serve.

Meanwhile, heat a barbecue to medium heat, then cook the chicken, turning regularly for about 25 minutes, or until tender and cooked through. The breast pieces may only take about 15 minutes so take them off first and keep warm.

Serve the chicken, rice, dipping sauce and cucumber on separate plates in the center of the table and allow your guests to help themselves.

Hainanese Chicken Rice

❋ SERVES 6
❋ PREPARATION TIME: 50 MINUTES
❋ COOKING TIME: 1 HOUR 30 MINUTES

4 lb 8 oz chicken
6 medium scallions
thick slices ginger
4 medium garlic cloves, bruised
1 teaspoon vegetable oil
1 teaspoon sesame oil

RICE
5 medium red Asian shallots, finely
   chopped
2 medium garlic cloves, crushed
1 tablespoon very finely chopped
   fresh ginger
1½ cups jasmine rice
½ cup long-grain glutinous rice
3 plum tomatoes, cut into thin wedges
3 short cucumbers, sliced diagonally
cilantro sprigs, to garnish

SAUCE
2 small red chilies, seeded and chopped
4 medium garlic cloves, roughly chopped
1½ tablespoons finely chopped
   fresh ginger
3 cilantro roots, chopped
2 tablespoons dark soy sauce
2 tablespoons lime juice
2 tablespoons sugar
pinch ground white pepper

Remove the excess fat from around the cavity of the chicken and reserve. Rinse and salt the inside of the chicken and rinse again. Insert the scallions, ginger slices and garlic into the chicken cavity then place, breast side down, in a large saucepan and cover with cold water. Add 1 teaspoon salt and bring to a boil over high heat, skimming the surface as required. Reduce the heat to low and simmer gently for 15 minutes, then carefully turn over without piercing the skin and cook for another 15 minutes, or until the thigh juices run clear when pierced.

Carefully lift the chicken out of the saucepan, draining any liquid from the cavity into the rest of the stock. Reserve 4 cups of the stock. Plunge the chicken into iced water for 5 minutes to stop the cooking process and to firm the skin. Rub the entire surface of the chicken with the combined vegetable and sesame oils and allow to cool while you make the rice.

To make the rice, cook the reserved chicken fat in a saucepan over medium heat for about 8 minutes, or until you have about 2 tablespoons of liquid fat, then discard the solids. (If you prefer, use vegetable oil.) Add the shallots and cook for a few minutes, or until lightly golden, then add the garlic and ginger and stir until fragrant. Add both rices and cook for 5 minutes, or until lightly golden, then pour in the reserved chicken stock and 1 teaspoon salt and bring to a boil. Cover and reduce the heat to low and cook for about 20 minutes, or until tender and the liquid has evaporated. Cool, covered, for 10 minutes, then fluff with a fork.

Meanwhile, to make the sauce, pound the chili, garlic, ginger and cilantro root into a paste using a mortar and pestle. Stir in the rest of the ingredients and season to taste.

Shred the chicken. Divide the rice into six slightly wetted Chinese soup bowls and press down firmly, then turn out onto serving plates. Serve the chicken on a platter with the tomato, cucumber and cilantro and pour the dipping sauce into a small bowl and let your guests help themselves.

Thai Green Chicken Curry

✳ SERVES 4
✳ PREPARATION TIME: 15 MINUTES
✳ COOKING TIME: 30 MINUTES

1 cup coconut cream
2¼ cups boneless, skinless chicken thighs,
    thinly sliced
1 cup sliced Chinese long beans
2 cups coconut milk
2½ cups small florets broccoli
1 tablespoon grated jaggery or unpacked
    brown sugar
2–3 tablespoons fish sauce
5 tablespoons cilantro leaves,
    plus extra, to garnish
steamed rice, to serve

CURRY PASTE
1 tablespoon shrimp paste
1 teaspoon coriander seeds, toasted
½ teaspoon cumin seeds, toasted
¼ teaspoon white peppercorns
5 cilantro roots
3 tablespoons chopped fresh galangal
10 long green chilies, chopped
1 medium lemongrass stem,
    white part only, chopped
6 medium red Asian shallots
3 medium garlic cloves
1 teaspoon grated lime zest
2 tablespoons peanut oil

To make the curry paste, preheat the broiler to high, wrap the shrimp paste in foil and put under the hot broiler for 5 minutes. Cool, remove the foil then put the shrimp paste in a food processor.

Put the coriander seeds, cumin seeds and peppercorns in a mortar and pestle and grind to a fine powder. Transfer to the food processor with ¼ teaspoon salt and the remaining paste ingredients. Blend until smooth.

Put the coconut cream in a wok over high heat, bring to a boil then simmer for 10 minutes, or until the oil starts to separate from the cream. Reduce the heat to medium. Stir in half the curry paste and cook for 2–3 minutes, or until fragrant. Add the chicken and cook for 3–4 minutes. Stir in the beans, coconut milk and broccoli. Bring to a boil then reduce the heat and simmer for 4–5 minutes, or until cooked. Stir in the sugar, fish sauce and cilantro leaves. Garnish with the extra cilantro and serve with steamed rice.

NOTE: Store the remaining curry paste in an airtight container in the refrigerator for up to 2 weeks.

Chicken, Thai Basil and Cashew Stir-Fry

❉ SERVES 4
❉ PREPARATION TIME: 15 MINUTES
❉ COOKING TIME: 15 MINUTES

4 cups boneless, skinless chicken breast,
  cut into strips
2 medium lemongrass stems, white part
  only, finely chopped
3 small red chilies, seeded and chopped
4 medium garlic cloves, crushed
1 tablespoon finely chopped fresh ginger
2 cilantro roots, finely chopped
2 tablespoons oil
2/3 cup cashew nuts
1 1/2 tablespoons lime juice
2 tablespoons fish sauce
1 1/2 tablespoons grated jaggery or
  unpacked brown sugar
2 very large handfuls Thai basil
2 teaspoons cornstarch

Put the chicken in a large bowl with the lemongrass, chili, garlic, ginger and cilantro root. Mix together well.

Heat a wok over medium heat, add 1 teaspoon of the oil and swirl to coat. Add the cashews and cook for 1 minute, or until lightly golden. Remove and drain on crumpled paper towels.

Heat the remaining oil in the wok, add the chicken in batches and stir-fry over medium heat for 4–5 minutes, or until browned. Return the chicken to the wok.

Stir in the lime juice, fish sauce, jaggery and basil, and cook for 30–60 seconds, or until the basil just begins to wilt. Mix the cornstarch with 1 tablespoon water, add to the wok and stir until the mixture thickens slightly. Stir in the cashews and serve with steamed rice.

Chicken Braised with Ginger and Star Anise

❉ SERVES 4
❉ PREPARATION TIME: 10 MINUTES
❉ COOKING TIME: 30 MINUTES

1 teaspoon sichuan peppercorns
2 tablespoons peanut oil
3/4 x 1 1/4 inch piece ginger, cut into thin
  batons
2 medium garlic cloves, chopped
2 lb 4 oz boneless, skinless chicken
  thighs, halved
1/3 cup Chinese rice wine
1 tablespoon honey
1/4 cup light soy sauce
1 star anise

Heat a wok over medium heat, add the peppercorns and cook, stirring often, for 2–4 minutes, or until fragrant. Remove and lightly crush with the back of a knife.

Reheat the wok, add the oil and swirl to coat. Add the ginger and garlic and cook over low heat for 1–2 minutes, or until lightly golden. Add the chicken, increase the heat to medium and cook for 3 minutes, or until browned all over.

Add the remaining ingredients, reduce the heat and simmer, covered, for 20 minutes, or until the chicken is tender. Serve with rice.

Chicken, Thai Basil and Cashew Stir-Fry

Chicken and Almond Pilaff

❀ SERVES 4–6
❀ PREPARATION TIME: 15 MINUTES
❀ COOKING TIME: 45 MINUTES

4 cups boneless, skinless chicken thighs,
   trimmed and cut into 1¼ inch wide
   strips
2 cups basmati rice
3 cups chicken stock
2 tablespoons ghee
1 large onion, chopped
1 medium garlic clove, finely chopped
1 teaspoon ground turmeric
1²⁄₃ cups canned chopped tomatoes
1 cinnamon stick
4 cardamom pods, bruised
4 whole cloves
½ teaspoon finely grated lemon zest
3 tablespoons chopped cilantro leaves
2 teaspoons lemon juice
⅓ cup toasted slivered almonds

BAHARAT
1½ tablespoons coriander seeds
3 tablespoons black peppercorns
1½ tablespoons cassia bark
1½ tablespoons whole cloves
2 tablespoons cumin seeds
1 teaspoon cardamom seeds
2 whole nutmegs
3 tablespoons paprika

To make the baharat, grind the coriander seeds, peppercorns, cassia bark, cloves, cumin seeds and cardamom seeds to a powder using a mortar and pestle or in a spice grinder — you may need to do this in batches. Grate the nutmegs on the fine side of a grater and add to the spice mixture with the paprika. Stir together.

Combine the chicken and 1 tablespoon of the baharat in a large bowl, cover with plastic wrap and refrigerate for 1 hour. Meanwhile, put the rice in a large bowl, cover with cold water and soak for at least 30 minutes. Rinse under cold running water until the water runs clear, then drain and set aside.

Bring the stock to a boil in a saucepan. Reduce the heat, cover and keep at a low simmer. Meanwhile, heat the ghee in a large heavy-based saucepan over medium heat. Add the onion and garlic and cook for 5 minutes, or until soft and golden. Add the chicken and turmeric and cook for 5 minutes, or until browned. Add the rice and cook, stirring, for 2 minutes.

Add the chopped tomato, simmering chicken stock, cinnamon stick, cardamom pods, cloves, lemon zest and 1 teaspoon salt. Stir well and bring to a boil, then reduce the heat to low and cover the saucepan with a tight-fitting lid. Simmer for 20 minutes, or until the stock is absorbed and the rice is cooked. Remove from the heat and allow to stand, covered, for 10 minutes.

Stir in the cilantro, lemon juice and almonds. Season to taste.

NOTE: Baharat is an aromatic spice blend used in Arabic cuisine to add depth of flavor to dishes such as soups, fish curries and tomato sauces. Baharat can be stored in an airtight jar for up to 3 months in a cool, dry place. It can be used in Middle Eastern casseroles and stews, rubbed on fish that is to be broiled, pan-fried or barbecued, or used with salt as a spice rub for lamb roasts, cutlets or chops.

Butter Chicken

❋ SERVES 4–6
❋ PREPARATION TIME: 10 MINUTES
❋ COOKING TIME: 35 MINUTES

2 tablespoons peanut oil
2 lb 4 oz boneless, skinless chicken
    thighs, quartered
¼ cup butter or ghee
2 teaspoons garam masala
2 teaspoons sweet paprika
2 teaspoons ground coriander
1 tablespoon finely chopped fresh ginger
¼ teaspoon chili powder
1 cinnamon stick
6 cardamom pods, bruised
1⅓ cups puréed tomatoes
1 tablespoon sugar
¼ cup plain yogurt
½ cup whipping cream
1 tablespoon lemon juice

Heat a wok to very hot, add 1 tablespoon oil and swirl to coat the base and side. Add half the chicken and stir-fry for about 4 minutes, or until nicely browned. Remove from the wok. Add a little extra oil, if needed, and brown the remaining chicken. Remove from the wok and set aside.

Reduce the heat to medium, add the butter and stir until melted. Add the garam masala, paprika, ground coriander, ginger, chili powder, cinnamon stick and cardamom pods, and stir-fry for 1 minute, or until the spices are fragrant. Return the chicken to the wok and mix in until coated in the spices. Add the puréed tomatoes and sugar and simmer, stirring, for 15 minutes, or until the chicken is tender and the sauce is thick.

Stir in the yogurt, cream and lemon juice and simmer for 5 minutes, or until the sauce has thickened slightly.

Roast Pheasant

❋ SERVES 4–6
❋ PREPARATION TIME: 20 MINUTES
❋ COOKING TIME: 1 HOUR

2 x 2 lb 4 oz pheasants
6 thin bacon slices
8 medium sprigs thyme
2 large pieces of muslin
1/3 cup melted butter
2 medium apples, cored and cut into
   thick wedges
1/4 cup apple cider
1/2 cup whipping cream
2 teaspoons thyme leaves
2–4 teaspoons apple cider vinegar

Preheat the oven to 450°F. Rinse the pheasants and pat dry. Tuck the wings underneath the pheasants and tie the legs together with kitchen string. Wrap the bacon around each pheasant and secure with toothpicks. Thread the thyme sprigs through the bacon. Dip the pieces of muslin into the melted butter and wrap one around each pheasant.

Place on a rack in an ovenproof dish and bake for 10 minutes. Reduce the oven to 400°F and bake for a further 35 minutes. About 20 minutes before the end of the cooking, add the apple wedges to the base of the dish. The pheasants are cooked when the juices run clear when pierced with a skewer. Remove the pheasants and apple wedges, discard the muslin and toothpicks, then cover and keep warm.

Place the ovenproof dish with the juices on the stovetop. Pour the apple cider into the pan and bring to a boil. Cook for 3 minutes, or until reduced by half. Strain into a clean saucepan. Add the cream to the saucepan and boil for 5 minutes, or until the sauce thickens slightly. Stir in the thyme leaves and season well. Add the apple cider vinegar, to taste. Serve with the pheasant and apple.

General Tso's Chicken

❋ SERVES 4–6
❋ PREPARATION TIME: 15 MINUTES
❋ COOKING TIME: 10 MINUTES

2 tablespoons Chinese rice wine
1 tablespoon cornstarch
$\frac{1}{3}$ cup dark soy sauce
3 teaspoons sesame oil
$3\frac{3}{4}$ cups cubed boneless, skinless chicken
    thighs
2 pieces dried citrus peel
$\frac{1}{2}$ cup peanut oil
$1\frac{1}{2}$–2 teaspoons chili flakes
2 tablespoons finely chopped fresh ginger
1 cup thinly sliced scallions, plus extra,
    to garnish
2 teaspoons sugar
steamed rice, to serve

Combine the rice wine, cornstarch, 2 tablespoons of the soy sauce and 2 teaspoons of the sesame oil in a large non-metallic bowl. Add the chicken, toss to coat in the marinade, then cover and marinate in the refrigerator for 1 hour.

Meanwhile, soak the dried citrus peel in warm water for 20 minutes. Remove from the water and finely chop — you will need $1\frac{1}{2}$ teaspoons chopped peel.

Heat the peanut oil in a wok over high heat. Using a slotted spoon, drain the chicken from the marinade, then add to the wok in batches and stir-fry for 2 minutes at a time, or until browned and just cooked through. Remove from the oil with a slotted spoon and leave to drain in a colander or sieve.

Drain all the oil except 1 tablespoon from the wok. Reheat the wok over high heat, then add the chili flakes and ginger. Stir-fry for 10 seconds, then return the chicken to the wok. Add the scallions, sugar, chopped citrus peel, remaining soy sauce and sesame oil and $\frac{1}{2}$ teaspoon salt and stir-fry for a further 2–3 minutes, or until well combined and warmed through. Garnish with the extra scallions and serve with steamed rice.

NOTE: This dish is named after a 19th-century Chinese general from Yunnan province.

Saltimbocca

❀ SERVES 4

❀ PREPARATION TIME: 15 MINUTES

❀ COOKING TIME: 20 MINUTES

4 thin veal steaks

2 medium garlic cloves, crushed

4 medium prosciutto slices

4 sage leaves

2 tablespoons butter

2/3 cup Marsala

Trim the meat of excess fat and sinew and flatten each steak to 1/4 inch thick. Nick the edges to prevent curling and pat the meat dry with paper towels. Combine the garlic with 1/4 teaspoon salt and 1/2 teaspoon ground black pepper and rub some of the mixture over one side of each veal steak. Place a slice of prosciutto on each and top with a sage leaf. The prosciutto should cover the veal completely but not overlap the edge.

Melt the butter in a large heavy-based frying pan, add the veal, prosciutto side up, and cook over heat for 5 minutes, or until the underside is golden brown. Do not turn the veal. Add the Marsala, without wetting the top of the veal. Reduce the heat and simmer very slowly for 10 minutes. Transfer the veal to warm serving plates. Boil the sauce for 2–3 minutes, or until syrupy, then spoon it over the veal.

Braised Lamb Shanks with Haricot Beans

❀ SERVES 4

❀ PREPARATION TIME: 10 MINUTES

❀ COOKING TIME: 2 HOURS 15 MINUTES

2 cups dried haricot beans

1/3 cup oil

4 lamb shanks, trimmed

2 2/3 tablespoons butter

2 medium garlic cloves, crushed

2 medium onions, finely chopped

1 1/2 tablespoons thyme

2 tablespoons concentrated tomato purée

3 1/4 cups canned crushed tomatoes

1 tablespoon paprika

1 dried jalapeño chili, roughly chopped

1 cup roughly chopped Italian parsley

Cover the beans with water and soak overnight.

In a large heavy-based saucepan, heat 3 tablespoons of the oil over medium heat and brown the lamb on all sides. Remove, set aside and drain the fat from the pan. Heat the butter and remaining oil in the pan and cook the garlic and onion over medium heat for 3–4 minutes, or until softened. Add the thyme, tomato purée, crushed tomato and paprika and simmer for 5 minutes. Add the lamb shanks and 2 cups hot water. Season and bring to a boil. Cover, reduce the heat and simmer gently for 30 minutes.

Drain the beans and add to the pan with the chili and 2 cups hot water. Bring to a boil, cover and simmer for another 1–1 1/2 hours, or until the beans and the meat are tender, adding more water, 1/2 cup at a time, if necessary. Adjust the seasoning if necessary and stir in half the parsley. Serve hot, sprinkled with parsley.

Saltimbocca

Chicken and Chorizo Paella

🌸 SERVES 6
🌸 PREPARATION TIME: 30 MINUTES
🌸 COOKING TIME: 1 HOUR 5 MINUTES

¼ cup olive oil
1 large red pepper, cut into ¼ inch strips
2½ cups cubed boneless, skinless chicken
    thighs
7 oz sliced chorizo
2¼ cups thinly sliced mushrooms
3 medium garlic cloves, crushed
1 tablespoon grated lemon zest
3½ cups roughly chopped ripe medium
    tomatoes
1⅔ cups trimmed green beans, cut into
    1¼ inch lengths
1 tablespoon chopped rosemary
2 tablespoons chopped Italian parsley
¼ teaspoon saffron threads dissolved in
    ¼ cup hot water
2 cups short-grain white rice
3 cups hot chicken stock
6 lemon wedges, to serve

Heat the olive oil in a paella pan or in a large heavy-based, deep frying pan over medium heat. Add the red pepper strips and cook, stirring, for about 6 minutes, or until softened, then remove from the pan.

Add the chicken to the pan and cook for 10 minutes, or until browned. Remove from the pan. Add the chorizo to the pan and cook for 5 minutes, or until golden. Remove from the pan. Add the mushrooms, garlic and lemon zest to the pan, and cook over medium heat for 5 minutes.

Stir in the tomato and red pepper, and cook for a further 5 minutes, or until the tomato is soft.

Add the beans, rosemary, parsley, saffron mixture, rice, chicken and chorizo. Stir briefly and add the stock. Do not stir at this point. Reduce the heat and simmer for 30 minutes. Remove from the heat, cover and leave to stand for 10 minutes. Serve with lemon wedges.

NOTE: Paella pans are available from specialist kitchenware shops.

Indonesian Spicy Chicken Soup

❊ SERVES 6

❊ PREPARATION TIME: OVERNIGHT
+ 30 MINUTES

❊ COOKING TIME: 2 HOURS

2 teaspoons coriander seeds
2 tablespoons vegetable oil
3 lb 2 oz whole chicken, jointed
  into 8 pieces
4 medium garlic cloves
1 medium onion, chopped
2 teaspoons finely sliced ginger
1 dried medium red chili, halved
2 medium lemongrass stems, white part
  only, roughly chopped
1 cup roughly chopped cilantro roots and
  stems, well rinsed
2 teaspoons ground turmeric
1 teaspoon galangal powder
1 teaspoon sugar
1 teaspoon ground coriander
4 cups chicken stock
2 tablespoons lemon juice
1¼ cups cellophane noodles
1½ tablespoons fish sauce
1 cup trimmed bean sprouts
3 tablespoons chopped cilantro leaves
4 medium scallions, thinly sliced
¼ cup crisp fried onions
1 tablespoon sambal oelek

Dry-fry the coriander seeds in a small frying pan over medium heat for 1 minute, or until fragrant. Cool, then finely grind using a mortar and pestle.

Heat a wok to very hot, add 2 teaspoons of the oil and swirl to coat the base and side. Add the chicken pieces and cook in batches for 3–4 minutes, or until browned all over. Remove from the wok and set aside.

Heat the remaining oil in the wok then add the garlic, onion, ginger and chili and stir-fry for 5 minutes, or until softened. Add the lemongrass, cilantro root and stem, turmeric, galangal, sugar and ground coriander and cook for 5 minutes. Return the chicken to the wok and pour in the stock, lemon juice and 2 cups water to cover the chicken. Cover the wok with a lid and simmer for 20 minutes, skimming the surface periodically to remove any scum that rises to the surface. Remove only the chicken breast pieces, then cover the wok and simmer (still skimming the surface occasionally) for 20 minutes before removing the rest of the chicken pieces. Cover and refrigerate the chicken until needed. Return the lid to the wok and simmer the broth over low heat for 1 hour. Strain through a fine sieve, and allow to cool to room temperature before covering with plastic wrap and refrigerating overnight.

Soak the cellophane noodles in boiling water for 3–4 minutes then drain and rinse.

Remove any fat from the top of the cold broth. Remove the flesh from the chicken and shred with a fork. Place the broth and chicken flesh in the wok, and place over medium heat. Bring to a boil, then stir in the fish sauce, bean sprouts, cilantro leaves and noodles. Season well, then ladle into large bowls. Sprinkle with scallions and crisp fried onion, and serve with sambal oelek.

Braised Duck with Mushrooms

❋ SERVES 6
❋ PREPARATION TIME: 20 MINUTES
❋ COOKING TIME: 1 HOUR 10 MINUTES

2/3 cup dried Chinese mushrooms
3 lb 5 oz whole duck
2 teaspoons oil
2 tablespoons soy sauce
2 tablespoons Chinese rice wine
2 teaspoons sugar
2 wide strips orange peel
4 1/4 cups watercress

Soak the mushrooms in hot water for 20 minutes. Drain well, discard the stems and thinly slice the caps.

Using a large heavy knife or cleaver, chop the duck into small pieces, cutting through the bone. Arrange the pieces on a rack and pour boiling water over them — the water will plump up the skin and help keep the duck succulent. Drain and pat dry with paper towel.

Heat the oil in a wok over medium heat and add the duck. Cook, in batches, for about 8 minutes, turning regularly, until browned. (The darker the browning at this stage, the better the color when finished.) Between each batch, wipe out the pan with crumpled paper towel to remove excess oil.

Wipe the pan with paper towel again and return all the duck to the pan. Add the mushrooms, soy sauce, wine, sugar and orange peel. Bring the mixture to a boil, reduce the heat, cover and simmer gently for 35 minutes or until the duck is tender. Season to taste and stand for 10 minutes, covered, before serving.

Remove the duck from the sauce and discard the orange peel. Pick off small sprigs of the watercress and arrange them on one side of a large serving platter. Carefully place the duck segments on the other side of the plate — try not to place the duck on the watercress as it will become soggy. Carefully spoon a little of the sauce over the duck and serve.

NOTE: Braising the duck over low heat produces tender, melt-in-the-mouth meat and a delicious sauce. If the heat is too high, the duck will dry out and lose its flavor.

Parmesan and Rosemary Crusted Veal Chops

※ SERVES 4
※ PREPARATION TIME: 15 MINUTES
※ COOKING TIME: 15 MINUTES

4 veal chops
1¾ cup fresh white breadcrumbs
¾ cup freshly grated parmesan cheese
1 tablespoon rosemary, finely chopped
2 eggs, lightly beaten, seasoned
¼ cup olive oil
¼ cup butter
4 medium garlic cloves

Trim the chops of excess fat and sinew and flatten to ½ inch thickness. Pat the meat dry with paper towels. Combine the breadcrumbs, parmesan and rosemary in a shallow bowl.

Dip each chop in the beaten egg, draining off excess. Press both sides of the chops firmly in the crumbs.

Heat the oil and butter in a heavy-based frying pan over low heat, add the garlic and cook until golden. Discard the garlic.

Increase the heat to medium, add the chops to the pan and cook for 4–5 minutes on each side, depending on the thickness of the chops, until golden and crisp. Transfer to a warm serving dish and season.

Shish Kebabs with Peppers and Herbs

❋ SERVES 4
❋ PREPARATION TIME: 20 MINUTES
❋ COOKING TIME: 5 MINUTES

2 lb 4 oz boneless leg of lamb
1 medium red bell pepper
1 medium green bell pepper
3 medium red onions
olive oil, for brushing

MARINADE
1 medium onion, thinly sliced
2 medium garlic cloves, crushed
$1/4$ cup lemon juice
$1/3$ cup olive oil
1 tablespoon chopped thyme
1 tablespoon paprika
$1/2$ teaspoon chili flakes
2 teaspoons ground cumin
$1/2$ cup chopped Italian parsley
$1/3$ cup chopped mint

If using wooden skewers, soak them in water for about 30 minutes to prevent them from burning during cooking.

Trim the sinew and most of the fat from the lamb and cut the meat into $1 1/4$ inch cubes. Mix all the ingredients for the marinade in a large bowl. Season well, add the meat and mix well. Cover and refrigerate for 4–6 hours, or overnight.

Remove the seeds and membrane from the peppers and cut the flesh into $1 1/4$ inch squares. Cut each red onion into six wedges. Remove the lamb from the marinade and reserve the liquid. Thread the meat onto the skewers, alternating with onion and pepper pieces. Broil the skewers for 5–6 minutes, brushing frequently with the marinade for the first couple of minutes. Serve immediately. These are delicious served with bread or pilaff.

Beef Wellington

* SERVES 6–8
* PREPARATION TIME: 25 MINUTES
* COOKING TIME: 1 HOUR 30 MINUTES

2 lb 12 oz beef fillet or rib-eye in 1 piece
1 tablespoon oil
1/2 cup pâté
2/3 cup sliced button mushrooms
2 sheets frozen puff pastry, thawed
1 egg, lightly beaten
1 sheet frozen puff pastry, thawed

Preheat the oven to 425°F. Trim the meat of any excess fat and sinew. Fold the thinner part of the tail end under the meat and tie securely with kitchen string at regular intervals to form an even shape.

Rub the meat with freshly ground black pepper. Heat the oil over high heat in a large frying pan. Add the meat and brown well all over. Remove from the heat and allow to cool. Remove the string.

Spread the pâté over the top and sides of the beef. Cover with the mushrooms, pressing them onto the pâté. Roll out the block pastry on a lightly floured surface to a rectangle large enough to completely enclose the beef.

Place the beef on the pastry, brush the edges with egg, and fold over to enclose the meat completely, brushing the edges of the pastry with the beaten egg to seal, and folding in the ends. Invert onto a greased baking sheet so the seam is underneath. Cut leaf shapes from the sheet of puff pastry and use to decorate the Wellington. Use the egg to stick on the shapes. Cut a few slits in the top to allow the steam to escape. Brush the top and sides of the pastry with egg, and cook for 45 minutes for rare, 1 hour for medium or 1 1/2 hours for well-done. Leave in a warm place for 10 minutes before cutting into slices for serving.

NOTE: Use a firm pâté, discarding any jelly. Cover the pastry loosely with foil if it begins to darken too much.

Stuffed Leg of Lamb

* SERVES 6–8
* PREPARATION TIME: 25 MINUTES
* COOKING TIME: 2 HOURS 15 MINUTES

1 large leg of lamb (6 lb 12 oz), boned
1 teaspoon sweet paprika
1 tablespoon all-purpose flour
4 medium garlic cloves, peeled
2 tablespoons olive oil
1 1/2 cups dry white wine
1 tablespoon lard
1/2 cup chicken stock

STUFFING
1 thick slice white bread, crusts removed
2 1/2 oz chicken livers, trimmed
1/3 cup tocino or bacon
1 tablespoon dry sherry
1 medium garlic clove, crushed
1 tablespoon chopped Italian parsley
1/2 tablespoon chopped chives
1 teaspoon finely chopped rosemary
1 tablespoon capers, finely chopped

To make the stuffing, break the bread into pieces and process with the chicken livers and tocino until medium-fine. Put in a bowl with the sherry, garlic, parsley, chives, rosemary and capers. Season and mix well.

Preheat the oven to 425°F. Lay the lamb out flat and put the filling down the center. Roll the meat up to encase the filling. Tie with kitchen string. Combine the paprika and flour with 1/4 teaspoon salt and rub all over the lamb. Put the garlic in a row in the center of an ovenproof dish and pour the oil over the top. Put the lamb on the garlic and pour the wine over the top. Spread the lard over the surface.

Bake for 20 minutes, then reduce the heat to 325°F. Baste, then bake for a further 1 hour 45 minutes, basting frequently, until the lamb is well cooked. Transfer to a carving tray and keep warm. Spoon off excess oil from the pan juices, then transfer the contents of the ovenproof dish to a saucepan; there will be about 1/2 cup. Add the stock and cook over high heat until slightly thickened. Slice the lamb and arrange on a serving platter. Pour the sauce over the lamb.

Lamb Tagine with Quince

※ SERVES 4–6
※ PREPARATION TIME: 20 MINUTES
※ COOKING TIME: 1 HOUR 40 MINUTES

3 lb 5 oz cubed lamb shoulder
2 large onions, diced
½ teaspoon ground ginger
½ teaspoon cayenne pepper
¼ teaspoon crushed saffron threads
1 teaspoon ground coriander
1 cinnamon stick
½ cup roughly chopped cilantro leaves
2⅔ tablespoons butter
1 lb 2 oz peeled, cored and quartered
    quinces
½ cup dried apricots
cilantro sprigs, extra, to garnish

Place the lamb in a heavy-based flameproof casserole dish and add half the onion, the ginger, cayenne pepper, saffron, ground coriander, cinnamon stick, cilantro leaves and some salt and pepper. Cover with cold water and bring to a boil over medium heat. Reduce the heat and simmer, partly covered, for ½ hours, or until the lamb is tender.

While the lamb is cooking, melt the butter in a heavy-based frying pan and cook the remaining onion and the quinces for 15 minutes over medium heat, or until lightly golden.

When the lamb has been cooking for 1 hour, add the quinces and apricots and continue cooking.

Taste the sauce and adjust the seasoning if necessary. Transfer to a warm serving dish and sprinkle with cilantro sprigs. Serve with couscous or rice.

Peppered Beef Fillet with Béarnaise Sauce

❋ SERVES 6
❋ PREPARATION TIME: 30 MINUTES
❋ COOKING TIME: 45 MINUTES

2 lb 4 oz beef tenderloin
1 tablespoon oil
2 medium garlic cloves, crushed
1 tablespoon cracked black peppercorns
2 teaspoons crushed coriander seeds

BÉARNAISE SAUCE
3 medium scallions, chopped
1/2 cup dry white wine
2 tablespoons tarragon vinegar
1 tablespoon chopped tarragon
1/2 cup butter
4 egg yolks
1 tablespoon lemon juice

Preheat the oven to 425°F. Trim the fillet, removing any excess fat. Tie at regular intervals with kitchen string. Combine the oil and garlic, brush over the fillet, then roll the fillet in the combined peppercorns and coriander seeds.

Put the meat on a rack in an ovenproof dish. Bake for 10 minutes, then reduce the oven to 350°F and cook for a further 15–20 minutes for a rare result, or until cooked according to taste. Cover and leave for 10–15 minutes.

To make the béarnaise sauce, put the scallions, wine, vinegar and tarragon in a saucepan. Boil the mixture until only 2 tablespoons of the liquid remains. Strain and set aside. Melt the butter in a small saucepan. Place the wine mixture in a food processor with the egg yolks, and process for 30 seconds. With the motor running, add the butter in a thin stream, leaving the milky white sediment behind in the saucepan. Process until thickened. Add the lemon juice, to taste, and season.

Pork Sausages with White Beans

❋ SERVES 4

❋ PREPARATION TIME: 25 MINUTES

❋ COOKING TIME: 1 HOUR 40 MINUTES

1³/₄ cups dried white haricot beans

5¹/₂ oz tocino, speck or pancetta, unsliced

¹/₂ leek, white part only, thinly sliced

2 medium garlic cloves

1 medium bay leaf

1 small red chili, split and seeded

1 small onion

2 whole cloves

1 medium rosemary sprig

3 medium thyme sprigs

1 medium Italian parsley sprig

¹/₄ cup olive oil

8 pork sausages

¹/₂ medium onion, finely chopped

1 medium green bell pepper, seeded and membrane removed, finely chopped

¹/₂ teaspoon paprika

¹/₂ cup puréed tomatoes

1 teaspoon cider vinegar

Soak the beans overnight in cold water. Drain and rinse the beans under cold water. Put them in a large saucepan with the tocino, leek, garlic, bay leaf and chili. Stud the onion with the cloves and add to the pan. Tie the rosemary, thyme and parsley together and add to the pan. Pour in 3 cups cold water and bring to a boil. Add 1 tablespoon of the oil, reduce the heat and simmer, covered, for 1 hour, or until the beans are tender. When necessary, add boiling water to keep the beans covered.

Prick each sausage five or six times and twist tightly in opposite directions in the middle to give two short fat sausages. Put in a single layer in a large frying pan and add enough cold water to reach halfway up their sides. Bring to a boil and simmer, turning a few times, until all the water has evaporated and the sausages brown lightly in the fat that is left in the pan. Remove from the pan and cut the short sausages apart. Add the remaining oil, the chopped onion and pepper to the pan and fry over medium heat for 5–6 minutes. Stir in the paprika, cook for 30 seconds, then add the puréed tomato and season. Cook, stirring, for 1 minute.

Remove the tocino, herb sprigs and any loose large pieces of onion from the bean mixture. Leave in any loose leaves from the herbs, and any small pieces of onion. Add the sausages and sauce to the pan and stir the vinegar through. Bring to a boil.

Rack of Lamb with Herb Crust

✳ SERVES 4
✳ PREPARATION TIME: 25 MINUTES
✳ COOKING TIME: 25 MINUTES

2 x 6–rib racks of lamb, French trimmed
1 tablespoon oil
1 cup fresh breadcrumbs
3 medium garlic cloves
3 tablespoons finely chopped Italian
    parsley
2 teaspoons thyme leaves
$1/2$ teaspoon finely grated lemon zest
$1/4$ cup softened butter
1 cup beef stock
1 medium garlic clove, extra,
    finely chopped
1 medium thyme sprig

Preheat the oven to 500°F. Score the fat on the lamb racks in a diamond pattern. Rub with a little oil and season.

Heat the oil in a frying pan over high heat, add the lamb racks and brown for 4–5 minutes. Remove and set aside. Do not wash the pan as you will need it later.

In a large bowl, mix the breadcrumbs, garlic, parsley, thyme leaves and lemon zest. Season, then mix in the butter to form a paste.

Firmly press a layer of breadcrumb mixture over the fat on the lamb racks, leaving the bones and base clean. Bake in a roasting tin for 12 minutes for medium-rare. Rest the lamb on a plate while you make the jus.

To make the jus, add the beef stock, extra garlic and thyme sprig to the roasting tin juices, scraping the pan. Return this liquid to the original frying pan and simmer over high heat for 5–8 minutes, or until the sauce has reduced. Strain and serve with the lamb.

Beef Provençale

- SERVES 6
- PREPARATION TIME: 20 MINUTES
- COOKING TIME: 2 HOURS 25 MINUTES

3 lb 5 oz chuck steak, cut into 1 1/2 inch pieces
2 tablespoons olive oil
1 small onion, sliced
1 1/2 cups red wine
2 tablespoons chopped Italian parsley
1 tablespoon chopped rosemary
1 tablespoon chopped thyme
9 oz speck, rind removed, cut into 1/2 x 3/4 inch pieces
1 2/3 cups canned crushed tomatoes
1 cup beef stock
30 baby carrots
1/3 cup pitted medium niçoise olives

In a bowl, combine the cubed beef with 1 tablespoon of the oil, the onion, 1 cup of the wine and half the herbs. Cover with plastic wrap and marinate in the refrigerator overnight. Drain the beef, reserving the marinade. Heat the remaining oil in a large heavy-based saucepan and brown the beef and onion in batches. Remove from the pan.

Add the speck to the saucepan and cook for 3–5 minutes, or until crisp. Return the beef to the pan with the remaining wine and marinade and cook, scraping the residue from the base of the pan for 2 minutes, or until the wine has slightly reduced. Add the tomato and stock and bring to a boil. Reduce the heat and add the remaining herbs. Season well, cover and simmer for 1 1/2 hours.

Add the carrots and olives to the saucepan and cook, uncovered, for another 30 minutes, or until the meat and the carrots are tender. Before serving, check the seasoning and adjust if necessary.

Pork with Apple and Prune Stuffing

❋ SERVES 8
❋ PREPARATION TIME: 35 MINUTES
❋ COOKING TIME: 2 HOURS

1 medium granny smith apple, chopped
$1/3$ cup chopped pitted prunes
2 tablespoons port
1 tablespoon chopped Italian parsley
4 lb 8 oz piece boned pork loin
olive oil and salt, to rub on pork

GRAVY WITH WINE
2 tablespoons all-purpose flour
2 teaspoons worcestershire sauce
2 tablespoons red or white wine
$2^1/4$ cups beef or chicken stock

Preheat the oven to 475°F. To make the stuffing, combine the apple, prunes, port and parsley. Lay the pork loin on a board with the rind underneath. Spread the stuffing over the meat side of the loin, roll up and secure with skewers or string at regular intervals. If some of the filling falls out while tying, carefully push it back in. Score the pork rind with a sharp knife at $1/2$ inch intervals (if the butcher hasn't already done so) and rub generously with oil and salt.

Place on a rack in an ovenproof dish. Bake for 15 minutes, then reduce the heat to 350°F and bake for $1^1/2$–2 hours, or until the pork is cooked through. The juices will run clear when a skewer is inserted into the thickest part of the meat. Cover and stand for 15 minutes before removing the skewers or string and carving. Reserve any pan juices for making the gravy.

To make the gravy, discard all but 2 tablespoons of the pan juices from the ovenproof dish the roast was cooked in. Heat the dish on the stovetop over medium heat, stir in the flour and cook, stirring, until well browned. Remove from the heat and gradually add the worcestershire sauce, wine and stock. Return to the heat. Stir until the mixture boils and thickens, then simmer for 2 minutes. Season with salt and pepper, to taste.

NOTE: If the rind fails to crackle, carefully remove it from the meat, cutting between the fat layer and the meat. Scrape off any excess fat and put the rind on a piece of foil. Place under a hot broiler, and broil until the rind has crackled. Alternatively, place between several sheets of paper towel and microwave on High (100%) in 1 minute bursts, for about 2–3 minutes altogether (depending on the thickness of the rind).

Chinese Beef and Black Bean Sauce

❋ SERVES 4–6
❋ PREPARATION TIME: 15 MINUTES
❋ COOKING TIME: 20 MINUTES

2 tablespoons rinsed and drained black
   beans, chopped
1 tablespoon dark soy sauce
1 tablespoon Chinese rice wine
1 medium garlic clove, finely chopped
1 teaspoon sugar
$1/4$ cup peanut oil
1 medium onion, cut into wedges
1 lb 2 oz lean beef fillet, thinly
   sliced across the grain
$1/2$ teaspoon finely chopped fresh ginger
1 teaspoon cornstarch
1 teaspoon sesame oil
steamed rice, to serve

Put the beans, soy sauce, rice wine and $1/4$ cup water in a small bowl and mix. In a separate bowl, crush the garlic and sugar to a paste, using a mortar and pestle.

Heat a wok over high heat, add 1 teaspoon of the peanut oil and swirl to coat the base and side. Add the onion and stir-fry for 1–2 minutes, then transfer to a bowl and set aside. Add 1 tablespoon of the peanut oil to the wok and swirl to coat the base and side, then add half the beef and stir-fry for 5–6 minutes, or until browned. Remove to the bowl with the onion. Repeat with the remaining beef.

Add the remaining peanut oil to the wok along with the garlic paste and ginger and stir-fry for 30 seconds, or until fragrant. Add the bean mixture, onion and beef. Bring to a boil, then reduce the heat and simmer, covered, for 2 minutes.

Combine the cornstarch with 1 tablespoon water, pour into the wok and stir until the sauce boils and thickens. Stir in the sesame oil and serve with steamed rice.

Rigatoni with Italian-Style Oxtail Sauce

❋ SERVES 4
❋ PREPARATION TIME: 25 MINUTES
❋ COOKING TIME: 2 HOURS

2 tablespoons olive oil
3 lb 5 oz oxtail, jointed
2 large onions, sliced
4 medium garlic cloves, chopped
2 medium celery stalks, sliced
2 medium carrots, thinly sliced
2 large rosemary sprigs
1/4 cup red wine
1/4 cup concentrated tomato purée
4 medium tomatoes, peeled and chopped
6 cups beef stock
7 1/2 cups rigatoni

Heat the oil in a large heavy-based saucepan. Brown the oxtail, remove from the pan and set aside. Add the onion, garlic, celery and carrot to the pan and stir for 3–4 minutes, or until the onion is lightly browned.

Return the oxtail to the pan and add the rosemary and red wine. Cover and cook for 10 minutes, shaking the pan occasionally to prevent the meat from sticking to the bottom. Add the concentrated tomato purée and chopped tomato to the pan with 2 cups of the beef stock and simmer, uncovered, for 30 minutes, stirring the mixture occasionally.

Add another 2 cups of beef stock to the pan and cook for 30 minutes. Add 1 cup of stock and cook for 30 minutes. Finally, add the remaining stock and cook until the oxtail is tender and the meat is falling from the bone. The liquid should have reduced to produce a thick sauce.

Just before the meat is cooked, cook the pasta in a large saucepan of rapidly boiling salted water until *al dente*. Serve the meat and sauce over the hot pasta.

NOTE: For a different flavor, you can add 9 oz bacon to the cooked onion, garlic and vegetables.

Surf 'n' Turf

❋ SERVES 4
❋ PREPARATION TIME: 20 MINUTES
❋ COOKING TIME: 15–20 MINUTES

1 large or 2 small raw lobster tails
2 tablespoons oil
4 x 7 oz beef tenderloin
1 cup fresh or frozen crabmeat
Italian parsley, to garnish

LEMON MUSTARD SAUCE
2 tablespoons butter
1 medium scallion, finely chopped
1 medium garlic clove, crushed
1 tablespoon all-purpose flour
1 cup whole milk
2 tablespoons whipping cream
1 tablespoon lemon juice
2 teaspoons dijon mustard

To make the sauce, melt the butter in a saucepan, add the scallion and garlic and stir over medium heat for 1 minute, or until the onion has softened. Stir in the flour and cook for 1 minute, or until pale and foaming. Remove from the heat and gradually stir in the milk. Return to the heat and stir constantly until the sauce boils and thickens. Reduce the heat and simmer for 2 minutes. Remove from the heat and stir in the cream, lemon juice and mustard. Keep warm.

Starting at the end where the head was, cut down each side of the lobster shell on the underside with kitchen scissors. Pull back the flap and remove the meat from the shell. Heat half the oil in a frying pan, add the lobster meat and cook over medium heat for 3 minutes each side (longer if using a large tail), or until just cooked through. Remove from the pan and keep warm. Reserve the oil in the pan.

Meanwhile, heat the remaining oil in a separate frying pan, add the steaks and cook over high heat for 2 minutes each side to seal, turning once. For rare steaks, cook each side 1 more minute. For medium and well-done steaks, reduce the heat to medium and continue cooking for 2–3 minutes each side for medium or 4–6 minutes each side for well-done. Remove from the pan and keep warm.

Add the crab to the reserved lobster pan and stir until heated through. To serve, place the steaks on plates. Top with crab followed by slices of lobster. Pour the sauce over the top and garnish with parsley.

Thai Beef Curry

❀ SERVES 6

❀ PREPARATION TIME: 15 MINUTES

❀ COOKING TIME: 1 HOUR

1 tablespoon tamarind pulp

$1/2$ cup boiling water

2 tablespoons vegetable oil

$3^3/4$ cups cubed lean stewing beef

2 cups coconut milk

4 cardamom pods, bruised

2 cups coconut cream

2 tablespoons ready-made Musaman
   curry paste

2 tablespoons fish sauce

8 pickling onions (see Notes)

8 baby potatoes (see Notes)

2 tablespoons grated jaggery or unpacked
   brown sugar

$1/2$ cup toasted and ground unsalted
   peanuts

Put the tamarind pulp and boiling water in a bowl and set aside to cool. Mash the pulp with your fingertips to dissolve the pulp, then strain and reserve the liquid, and discard the pulp.

Heat a non-stick wok over high heat, add the oil and swirl to coat the base and side. Add the beef in batches and cook over high heat for 5 minutes, or until browned all over. Reduce the heat, add the coconut milk and cardamom pods, and simmer for 1 hour, or until the beef is tender. Remove the beef from the wok. Strain the cooking liquid into a bowl and reserve.

Heat the coconut cream in the cleaned wok and stir in the curry paste. Cook for 10 minutes, or until the oil starts to separate from the cream. Add the fish sauce, onions, potatoes, beef mixture, jaggery, peanuts, tamarind water and the reserved cooking liquid. Simmer for about 30 minutes, or until the sauce has thickened and the meat is tender.

NOTES: It is important that the pickling onions and baby potatoes are small and similar in size to ensure that they cook evenly.
Also, use a non-stick or stainless-steel wok as the tamarind purée will react with the metal in a regular wok and badly taint the dish.

Roast Beef with Yorkshire Puddings

❋ SERVES 6
❋ PREPARATION TIME: 15 MINUTES
❋ COOKING TIME: 1 HOUR 40 MINUTES

4 lb 8 oz piece roasting beef
    (scotch fillet, rump or sirloin)
2 medium garlic cloves, crushed

YORKSHIRE PUDDINGS
3/4 cup all-purpose flour
1/2 cup whole milk
2 eggs

RED WINE GRAVY
2 tablespoons all-purpose flour
1/3 cup red wine
2 1/2 cups beef stock

Preheat the oven to 475°F. Rub the piece of beef with the crushed garlic and some freshly cracked black pepper and drizzle with oil. Bake on a rack in an ovenproof dish for 20 minutes.

To make the Yorkshire puddings, sift the flour and 1/2 teaspoon salt into a large bowl, then make a well in the center and whisk in the milk. In a separate bowl, whisk the eggs together until fluffy, then add to the batter and mix well. Add 1/2 cup water and whisk until large bubbles form on the surface. Cover the bowl with plastic wrap and refrigerate for 1 hour.

Reduce the oven to 350°F and continue to roast the meat for 1 hour for rare, or longer for well-done. Cover loosely with foil and leave in a warm place while making the Yorkshire puddings.

Increase the oven to 425°F. Pour off all the pan juices into a cup and spoon 1/2 teaspoon of the juices into 12 1/3-cup muffin tins. (Reserve the remaining juice for the gravy.) Heat the muffin tins in the oven until the fat is almost smoking. Whisk the batter again until bubbles form on the surface. Pour into each muffin tin to three-quarters full. Bake for 20 minutes, or until puffed and lightly golden. Make the gravy while the Yorkshire puddings are baking.

To make the gravy, heat 2 tablespoons of the reserved pan juices in the ovenproof dish on the stovetop over low heat. Add the flour and stir well, scraping the dish to incorporate all the sediment. Cook over medium heat for 1–2 minutes, stirring constantly, until the flour is well browned. Remove from the heat and gradually stir in the wine and stock. Return to the heat, stirring constantly, until the gravy boils and thickens. Simmer for 3 minutes, then season, to taste, with salt and freshly ground black pepper. Strain, if desired.

Serve the beef with the hot Yorkshire puddings and red wine gravy.

Rabbit with Rosemary and White Wine

❋ SERVES 4
❋ PREPARATION TIME: 25 MINUTES
❋ COOKING TIME: 2 HOURS

1 large rabbit (about 3 lb 8 oz)
$^1/_4$ cup seasoned flour
$^1/_4$ cup olive oil
2 medium onions, thinly sliced
1 large rosemary sprig
1 small sage sprig
2 medium garlic cloves, crushed
2 cups dry white wine
1$^2/_3$ cups canned chopped tomatoes
good pinch of cayenne pepper
$^1/_2$ cup chicken stock
12 small black olives such as niçoise or
    ligurian, optional
3 small rosemary sprigs, extra

Cut the rabbit into large pieces and dredge the pieces in the flour. Heat the oil in a large heavy-based saucepan over heat. Brown the rabbit pieces on all sides, then remove from the saucepan.

Reduce the heat and add the onion, rosemary and sage to the saucepan. Cook gently for 10 minutes, then stir in the garlic and return the rabbit to the saucepan.

Increase the heat to high, add the wine to the pan and cook for 1 minute. Stir in the tomato, cayenne and half the stock. Reduce the heat, cover and simmer over low heat for about 1$^1/_2$ hours, until the rabbit is tender. Halfway through cooking, check the sauce and if it seems too dry, add $^1/_4$ cup water.

Discard the herb sprigs. If necessary, thicken the sauce by transferring the rabbit to a serving plate and cooking the sauce, uncovered, over high heat for about 5 minutes. Check the seasoning and adjust if necessary. Pour over the rabbit and garnish with the olives and extra rosemary. Polenta makes an excellent accompaniment to this dish.

Roast Sirloin with Mustard Sauce

※ SERVES 6
※ PREPARATION TIME: 15 MINUTES
※ COOKING TIME: 1 HOUR 30 MINUTES

3 lb 5 oz beef sirloin
1/3 cup wholegrain mustard
1 tablespoon dijon mustard
1 teaspoon honey
1 medium garlic clove, crushed
1 tablespoon oil

MUSTARD SAUCE
1 cup white wine
1 tablespoon dijon mustard
1/4 cup wholegrain mustard
2 tablespoons honey
3/4 cup cubed chilled butter

Preheat the oven to 425°F. Cut most of the fat from the piece of beef sirloin, leaving a thin layer. Mix together the mustards and add the honey and garlic. Spread over the sirloin in a thick layer. Place the oil in an ovenproof dish and heat it in the oven for 2 minutes. Place the meat in the hot dish and roast for 15 minutes. Reduce the oven to 400°F and cook for 45–50 minutes for medium-rare, or until cooked to your liking.

To make the sauce, pour the wine into a saucepan and cook over high heat for 5 minutes, or until reduced by half. Add the mustards and honey. Reduce the heat and whisk in the butter. Remove from the heat and season. Serve thin slices of the meat with the sauce and roast vegetables.

Lamb Crown Roast with Sage Stuffing

※ SERVES 4–6
※ PREPARATION TIME: 30 MINUTES
※ COOKING TIME: 50 MINUTES

1 crown roast of lamb (12 cutlets)
1 1/3 tablespoons butter
2 medium onions, chopped
1 medium granny smith apple, peeled and
    chopped
2 cups fresh breadcrumbs
2 tablespoons chopped sage
1 tablespoon chopped Italian parsley
1/4 cup unsweetened apple juice
2 eggs, separated

Preheat the oven to 425°F. Trim the meat of excess fat and sinew.

Melt the butter in a saucepan. Add the onion and apple and cook over medium heat until soft. Remove from the heat and stir into the combined breadcrumbs, sage and parsley. Whisk the apple juice and egg yolks together, then stir into the breadcrumb mixture. Beat the egg whites using electric beaters until soft peaks form. Fold into the stuffing mixture.

Place the roast on a sheet of greased foil in an ovenproof dish. Wrap some foil around the tops of the bones to prevent burning. Spoon the stuffing into the cavity. Roast for 45 minutes for medium, or until cooked to your liking. Leave for 10 minutes before cutting between the cutlets.

Roast Sirloin with Mustard Sauce

Mexican Beef Chili with Beans and Rice

❋ SERVES 4–6
❋ PREPARATION TIME: 20 MINUTES
❋ COOKING TIME: 2 HOURS

2 cups long-grain white rice
2 tablespoons olive oil
1 lb 5 oz chuck steak, cut into ¾ inch
   cubes
1 medium red onion, chopped
3 medium garlic cloves, crushed
1 long green chili, finely chopped
2½ teaspoons ground cumin
2 teaspoons ground coriander
1 teaspoon chili powder
3 teaspoons dried oregano
1⅔ cups canned chopped tomatoes
2 tablespoons concentrated tomato purée
3 cups beef stock
1½ cups canned kidney beans, drained
   and rinsed
2 tablespoons oregano, chopped
burritos, to serve
sour cream, to serve

Put the rice in a heatproof bowl, add enough boiling water to cover it and leave it to soak until cool.

Meanwhile, heat 1 tablespoon of the oil in a large heavy-based saucepan. Cook the beef in two batches until browned, then remove from the pan.

Heat the remaining oil in the pan and cook the onion for 2 minutes, or until softened but not browned. Add the garlic and chili and cook for a further minute, then add the cumin, ground coriander, chili powder and dried oregano and cook for a further 30 seconds. Return the beef to the pan and add the chopped tomato, concentrated tomato purée and 1 cup of the stock. Bring to a boil, then reduce the heat and simmer, covered, for 1½ hours, or until the beef is tender.

Drain the rice and stir it into the beef mixture along with the kidney beans and remaining stock. Bring the mixture to a boil, then reduce the heat and simmer, covered, for 20 minutes, or until the rice is tender and all the liquid has been absorbed. Stir in the oregano and serve with warmed burritos and a dollop of sour cream. Let your guests assemble their own burritos at the table.

Steak and Kidney Pie

❀ SERVES 6

❀ PREPARATION TIME: 20 MINUTES

❀ COOKING TIME: 1 HOUR 50 MINUTES

1 lb 10 oz round steak, trimmed of
    excess fat and sinew
4 lamb kidneys
2 tablespoons all-purpose flour
1 tablespoon oil
1 medium onion, chopped
2 tablespoons butter
1 tablespoon worcestershire sauce
1 tablespoon concentrated tomato purée
$1/2$ cup red wine
1 cup beef stock
$1^1/3$ cups sliced button mushrooms
$1/2$ teaspoon dried thyme
4 tablespoons chopped Italian parsley
2 sheets frozen puff pastry, thawed
1 egg, lightly beaten

Cut the steak into $3/4$ inch cubes. Peel the skin from the kidneys, quarter them and trim away any fat or sinew. Put the flour in a plastic bag with the meat and kidneys and toss gently. Heat the oil in a frying pan, add the onion and fry for 5 minutes, or until soft. Remove from the pan with a slotted spoon. Add the butter to the pan, brown the steak and kidneys in batches and then return the steak, kidneys and onion to the pan.

Add the worcestershire sauce, concentrated tomato purée, wine, stock, mushrooms and herbs to the pan. Bring to a boil, reduce the heat and simmer, covered, for 1 hour, or until the meat is tender. Season to taste and allow to cool. Spoon into a 6-cup pie dish.

25°F. Roll the pastry between two sheets of baking paper, to a size $1^1/2$ inches larger than the pie dish. Cut thin strips from the edge of the pastry and press onto the rim of the dish, sealing the joins. Place the pastry on the pie, trim the edges and cut two steam holes in the pastry. Decorate the pie with leftover pastry and brush the top with egg. Bake for 35–40 minutes, or until the pastry is golden.

Veal Osso Bucco alla Milanese

❈ SERVES 4
❈ PREPARATION TIME: 30 MINUTES
❈ COOKING TIME: 1 HOUR 40 MINUTES

12 pieces veal shank, about 1 1/2 inch thick
all-purpose flour, seasoned, for dusting
1/4 cup olive oil
1/4 cup butter
1 medium garlic clove, finely chopped
1 medium onion, finely chopped
1 medium celery stalk, finely chopped
1 cup dry white wine
1 medium bay leaf or lemon leaf
pinch ground allspice
pinch ground cinnamon

GREMOLATA
2 teaspoons grated lemon zest
2 tablespoons finely chopped Italian
    parsley
1 medium garlic clove, finely chopped

Dust each piece of veal shank with seasoned flour. Heat the oil, butter, garlic, onion and celery in a heavy-based frying pan or saucepan that is big enough to hold the shanks in a single layer (but don't add the shanks yet). Cook for about 5 minutes over low heat until softened but not browned. Add the shanks to the pan and cook for 12–15 minutes, or until well browned all over. Arrange the shanks in the pan, standing them up in a single layer. Pour in the wine and add the bay leaf, allspice and cinnamon. Bring to a boil and cover the pan. Turn the heat down to low.

Cook at a low simmer for 15 minutes, then add 1/2 cup warm water. Continue cooking, covered, for 45–60 minutes (the timing will depend on the age of the veal) or until the meat is tender and you can cut it with a fork. Check the volume of liquid once or twice during cooking time and add more warm water as needed.

To make the gremolata, mix together the lemon zest, parsley and garlic.

Transfer the veal shanks to a plate and keep warm. Discard the bay leaf. Increase the heat under the pan and stir for 1–2 minutes until the sauce has thickened, scraping up any bits off the bottom of the pan as you stir. Season to taste and return the veal shanks to the sauce. Heat everything through, then stir in half the gremolata. Serve sprinkled with the remaining gremolata.

Tagliatelle with Veal, Wine and Cream

✳ SERVES 4
✳ PREPARATION TIME: 15 MINUTES
✳ COOKING TIME: 20 MINUTES

1 lb 2 oz thin strips veal scaloppine or
    escalopes
all-purpose flour, seasoned
1/4 cup butter
1 medium onion, sliced
1/2 cup dry white wine
1/4 cup beef stock or chicken stock
2/3 cup whipping cream
1 lb 5 oz fresh plain or spinach
    tagliatelle (or a mixture of both)
1 tablespoon freshly grated parmesan
    cheese, plus extra, to serve, optional
Italian parsley, to garnish

Coat the veal strips with the seasoned flour. Melt the butter in a frying pan. Add the veal strips and fry quickly until browned. Remove with a slotted spoon and set aside.

Add the onion to the pan and stir until soft and golden. Pour in the wine and cook rapidly to reduce the liquid. Add the stock and cream and season to taste. Reduce the sauce again, and add the veal towards the end.

Meanwhile, cook the tagliatelle in a large saucepan of rapidly boiling salted water until *al dente*. Drain and transfer to a warm serving dish.

Stir the parmesan through the sauce. Pour the sauce over the pasta. Serve with extra parmesan, if desired, and garnish with parsley.

Slow-Roasted Lamb with Cumin and Paprika

✳ SERVES 6
✳ PREPARATION TIME: 15 MINUTES
✳ COOKING TIME: 3 HOURS 30 MINUTES

5 lb leg of lamb
1/3 cup softened butter
3 medium garlic cloves, crushed
2 teaspoons ground cumin
3 teaspoons ground coriander
1 teaspoon paprika
1 tablespoon ground cumin, extra,
    for dipping

Preheat the oven to 425°F. With a small sharp knife, cut small deep slits in the top and sides of the lamb.

Mix the butter, garlic, spices and 1/4 teaspoon salt in a bowl until a smooth paste forms.

With the back of a spoon, rub the paste all over the lamb, then use your fingers to spread the paste and make sure all the lamb is covered.

Put the lamb, bone side down, in a deep roasting tin and place on the top shelf of the oven. Bake for 10 minutes, then baste and return to the oven. Reduce the temperature to 325°F. Bake for 3 hours 20 minutes, basting every 20–30 minutes. Basting makes the lamb tender and flavorsome. Carve the lamb into chunky slices. Mix the cumin with 1 1/2 teaspoons salt and serve on the side for dipping.

Tagliatelle with Veal, Wine and Cream

Filo Risotto Pie

❋ SERVES 8

❋ PREPARATION TIME: 45 MINUTES

❋ COOKING TIME: 1 HOUR 45 MINUTES

2 large red bell peppers
10 sheets filo pastry
$1/4$ cup olive oil
$2^1/2$ cups spinach, blanched
$1^3/4$ cups sliced feta cheese
1 tablespoon sesame seeds

RISOTTO
1 cup white wine
4 cups vegetable stock
2 tablespoons oil
1 medium garlic clove, crushed
1 leek, white part only, sliced
1 fennel bulb, thinly sliced
2 cups risotto rice
$2/3$ cup freshly grated parmesan cheese

Cut the red peppers in half. Remove the seeds and membrane and then cut into large, flattish pieces. Broil until the skin blackens and blisters. Place on a cutting board, cover with a dish towel and allow to cool. Peel the peppers and cut the flesh into smaller pieces.

To make the risotto, put the wine and stock into a large saucepan. Bring to a boil and reduce the heat.

Heat the oil and garlic in a large heavy-based saucepan. Add the leek and fennel, cook over medium heat for 5 minutes, or until lightly browned. Add the rice and stir for 3 minutes, or until the rice is translucent.

Add 1 cup of the stock mixture to the rice and stir constantly until the liquid is absorbed. Continue adding liquid, $1/2$ cup at a time, stirring constantly until all the stock mixture has been used and the rice is tender. (This will take about 40 minutes.) Make sure the liquid stays hot as the risotto will become gluggy if it isn't. Remove from the heat, stir in the parmesan and season. Set aside until cooled slightly.

Brush each sheet of filo with olive oil and fold in half lengthways. Arrange like overlapping spokes on a wheel, in a 9 inch spring-form pan, with one side of the pastry hanging over the side of tin.

Preheat the oven to 350°F. Spoon half the risotto mixture over the pastry and top with half the red pepper, half the spinach and half the feta. Repeat with the remaining risotto, pepper, spinach and feta.

Fold the pastry over the filling, brush lightly with oil and sprinkle with sesame seeds. Bake for 50 minutes, or until the pastry is crisp and golden and the pie is heated through.

Spinach and Ricotta Cannelloni

✳ SERVES 6

✳ PREPARATION TIME: 1 HOUR

✳ COOKING TIME: 1 HOUR 15 MINUTES

1 large onion
20 cups firmly packed spinach
13 oz fresh lasagne sheets
2 tablespoons olive oil
1–2 medium garlic cloves, crushed
2⅓ cups beaten ricotta cheese
2 eggs, beaten
¼ teaspoon freshly grated nutmeg

TOMATO SAUCE
1 medium onion
1 lb 2 oz very ripe medium tomatoes
1 tablespoon olive oil
2 medium garlic cloves, finely chopped
2 tablespoons concentrated tomato purée
1 teaspoon unpacked brown sugar
1 cup grated mozzarella cheese

Finely chop the onion and spinach. Cut the lasagne sheets into 15 even-sized pieces and trim lengthways so that they will fit neatly into a deep-sided, rectangular ovenproof dish when filled. Bring a large saucepan of water to a rapid boil and cook 1–2 lasagne sheets at a time until just softened. The amount of time will differ, depending on the type and brand of lasagne, but is usually about 2 minutes. Remove the sheets carefully with a wide strainer or sieve and lay out flat on a clean, damp dish towel. Return the water to a boil and repeat the process with the remaining pasta sheets.

Heat the oil in a heavy-based frying pan. Cook the onion and garlic until golden, stirring regularly. Add the washed spinach, cook for 2 minutes, cover with a tight-fitting lid and steam for 5 minutes. Drain, removing as much liquid as possible. The spinach must be quite dry or the pasta will be soggy. Combine the spinach with the ricotta, eggs and nutmeg, and season to taste. Mix well and set aside.

To make the tomato sauce, chop the onion and tomatoes. Heat the oil in a frying pan and cook the onion and garlic for 10 minutes over low heat, stirring occasionally. Add the tomato including the juice, the concentrated tomato purée, sugar, ½ cup water and season. Bring the sauce to a boil, reduce the heat and simmer for 10 minutes.

Preheat the oven to 350°F. Lightly brush the ovenproof dish with melted butter or oil. Spread about one-third of the tomato sauce over the base of the dish. Working with one piece of lasagne at a time, spoon 2½ tablespoons of the spinach mixture down the center of the sheet, leaving a border at each end. Roll up and place, seam side down, in the dish. Repeat with the remaining pasta and filling. Spoon the remaining tomato sauce over the cannelloni and scatter the mozzarella over the top. Bake for 30–35 minutes, or until golden brown and bubbling. Set aside for 10 minutes before serving. Garnish with fresh herb sprigs if desired.

Giant Shell Pasta with Ricotta and Arugula

🌿 SERVES 6

🌿 PREPARATION TIME: 50 MINUTES

🌿 COOKING TIME: 1 HOUR

40 giant shell pasta
2⅓ cups bottled pasta sauce
2 tablespoons oregano, chopped
2 tablespoons basil

FILLING
2 cups ricotta cheese
1 cup grated parmesan cheese
3 cups finely shredded arugula
1 egg, lightly beaten
¾ cup finely chopped marinated
    artichokes
½ cup finely chopped sun-dried tomatoes
⅔ cup finely chopped sun-dried bell
    peppers

CHEESE SAUCE
¼ cup butter
¼ cup all-purpose flour
3 cups whole milk
¾ cup grated gruyère cheese
2 tablespoons chopped basil

Cook the giant shell pasta in a large saucepan of rapidly boiling salted water until *al dente*. Drain and arrange the shells on two non-stick baking sheets to prevent them sticking together. Cover lightly with plastic wrap.

To make the filling, combine all the ingredients in a large bowl. Spoon the filling into the shells, taking care not to overfill them or they will split.

To make the cheese sauce, melt the butter in a small saucepan over low heat. Add the flour and stir for 1 minute, or until golden and smooth. Remove from the heat and gradually stir in the milk. Return to the heat and stir constantly until the sauce boils and begins to thicken. Simmer for a further minute. Remove from the heat and stir in the gruyère cheese with the basil and season to taste.

Preheat the oven to 350°F. Spread 1 cup of the cheese sauce over the base of a 3 quart capacity ovenproof dish. Arrange the filled shell pasta over the sauce, top with the remaining sauce and bake for 30 minutes, or until the sauce is golden.

Pour the bottled pasta sauce in a saucepan and add the oregano. Cook over medium heat for 5 minutes, or until heated through. To serve, divide the sauce among the warmed serving plates, top with the shell pasta and sprinkle with the basil leaves.

Tofu, Peanut and Noodle Stir-Fry

❋ SERVES 4
❋ PREPARATION TIME: 15 MINUTES
❋ COOKING TIME: 5 MINUTES

1 medium red bell pepper
1 1/3 cups firm tofu
1 medium onion
2 cups broccoli
2 medium garlic cloves, crushed
1 teaspoon grated fresh ginger
1/3 cup kecap manis
1/3 cup peanut butter
2 tablespoons peanut or vegetable oil
1 lb 2 oz hokkien (egg) noodles

Cut the pepper in half, remove the seeds and membrane and chop. Cut the tofu into 5/8 inch cubes. Chop the onion and cut the broccoli into small florets. Combine the tofu with the garlic, ginger and half the kecap manis in a small bowl. Put the peanut butter, 1/2 cup water and remaining kecap manis in another bowl and mix.

Heat a wok over high heat, add the oil and swirl to coat the base and side. Drain the tofu and reserve the marinade. Cook the tofu in two batches in the hot oil until well browned. Remove from the wok.

Put the noodles in a large heatproof bowl. Cover with boiling water and leave for 1 minute. Drain and gently separate the noodles. Add the vegetables to the wok (add a little more oil if necessary) and stir-fry until just tender. Add the tofu, reserved marinade and noodles to the wok. Add the peanut butter mixture and toss until heated through.

Linguine with Roasted Vegetable Sauce

❋ SERVES 4
❋ PREPARATION TIME: 30 MINUTES
❋ COOKING TIME: 50 MINUTES

4 large red bell peppers
1 lb 2 oz firm ripe medium tomatoes
3 large red onions
1 bulb garlic
1/2 cup balsamic vinegar
1/4 cup olive oil
2 teaspoons sea salt
2 teaspoons freshly ground black pepper
1 lb 2 oz linguine
1 cup shaved parmesan cheese
1/2 cup medium black olives

Preheat the oven to 350°F. Cut the peppers in half and remove the seeds and membrane. Cut the tomatoes and onions in half and separate and peel the garlic cloves.

Arrange the vegetables in a large ovenproof dish in a single layer. Pour the vinegar and oil over them and sprinkle with the sea salt and pepper. Bake for 50 minutes. Allow to cool for 5 minutes before puréeing in a food processor for 3 minutes, or until the mixture is smooth. Season with more salt and pepper, if necessary.

When the vegetables are almost cooked, cook the linguine in a large saucepan of rapidly boiling salted water until *al dente*. Drain. Serve the roasted vegetable sauce over the linguine with the parmesan cheese, olives and some extra black pepper.

Tofu, Peanut and Noodle Stir-Fry

Pea, Egg and Ricotta Curry

❋ SERVES 4
❋ PREPARATION TIME: 15 MINUTES
❋ COOKING TIME: 30 MINUTES

4 hard-boiled eggs
$\frac{1}{2}$ teaspoon ground turmeric
2 small onions
$4\frac{1}{2}$ oz baked ricotta cheese (see Note)
3 tablespoons ghee or oil
1 medium bay leaf
1 teaspoon finely chopped garlic
$1\frac{1}{2}$ teaspoons ground coriander
$1\frac{1}{2}$ teaspoons garam masala
$\frac{1}{2}$ teaspoon chili powder, optional
$\frac{1}{2}$ cup canned chopped tomatoes
1 tablespoon concentrated tomato purée
1 tablespoon plain yogurt
$\frac{1}{2}$ cup frozen peas
2 tablespoons finely chopped cilantro
    leaves

Peel the eggs and coat them with the turmeric. Finely chop the onion and cut the ricotta into $\frac{1}{2}$ inch cubes.

Melt the ghee in a large saucepan and cook the eggs over moderate heat for 2 minutes until they are light brown, stirring constantly. Set aside.

Add the bay leaf, onion and garlic to the pan and cook over moderately high heat, stirring frequently, until the mixture is well reduced and pale gold. Lower the heat if the mixture is browning too quickly. Add the ground coriander, garam masala and chili powder, if using, and cook until fragrant.

Add the chopped tomato, concentrated tomato purée and $\frac{1}{2}$ cup water. Cover and simmer for 5 minutes. Return the eggs to the pan with the ricotta, yogurt, peas and $\frac{1}{4}$ teaspoon salt and cook for 5 minutes. Remove the bay leaf, sprinkle with the cilantro and serve immediately.

NOTE: Baked ricotta cheese is available from delicatessens and some supermarkets, but it is easy to prepare your own. Preheat the oven to 325°F. Slice the required amount of fresh ricotta (not cottage cheese or blended ricotta) into $1\frac{1}{4}$ inch thick slices. Place the ricotta on a lightly greased baking sheet and bake for 25 minutes.

Lemon and Herb Risotto with Fried Mushrooms

* SERVES 4
* PREPARATION TIME: 30 MINUTES
* COOKING TIME: 50 MINUTES

4 cups chicken or vegetable stock
pinch saffron threads
2 tablespoons olive oil
2 leeks, thinly sliced
2 medium garlic cloves, crushed
2 cups risotto rice
2–3 teaspoons finely grated lemon zest
2 tablespoons lemon juice
2 tablespoons chopped Italian parsley
2 tablespoons snipped chives
2 tablespoons chopped oregano
$3/4$ cup freshly grated parmesan cheese
$1/2$ cup mascarpone cheese
2 tablespoons butter
1 tablespoon olive oil
$2^1/4$ cups thickly sliced small flat
   mushrooms
1 tablespoon balsamic vinegar

Pour the stock into a saucepan and add the saffron threads. Bring to a boil, then reduce the heat, cover and keep at a low simmer.

Heat the olive oil in a large saucepan over medium heat. Add the leek, cook for 5 minutes, then add the garlic and cook for a further 5 minutes, or until golden. Add the rice and stir until well coated. Add half the lemon zest and half the juice, then add $1/2$ cup of the hot stock. Stir constantly over medium heat until all the liquid has been absorbed. Continue adding more liquid, $1/2$ cup at a time, until all the liquid is absorbed and the rice is tender and creamy. (You may not need to use all the stock, or you may need a little extra — every risotto will be slightly different.)

Remove the pan from the heat. Stir in the herbs, parmesan, mascarpone and the remaining lemon zest and lemon juice. Cover and keep warm.

To cook the mushrooms, melt the butter and olive oil in a large frying pan, add the mushroom slices and vinegar and cook, stirring, over high heat for 5–7 minutes, or until the mushrooms are tender and all the liquid has been absorbed.

Serve the risotto in large bowls topped with the mushrooms.

Spicy Chickpea and Vegetable Casserole

✳ SERVES 4
✳ PREPARATION TIME: 25 MINUTES
✳ COOKING TIME: 1 HOUR 30 MINUTES

1½ cups dried chickpeas (see Note)
1 large onion
2 cups winter squash
1¼ cups green beans
7 oz button squash
2 tablespoons oil
1 medium garlic clove, crushed
3 teaspoons ground cumin
½ teaspoon chili powder
½ teaspoon ground allspice
1¾ cups canned crushed tomatoes
1½ cups vegetable stock
2 tablespoons concentrated tomato purée
1 teaspoon dried oregano

Put the chickpeas in a large bowl. Cover with cold water and soak overnight. Drain.

Chop the onion. Cut the winter squash into large cubes. Top and tail the beans. Cut the button squash into quarters.

Heat the oil in a large saucepan. Add the onion and garlic and stir-fry for 2 minutes, or until tender. Add the cumin, chili powder and allspice. Stir-fry for 1 minute. Add the chickpeas, tomatoes and vegetable stock to the pan. Bring to a boil, then reduce the heat and simmer, covered, for 1 hour, stirring occasionally.

Add the winter squash, beans, button squash, concentrated tomato purée and oregano. Stir to combine. Simmer, covered, for another 15 minutes. Remove the lid from the pan and simmer, uncovered, for another 10 minutes to reduce and slightly thicken the sauce.

NOTE: A quick way to soak chickpeas is to place them in a large saucepan and cover with cold water. Bring to a boil, then remove from the heat and soak for 2 hours. If you are in a hurry, substitute canned chickpeas. Drain and rinse thoroughly before use.

Baked Eggplant with Tomato and Mozzarella

❋ SERVES 6
❋ PREPARATION TIME: 20 MINUTES
❋ COOKING TIME: 40 MINUTES

6 large slender eggplants, halved
  lengthways, leaving the stems attached
1/2 cup olive oil
2 medium onions, finely chopped
2 medium garlic cloves, crushed
1²/₃ cups canned chopped tomatoes
1 tablespoon concentrated tomato purée
3 tablespoons chopped Italian parsley
1 tablespoon chopped oregano
1 cup grated mozzarella cheese

Preheat the oven to 350°F. Score the eggplant flesh by cutting a criss-cross pattern with a sharp knife, being careful not to cut through the skin. Heat 2 tablespoons of the oil in a large frying pan, add three eggplants and cook for 2–3 minutes each side, or until the flesh is soft. Remove. Repeat with another 2 tablespoons of the oil and the remaining eggplants. Cool slightly and scoop out the flesh, leaving a 1/16 inch border. Finely chop the flesh and reserve the shells.

In the same pan, heat the remaining oil and cook the onion over medium heat for 5 minutes. Add the garlic and cook for 30 seconds, then add the tomato, concentrated tomato purée, herbs and eggplant flesh, and cook, stirring occasionally, over low heat for 8–10 minutes, or until the sauce is thick and pulpy. Season well. Arrange the eggplant shells in a lightly greased ovenproof dish and spoon in the tomato filling. Sprinkle with mozzarella and bake for 5–10 minutes, or until the cheese has melted.

Chili Satay Noodles

❋ SERVES 4–6
❋ PREPARATION TIME: 10 MINUTES
❋ COOKING TIME: 10 MINUTES

4 slender eggplants
1 lb 2 oz thin fresh egg noodles
1 tablespoon oil
1 teaspoon sesame oil
1/3 cup peanuts
2 small red chilies
3 cups sugarsnap peas
1 cup trimmed bean sprouts
1/4 cup crunchy peanut butter
1 tablespoon hoisin sauce
1/3 cup coconut milk
2 tablespoons lime juice
1 tablespoon Thai sweet chili sauce

Slice the eggplants. Add the noodles to a large saucepan of boiling water and cook for 3 minutes. Drain, rinse well under cold running water and drain again. Heat the oils in a wok or frying pan. Add the peanuts and toss over high heat for 1 minute, or until golden. Add the chilies, eggplant and sugarsnap peas and cook over high heat for 2 minutes. Reduce the heat to medium and add the noodles and the sprouts. Toss for 1 minute, or until combined.

Blend the peanut butter, hoisin sauce, coconut milk and lime juice until almost smooth. Add to the noodles. Toss over medium heat until the noodles are coated and the sauce is heated.

Baked Eggplant with Tomato and Mozzarella

Mushroom Nut Roast with Tomato Sauce

* SERVES 6
* PREPARATION TIME: 30 MINUTES
* COOKING TIME: 1 HOUR

1 large onion
$10^1/_2$ oz cap mushrooms
2 tablespoons olive oil
2 medium garlic cloves, crushed
$^1/_4$ cup cashew nuts
$^1/_4$ cup brazil nuts
1 cup grated cheddar cheese
$^1/_4$ cup freshly grated parmesan cheese
1 egg, lightly beaten
2 tablespoons snipped chives
1 cup fresh whole-wheat breadcrumbs
chives, extra, to garnish

TOMATO SAUCE
1 medium onion
$1^1/_2$ tablespoons olive oil
1 medium garlic clove, crushed
14 oz canned chopped tomatoes
1 tablespoon concentrated tomato purée
1 teaspoon sugar

Grease a $5^1/_2$ x $8^1/_4$ inch bar tin and line the base with baking paper.

Dice the onion and finely chop the mushrooms. Heat the oil in a frying pan and add the onion, garlic and mushrooms. Fry until soft, then cool.

Process the nuts in a food processor until finely chopped, but do not overprocess. Preheat the oven to 350°F.

Combine the cooled mushroom mixture, chopped nuts, cheddar, parmesan, egg, chives and breadcrumbs in a bowl. Mix well and season to taste. Press into the bar tin and bake for 45 minutes, or until firm. Leave for 5 minutes, then turn out and garnish with the extra chives. Cut into slices to serve.

Meanwhile, to make the tomato sauce, finely chop the onion. Heat the oil in a saucepan, add the onion and garlic and cook, stirring frequently, for 5 minutes, or until soft but not brown. Stir in the tomato, concentrated tomato purée, sugar and $^1/_3$ cup water. Simmer gently for 3–5 minutes, or until slightly thickened. Season. Serve the tomato sauce with the sliced nut roast.

NOTE: For a variation, use a different mixture of nuts and add some seeds. You can use nuts such as pecans, almonds, hazelnuts (without skins) and pine nuts. Suitable seeds to use include sesame, pumpkin or sunflower seeds.

desserts

Ice Cream Cassata

❋ SERVES 10
❋ PREPARATION TIME: 50 MINUTES
❋ COOKING TIME: NIL

FIRST LAYER

2 eggs, at room temperature, separated
1/3 cup confectioners' sugar
3/4 cup whipping cream
1/2 cup toasted flaked almonds

SECOND LAYER

3/4 cup chopped dark chocolate
1 tablespoon dark unsweetened cocoa
    powder
2 eggs, at room temperature, separated
1/3 cup confectioners' sugar
3/4 cup whipping cream

THIRD LAYER

2 eggs, at room temperature, separated
1/4 cup confectioners' sugar
1/4 cup whipping cream
1/2 cup ricotta cheese
1 cup finely chopped candied glacé fruit
    (pineapple, apricot, cherries,
    fig and peach)
1 teaspoon natural vanilla essence

Line the base and sides of a deep 8 inch square tin with foil.

To make the first layer, beat the egg whites with electric beaters until soft peaks form. Add the confectioners' sugar gradually, beating well after each addition. In a separate bowl, beat the cream until firm peaks form. Using a metal spoon, fold the yolks and beaten egg whites into the cream. Stir in the almonds. Spoon into the tin and smooth the surface. Tap the tin gently on the bench to level the surface, then freeze for 30–60 minutes, or until firm.

To make the second layer, melt the chocolate by stirring in a heatproof bowl over a saucepan of steaming water, off the heat. Make sure the base of the bowl does not touch the water. Stir in the cocoa until smooth. Cool slightly, then proceed as for step 1, beating the egg whites and confectioners' sugar and then the cream. Using a metal spoon, fold the chocolate into the cream. Fold in the yolks and beaten egg whites and stir until smooth. Spoon over the frozen first layer. Tap the tin on the bench to smooth the surface. Freeze for 30–60 minutes, or until firm.

To make the third layer, proceed as for the first layer, beating the egg whites with the confectioners' sugar and then the cream. Stir the ricotta into the cream. With a metal spoon, fold the yolks and egg white into the cream, then stir in the fruit and vanilla essence. Spoon over the chocolate layer, cover the surface with baking paper, then freeze overnight. Slice to serve.

Chocolate Cherry Trifle

※ SERVES 6
※ PREPARATION TIME: 30 MINUTES
※ COOKING TIME: 10 MINUTES

11 oz chocolate cake
2 x 14 oz cans pitted dark cherries
¼ cup kirsch
¼ cup toasted slivered almonds, to serve
whipped cream, to serve

CUSTARD
2 egg yolks, at room temperature
2 tablespoons sugar
1 tablespoon cornstarch
1 cup whole milk
1 teaspoon natural vanilla essence
¾ cup whipping cream, lightly whipped

Cut the cake into thin strips. Line the base of a 7-cup serving bowl with one-third of the cake.

Drain the cherries, reserving the juice. Combine 1 cup of the juice with the kirsch and sprinkle some liberally over the cake. Spoon some cherries over the cake.

To make the custard, whisk the egg yolks, sugar and cornstarch in a heatproof bowl until thick and pale. Heat the milk in a pan until almost boiling. Remove from the heat and add gradually to the egg mixture, beating constantly. Return to a clean pan and stir over medium heat for 5 minutes, or until the custard boils and thickens. Remove from the heat and add the vanilla essence. Cover the surface with plastic wrap and allow to cool, then fold in the whipped cream.

To assemble, spoon a third of the custard over the cherries and cake in the bowl. Top with more cake, syrup, cherries and custard. Repeat the layering process, ending with custard on top. Cover and refrigerate for 3–4 hours. Decorate with almonds and whipped cream.

Devil's Food Cake

✳ SERVES 8–10
✳ PREPARATION TIME: 30 MINUTES
✳ COOKING TIME: 35 MINUTES

1 1/2 cups unpacked brown sugar
1/3 cup unsweetened cocoa powder
1 cup whole milk
2/3 cup chopped dark chocolate
1/2 cup softened unsalted butter
1 teaspoon natural vanilla essence
2 eggs, at room temperature, separated
1 1/2 cups all-purpose flour
1 teaspoon baking soda

CHOCOLATE ICING
1/3 cup chopped dark chocolate
2 tablespoons unsalted butter
1 tablespoon confectioners' sugar

FILLING
1 cup whipping cream
1 tablespoon confectioners' sugar
1 teaspoon natural vanilla essence

Preheat the oven to 325°F. Lightly grease two deep 8 inch round cake tins and line the bases with baking paper. Combine one-third of the brown sugar with the cocoa and milk in a small saucepan. Stir over low heat until the sugar and cocoa have dissolved. Remove from the heat and stir in the chocolate, stirring until it is melted. Cool.

Cream the remaining brown sugar with the butter in a small bowl with electric beaters until light and fluffy. Beat in the vanilla essence and egg yolks and the cooled chocolate mixture. Transfer to a large bowl, and stir in the sifted flour and baking soda.

Beat the egg whites in a small bowl until soft peaks form. Fold into the chocolate mixture. Divide the mixture evenly between the tins. Bake for 35 minutes, or until a skewer inserted in the center of the cakes comes out clean. Leave in the tins for 5 minutes before turning out onto a wire rack to cool.

To make the icing, put the chocolate and butter in a heatproof bowl. Place the bowl over a pan of simmering water, making sure it does not touch the water, and stir until the mixture is melted and smooth. Gradually add the sifted confectioners' sugar and stir until smooth.

To make the filling, whip the cream, confectioners' sugar and vanilla essence in a small bowl with electric beaters until stiff peaks form. Spread over one of the cold cakes, top with the second cake and spread with icing, over the top or top and sides.

Chocolate Pots

❋ SERVES 8
❋ PREPARATION TIME: 20 MINUTES
❋ COOKING TIME: 1 HOUR

²/₃ cup heavy cream
¹/₂ vanilla bean, split lengthways
1 cup chopped good-quality dark
    chocolate
¹/₃ cup whole milk
2 egg yolks, at room temperature
¹/₄ cup sugar
whipped cream and unsweetened cocoa
    powder, to serve

Lightly brush eight ¹/₃-cup ramekins with melted butter and put in a deep ovenproof dish. Preheat the oven to 275°F. Heat the cream and vanilla bean in a small saucepan until the cream is warm. Leave to infuse. Combine the chocolate and milk in a small saucepan. Stir constantly over low heat until the chocolate has just melted.

Put the egg yolks in a small bowl and slowly whisk in the sugar until it has dissolved and the mixture is light and creamy. Scrape the seeds out of the vanilla bean into the cream and discard the bean. Add the vanilla cream and the melted chocolate mixture to the beaten egg yolks and mix well.

Pour the mixture into the ramekins, filling about two-thirds of the way. Fill the ovenproof dish with enough boiling water to come halfway up the ramekins. Bake for 45 minutes, or until the pots have puffed up slightly and feel spongy. Remove from the dish and cool. Cover and refrigerate for 6 hours before serving. Serve with cream and a sprinkle of sifted cocoa powder.

Espresso Granita

❋ SERVES 6
❋ PREPARATION TIME: 10 MINUTES
❋ COOKING TIME: NIL

2 tablespoons sugar
2 cups hot espresso coffee
lightly whipped cream, to serve

Dissolve the sugar in the coffee and stir thoroughly until dissolved. Pour into a shallow metal container or tray and cool completely. Freeze for 30 minutes, then scrape with a fork to distribute the ice crystals evenly. Freeze again for 30 minutes.

Using a fork, scrape the granita into fine crystals and return to the freezer for 1 hour before serving. Spoon into glasses and top with a dollop of lightly whipped cream.

> NOTE: Use a shallow tray and break the granita up when partially frozen. It is difficult to break up if made in a deep container.

Chocolate Pots

Praline Ice Cream with Caramel Bark

❋ SERVES 4
❋ PREPARATION TIME: 25 MINUTES
❋ COOKING TIME: 7 MINUTES

½ cup toasted blanched almonds
¼ cup sugar
¾ cup whipping cream
1 cup 2 tablespoons mascarpone
1 cup melted and cooled white chocolate
2 tablespoons sugar, extra
fresh medium figs and dessert wafers,
    to serve, optional

Line a flat baking sheet with foil, brush the foil lightly with oil and put the almonds on the foil. Place ¼ cup sugar in a small pan over low heat. Tilt the pan slightly (do not stir) and watch until the sugar melts and turns golden — this should take about 3–5 minutes.

Pour the caramel over the almonds and leave until set and cold. Break into chunks, put in a plastic bag and crush with a rolling pin, or crush briefly in a food processor until crumbly.

Whip the cream until stiff peaks form. Stir the mascarpone and chocolate in a large bowl to combine. Using a metal spoon, fold in the whipped cream and crushed praline. Transfer to a 4-cup metal tray, cover the surface with a piece of baking paper and freeze for 6 hours, or overnight. Remove from the freezer 15 minutes before serving, to soften slightly.

To make the caramel bark, line a baking sheet with foil and brush lightly with oil. Sprinkle 2 tablespoons sugar evenly onto the tray and place under a hot broiler for 2 minutes, until the sugar is melted and golden. Check frequently towards the end of cooking time, as the sugar may burn quickly. Remove from the heat, leave until set and completely cold, then break into shards. Serve with the ice cream, perhaps with fresh figs and dessert wafers.

Chilled Lime Soufflé

- SERVES 4
- PREPARATION TIME: 35 MINUTES + CHILLING
- COOKING TIME: NIL

5 eggs, at room temperature, separated
1 cup sugar
2 teaspoons finely grated lime rind
3/4 cup lime juice, strained
1 tablespoon gelatin
1 1/4 cups whipping cream, lightly whipped

Cut four strips of baking paper or foil long enough to fit around 1-cup soufflé dishes. Fold each in half lengthways, wrap one around each dish, extending 1 1/2 inches above the rim, then secure with string. Brush the inside of the collar with melted butter, sprinkle with sugar, shake to coat, then tip out excess.

Using electric beaters, beat the egg yolks, sugar and lime rind in a small bowl for 3 minutes, until the sugar has dissolved and the mixture is thick and pale. Heat the lime juice in a small pan, then gradually add to the yolk mixture while beating, until well mixed.

Pour 1/4 cup water into a small heatproof bowl, sprinkle the gelatin in an even layer over the surface and leave to go spongy. Bring a large pan filled with about 1 1/2 inches water to a boil, remove from the heat, carefully lower the gelatin bowl into the water (it should come halfway up the side of the bowl), then stir until dissolved. Cool slightly, then add gradually to the lime mixture, beating on low speed until combined. Transfer to a large bowl, cover with plastic wrap and refrigerate for 15 minutes, or until thickened but not set. Using a metal spoon, fold the cream into the lime mixture until almost combined.

Using electric beaters, beat the egg whites in a clean, dry bowl until soft peaks form. Fold the egg white quickly and lightly into the lime mixture, using a large metal spoon, until just combined with no lumps of egg white remaining. Spoon gently into the soufflé dishes and chill until set. Remove the collars when ready to serve. Can be served with whipped cream.

Hazelnut Torte

* SERVES 8–10
* PREPARATION TIME: 1 HOUR
* COOKING TIME: 20 MINUTES

6 egg whites, at room temperature
1¼ cups sugar
1⅓ cups ground hazelnuts
2 tablespoons all-purpose flour, sifted
6½ tablespoons white rum
chopped toasted hazelnuts, to decorate

CHOCOLATE LEAVES
1 cup white chocolate
non-toxic leaves (choose leaves with
    prominent veins such as ivy or rose —
    you can also check with your florist or
    local nursery for appropriate leaves)

WHITE CHOCOLATE CREAM
1 cup white chocolate
1¾ cups whipping cream

DARK CHOCOLATE CREAM
¼ cup dark chocolate
½ cup whipping cream

Lightly grease two 8 inch round cake tins. Line the bases with baking paper and then grease the paper. Dust the tins lightly with flour, shaking off any excess. Preheat the oven to 350°F.

Beat the egg whites in a clean, dry bowl, with electric beaters, until stiff peaks form. Gradually add the sugar, beating until thick and glossy. Fold in the ground hazelnuts and flour. Divide evenly between the tins and smooth the tops. Bake for 15–20 minutes, or until the cakes feel spongy to touch. Leave to cool a little before turning onto wire racks. Cut in half horizontally with a serrated knife.

To make the chocolate leaves, chop the white chocolate into small even-sized pieces and place in a heatproof bowl. Bring a saucepan of water to a boil, then remove from the heat. Sit the bowl over the pan, making sure the base of the bowl doesn't sit in the water. Stir occasionally until the chocolate has melted. Use a brush to paint the chocolate over the underside of the leaves. Leave to set, then peel away the leaf. If the chocolate is too thin, it will break when the leaf is removed.

For the white chocolate cream, bring a saucepan of water to a boil and remove the pan from the heat. Place the white chocolate in a heatproof bowl and sit the bowl over the water, making sure the bowl does not touch the water. Stir occasionally until the chocolate melts, then allow to cool. Whip the cream in a bowl, with beaters, until it begins to hold its shape. Add the chocolate and beat it in, then allow to cool. Make the dark chocolate cream in the same way.

Put a layer of cake on a plate, brush the cut surface with rum and spread with a quarter of the white chocolate cream. Top with a second cake layer. Brush with rum and spread with all the dark chocolate cream. Add another layer of cake and spread with rum and a quarter of the white chocolate cream. Top with the final cake layer and spread the remaining white chocolate cream over the top and side of the cake. Decorate with chopped hazelnuts and chocolate leaves.

Pears Poached in Wine

✳ SERVES 4
✳ PREPARATION TIME: 20 MINUTES
✳ COOKING TIME: 45 MINUTES

4 firm medium pears
3 cups good-quality red wine
¾ cup sugar
1 cinnamon stick
¼ cup orange juice
2 inch piece orange peel
1 cup mascarpone cheese, to serve

Peel the pears, being careful to keep the pears whole with the stalks still attached.

Put the wine, sugar, cinnamon stick, orange juice and peel in a saucepan that is large enough for the pears to stand upright. Stir over medium heat until the sugar is dissolved. Add the pears to the saucepan and stir gently to coat. The pears should be almost covered with the wine mixture. Cover the pan and simmer for 20–25 minutes, or until the pears are cooked. Allow to cool in the syrup.

Remove the pears with a slotted spoon. Bring the liquid to a boil and boil rapidly until about ¾ cup of liquid remains. Serve the pears with a little syrup and some mascarpone.

Tapioca Pudding

✳ SERVES 6
✳ PREPARATION TIME: 20 MINUTES
✳ COOKING TIME: 20 MINUTES

1 cup tapioca
1 cup unpacked brown sugar
1 cup coconut cream, well chilled

Soak the tapioca in 3 cups water for 1 hour. Pour into a saucepan, add 2 tablespoons of the sugar and bring to a boil over low heat, stirring constantly. Reduce the heat and simmer, stirring occasionally, for 8 minutes. Cover and cook for 2–3 minutes, until the mixture becomes thick and the tapioca grains are translucent.

Half-fill six wet ½-cup molds with the tapioca mixture. Refrigerate for 2 hours, or until set.

Combine the remaining sugar with 1 cup water in a small saucepan and cook over low heat until the sugar dissolves. Simmer for 5–7 minutes, or until the syrup thickens. Remove from the heat and cool.

To serve, unmold the tapioca by wiping a cloth dipped in hot water over the mold and turn out onto the plate. Top with the sugar syrup and coconut cream.

Pears Poached in Wine

Macerated Oranges

❋ SERVES 4
❋ PREPARATION TIME: 10 MINUTES
❋ COOKING TIME: NIL

4 medium oranges
1 teaspoon grated lemon zest
¼ cup sugar
1 tablespoon lemon juice
2 tablespoons orange-flavored liqueur or
   maraschino liqueur, to serve, optional

Cut a thin slice off the top and bottom of the oranges. Using a small sharp knife, slice off the skin and pith, removing as much pith as possible. Slice down the side of a segment between the flesh and the membrane. Repeat on the other side and lift the segment out. Do this over a bowl to catch the juice. Repeat with all the segments. Squeeze out any juice remaining in the membranes.

Place the segments on a shallow dish and sprinkle with the lemon zest, sugar and lemon juice. Toss carefully. Cover and refrigerate for at least 2 hours. Toss again. Serve chilled. Add orange or maraschino liqueur just before serving, if desired.

Black Forest Gateau

* SERVES 8–10
* PREPARATION TIME: 1 HOUR
* COOKING TIME: 60 MINUTES

½ cup unsalted butter
1 cup sugar
2 eggs, at room temperature, lightly beaten
1 teaspoon natural vanilla essence
⅓ cup self-rising flour
1 cup all-purpose flour
1 teaspoon baking soda
½ cup unsweetened cocoa powder
¾ cup buttermilk

TOPPING
⅔ cup dark chocolate
⅔ cup milk chocolate
cherries with stalks, to decorate

FILLING
¼ cup kirsch
3 cups whipping cream, whipped
2¼ cups canned pitted morello or
    black cherries, drained

Preheat the oven to 350°F. Lightly grease a deep, 8 inch round cake tin. Line the base and side with baking paper. Using electric beaters, beat the butter and sugar until light and creamy. Add the egg gradually, beating thoroughly after each addition. Add the vanilla essence and beat until well combined. Transfer to a large bowl. Using a metal spoon, fold in the sifted flours, baking soda and cocoa alternately with the buttermilk. Mix until combined and the mixture is smooth.

Pour the mixture into the tin and smooth the surface. Bake the cake for 50–60 minutes, or until a skewer inserted into the center of the cake comes out clean. Leave the cake in the tin for 30 minutes before turning out onto a wire rack to cool. When cold, cut horizontally into three layers, using a long serrated knife. The easiest way to do this is to rest the palm of one hand lightly on top of the cake while cutting into it. Turn the cake every few strokes so the knife cuts in evenly all the way around the edge. When you have gone the whole way round, cut through the middle. Remove the first layer so it will be easier to see what you are doing while cutting the next one.

To make the topping, leave the chocolate in a warm place for 10–15 minutes, or until soft but still firm. With a vegetable peeler, and using long strokes, shave curls of chocolate from the side of each block. If the block is too soft, chill it to firm it up.

To assemble, place one cake layer on a serving plate and brush liberally with kirsch. Spread evenly with one-fifth of the whipped cream. Top with half the cherries. Continue layering with the remaining cake, cream and liqueur cherries, finishing with the cream on top. Spread the cream evenly on the outside of the cake. Coat the side with chocolate shavings by placing the shavings on a small piece of baking paper and then gently pressing them into the cream. If you use your hands, they will melt, so the paper acts as a barrier. Pipe rosettes of cream around the top edge of the cake and decorate with fresh or maraschino cherries on stalks and more chocolate shavings.

Chocolate Hazelnut Torte

※ SERVES 10
※ PREPARATION TIME: 1 HOUR
※ COOKING TIME: 1 HOUR 15 MINUTES

3⅓ cups chopped dark chocolate
6 eggs, at room temperature
2 tablespoons hazelnut liqueur
1½ cups ground hazelnuts
1 cup whipping cream
12 whole hazelnuts, lightly toasted

CHOCOLATE TOPPING
⅓ chopped dark chocolate
¾ cup whipping cream
1 tablespoon hazelnut liqueur

Preheat the oven to 300°F. Grease a deep 8 inch round cake tin and line with baking paper.

Put the chocolate in a heatproof bowl. Half-fill a saucepan with water and bring to a boil. Remove from the heat and place the bowl over the pan, making sure it is not touching the water. Stir occasionally until the chocolate is melted. Break the eggs into a large heatproof bowl and add the hazelnut liqueur. Place the bowl over a saucepan of barely simmering water over low heat, making sure it does not touch the water. Beat with electric beaters on high speed for 7 minutes, or until the mixture is light and foamy. Remove from the heat. Using a metal spoon, quickly and lightly fold the melted chocolate and ground nuts into the egg mixture until just combined. Fold in the cream and pour the mixture into the cake tin. Place the tin in a shallow ovenproof dish. Pour in enough hot water to come halfway up the side of the tin.

Bake for 1 hour, or until just set. Remove the tin from the ovenproof dish. Cool to room temperature, cover with plastic wrap and refrigerate overnight.

Cut a 7 inch circle from heavy cardboard. Invert the chilled cake onto the disc so that the base of the cake becomes the top. Place on a wire rack over a baking sheet and remove the baking paper. Allow the cake to return to room temperature before you start to decorate.

To make the topping, combine the chopped chocolate, cream and hazelnut liqueur in a small pan. Heat gently over low heat, stirring, until the chocolate is melted and the mixture is smooth. Pour the chocolate mixture over the cake in the center, tilting slightly to cover the cake evenly. Tap the baking sheet gently on the bench so that the top is level and the icing runs completely down the side of the cake. Place the hazelnuts around the edge of the cake. Refrigerate just until the topping has set and the cake is firm. Carefully transfer the cake to a serving plate, and cut into thin wedges to serve.

Summer Berry Tart

PASTRY
1 cup all-purpose flour
1/3 cup cubed chilled unsalted butter
2 tablespoons confectioners' sugar
1–2 tablespoons iced water

FILLING
3 egg yolks, at room temperature
2 tablespoons sugar
2 tablespoons cornstarch
1 cup whole milk
1 teaspoon natural vanilla essence
1 2/3 cups halved medium strawberries
3/4 cup medium blueberries
1 cup medium raspberries
1–2 tablespoons apple jelly

Preheat the oven to 350°F. Lightly grease an 8 inch round, loose-based, fluted tart tin.

To make the pastry, sift the flour into a bowl. Using your fingertips, rub in the butter until the mixture resembles fine breadcrumbs. Mix in the sugar. Make a well in the center and add almost all the water. Mix with a flat-bladed knife, using a cutting action, until the mixture comes together in beads. Add more water if the dough is too dry.

Roll out the pastry between two sheets of baking paper to fit the base and side of the tin. Line the tin with the pastry and trim away any excess. Refrigerate for 20 minutes. Line the tin with baking paper and spread a layer of baking beads or uncooked rice evenly over the paper. Bake for 15 minutes, remove the paper and beads and bake for another 15 minutes, or until golden.

To make the filling, put the egg yolks, sugar and cornstarch in a bowl and whisk until pale. Heat the milk in a small saucepan until almost boiling, then remove from the heat and add gradually to the egg mixture, beating constantly. Strain into the pan. Stir constantly over low heat for 3 minutes, or until the mixture boils and thickens. Remove from the heat and add the vanilla essence. Transfer to a bowl, cover with plastic wrap and set aside to cool.

Spread the filling in the pastry shell and top with the berries. Heat the apple jelly in a heatproof bowl in a saucepan of simmering water, or in the microwave, until it liquefies. Brush over the fruit with a pastry brush. Allow to set before cutting.

Crème Brûlée

❋ SERVES 6
❋ PREPARATION TIME: 5 MINUTES
❋ COOKING TIME: 20 MINUTES

4 cups whole milk
1 vanilla bean
1 cinnamon stick
zest of 1 small lemon, sliced into strips
2 strips orange zest (³⁄4 x 1¹⁄2 inches)
8 egg yolks, at room temperature
¹⁄2 cup sugar
¹⁄3 cup cornstarch
¹⁄4 cup unpacked brown sugar

Put the milk in a saucepan. Split the vanilla bean lengthways, scrape the seeds into the milk and put the bean in too. Add the cinnamon stick and lemon and orange zest and bring to a boil. Simmer for 5 minutes, then strain and set aside.

Whisk the egg yolks with the sugar in a bowl for about 5 minutes, or until pale and creamy. Add the cornstarch and mix well. Slowly add the warm milk mixture to the egg and whisk continuously. Return to the pan and cook over medium–low heat, stirring constantly, for 5–10 minutes, or until the mixture is thick and creamy. Do not boil as it will curdle. Pour into six 1-cup ramekins and refrigerate for 6 hours, or overnight.

When ready to serve, sprinkle the custards evenly with brown sugar and broil for 3 minutes, or until the sugar caramelizes.

Chocolate Bavarois

❋ SERVES 6
❋ PREPARATION TIME: 30 MINUTES
  + CHILLING
❋ COOKING TIME: 5 MINUTES

1 1/3 cups chopped good-quality dark
   chocolate
1 1/2 cups whole milk
4 egg yolks, at room temperature
1/3 cup sugar
1 tablespoon gelatin
1 1/4 cups whipping cream

Combine the chocolate and milk in a small saucepan. Stir over low heat until the chocolate has melted and the milk just comes to a boil. Remove from the heat.

Beat the egg yolks and sugar until combined. Gradually add the hot chocolate milk, whisking until combined. Return to a clean saucepan and cook over low heat until the mixture thickens enough to coat the back of a wooden spoon. Do not allow to boil. Remove from the heat.

Put 2 tablespoons water in a small heatproof bowl, sprinkle the gelatin in an even layer over the surface and leave to go spongy. Stir into the hot chocolate mixture until dissolved.

Refrigerate until the mixture is cold but not set, stirring occasionally. Beat the cream until soft peaks form, then fold into the chocolate mixture in two batches. Pour into six 1-cup glasses and refrigerate for several hours or overnight, or until set.

Fresh Fruit Pavlova

* SERVES 6–8
* PREPARATION TIME: 30 MINUTES
* COOKING TIME: 55 MINUTES

6 egg whites, at room temperature
$2^{1}/_3$ cups sugar
$1^{1}/_2$ tablespoons cornstarch
$1^{1}/_2$ teaspoons vinegar
2 cups whipping cream, whipped
2 medium bananas, sliced
$3^{1}/_3$ cups sliced medium strawberries
4 medium kiwi fruit, sliced
4 medium passionfruit

Preheat the oven to 300°F. Line a large baking sheet with baking paper and draw a $10^{1}/_2$ inch circle on the paper. Turn the paper over and place on the tray. Beat the egg whites with electric beaters in a large dry bowl until soft peaks form. Gradually add all but 2 tablespoons of the sugar, beating well after each addition. Combine the cornstarch and vinegar with the last of the sugar and beat for 1 minute before adding it to the bowl. Beat for 5–10 minutes, or until all the sugar has dissolved and the meringue is stiff and glossy. Spread onto the paper inside the circle. Shape the meringue evenly, running the flat side of a palette knife along the edge and over the top.

Bake for 40 minutes, or until pale and crisp. Reduce the heat to 250°F and bake for 15 minutes. Turn off the oven and cool the pavlova in the oven, keeping the door slightly ajar. When cooled, top with cream and fruit. Drizzle with passionfruit pulp and serve.

Green Tea Ice Cream

※ SERVES 4
※ PREPARATION TIME: 15 MINUTES
※ COOKING TIME: 20 MINUTES

4 tablespoons Japanese green tea leaves
2 cups whole milk
6 egg yolks, at room temperature
½ cup sugar
2 cups whipping cream

Combine the green tea leaves with the milk in a saucepan and slowly bring to simmering point. This step should not be rushed — the longer the milk takes to come to a simmer, the better the infusion of flavor. Set aside for 5 minutes before straining.

Whisk the egg yolks and sugar in a heatproof bowl until thick and pale, then add the infused milk. Place the bowl over a saucepan of simmering water, making sure that the base of the bowl does not touch the water. Stir the custard until it is thick enough to coat the back of spoon, then remove from the heat and allow to cool slightly before stirring through the cream. Transfer to an ice cream machine and freeze according to manufacturer's instructions. Alternatively, transfer to a shallow metal tray and freeze, whisking every couple of hours until frozen and creamy. Freeze overnight.

NOTE: If you prefer your green tea ice cream pale green, add a few drops of green food coloring.

Mango Fool

※ SERVES 6
※ PREPARATION TIME: 20 MINUTES
  + CHILLING
※ COOKING TIME: NIL

3 large mangoes
1 cup custard
1⅔ cups whipping cream

Peel and pit the mangoes and purée the flesh in a food processor. Add the custard and blend to combine.

Whip the cream until soft peaks form, then gently fold into the mango mixture until just combined — do not overmix as you want to end up with a decorative marbled effect.

Pour the mixture into a serving dish or individual glasses. Gently smooth the top or tops, then refrigerate for at least 1 hour before serving.

NOTE: Fresh fruit can be served with fool.

Green Tea Ice Cream

Orange and Lemon Syrup Cake

🌸 SERVES 10–12
🌸 PREPARATION TIME: 40 MINUTES
🌸 COOKING TIME: 1 HOUR 50 MINUTES

BUTTER CAKE
1 1/2 cups self-rising flour
1 1/2 cups all-purpose flour
3/4 cup chopped and softened unsalted
  butter
3/4 cup sugar
3 eggs, at room temperature, lightly beaten
1 teaspoon natural vanilla essence
1 teaspoon grated orange zest
1/4 cup whole milk

SYRUP
2 medium oranges
2 medium lemons
2 1/4 cups sugar

Preheat the oven to 350°F. Lightly grease an 8 inch kugelhopf tin. Dust lightly with flour.

Sift the flours into a bowl. Cream the butter and sugar in a small bowl using electric beaters until light and fluffy. With the beaters still running, add the egg gradually, a little at a time, beating thoroughly after each addition. Add the vanilla essence and beat well to combine. Transfer the mixture to a large bowl and, using a large metal spoon, gently fold in the sifted flour, orange zest and milk. Stir until combined and almost smooth. Spoon the mixture into the tin and cook for 1 hour 5 minutes, or until a skewer inserted into the center of the cake comes out clean.

Cut the oranges and lemons into thin slices, without peeling them. To make the syrup, place 1 cup of the sugar in a heavy-based frying pan with 1/3 cup water. Stir over low heat until the sugar has completely dissolved. Bring to a boil, then reduce the heat and simmer. Add a quarter of the sliced fruit to the syrup and leave to simmer for 5–10 minutes, or until transparent and toffee-like. Lift out the fruit with tongs and cool on a wire rack. Add an extra 1/3 cup of sugar to the syrup and stir gently to dissolve – the juice from the fruit breaks down the concentrated syrup and the fruit won't candy properly unless you add the sugar. Simmer the second batch of sliced fruit. Add 1/3 cup of sugar to the syrup before cooking each batch.

When all the fruit has been candied, turn the cake out onto a wire rack over a tray and pour the hot syrup over the warm cake, allowing it to soak in – if the syrup is too thick, thin it with a little orange juice. Put the cake on a serving plate. When the fruit slices have firmed, arrange them on top of the cake (you can cut and twist some of the slices).

NOTE: The candied fruit can be kept between layers of baking paper in an airtight container for up to 2 days. The cake should be served within a few hours of decorating. If you prefer, you can bake the cake in an 8 inch round tin.

Raspberry Cranachan

2 tablespoons medium oatmeal
1 cup whipping cream
2 tablespoons honey
1 tablespoon whiskey
4 cups medium raspberries or 3½ cups
   medium strawberries
2 tablespoons toasted rolled oats, to serve

Put the oatmeal in a small pan. Stir over low heat for 5 minutes, or until lightly toasted. Remove from the heat and cool completely.

Using electric beaters, beat the cream in a small bowl until soft peaks form. Add the honey and whiskey and beat until just combined.

Fold the cooled, toasted oatmeal into the cream mixture with a metal spoon.

Begin layering the raspberries and cream evenly into six tall dessert glasses, ending with the cream. Refrigerate for 2 hours and serve sprinkled with toasted oats.

NOTES: In Scotland, charms are placed into cranachan at Halloween, somewhat like the customary coins in English Christmas puddings. This dessert is also known as cream crowdie.

English Trifle (Zuppa Inglese)

❋ SERVES 6
❋ PREPARATION TIME: 25 MINUTES
❋ COOKING TIME: 5 MINUTES

2 cups whole milk
1 vanilla bean, split lengthways
4 egg yolks, at room temperature
1/2 cup sugar
2 tablespoons all-purpose flour
10 1/2 oz Madeira cake, cut into
    1/2 inch slices
1/3 cup rum
1/4 cup grated or shaved chocolate
1/2 cup flaked toasted almonds

Heat the milk and vanilla bean in a saucepan over low heat until bubbles appear around the edge of the pan.

Whisk the egg yolks, sugar and flour together in a bowl until thick and pale.

Discard the vanilla bean and whisk the warm milk slowly into the egg mixture, then blend well. Return to a clean pan and stir over medium heat until the custard boils and thickens. Allow to cool slightly.

Line the base of a 6-cup serving dish with one-third of the cake slices and brush well with the rum combined with 1 tablespoon water. Spread one-third of the custard over the cake, top with cake slices and brush with rum mixture. Repeat this process, finishing with a layer of custard. Cover and refrigerate for 3 hours. Sprinkle with chocolate and almonds just before serving.

Orange Sorbet

❋ SERVES 4
❋ PREPARATION TIME: 20 MINUTES
  + FREEZING
❋ COOKING TIME: 15 MINUTES

10–12 medium oranges
¾ cup confectioners' sugar
2 teaspoons lemon juice

Cut the oranges in half and carefully squeeze out the juice, taking care not to damage the skins. Dissolve the confectioners' sugar in the orange juice, add the lemon juice and pour into a freezer container. Cover the surface with baking paper and freeze for 1 hour.

Scrape the remaining flesh and membrane out of six of the orange halves, cover the skins with plastic wrap and refrigerate.

After 1 hour, stir any frozen juice that has formed around the edge of the sorbet into the center and return to the freezer. Repeat every hour, or until nearly frozen. Freeze overnight. Divide the sorbet among the orange skins and freeze until ready to serve. This sorbet may seem very hard when it has frozen overnight but it will melt quickly, so work fast.

Melon Medley

❋ SERVES 4
❋ PREPARATION TIME: 10 MINUTES
❋ COOKING TIME: NIL

½ medium canteloupe or any orange-
  fleshed melon
½ medium honeydew melon
¼ medium watermelon
2 medium passionfruit

Cut the melons into bite-sized pieces or use a melon baller to scoop the flesh into balls. Chill, covered, for 30 minutes.

Divide among serving bowls and drizzle with the passionfruit pulp.

Orange Sorbet

Lemon Passionfruit Syllabub with Berries

❉ SERVES 8–10

❉ PREPARATION TIME: 40 MINUTES
  + STANDING + CHILLING

❉ COOKING TIME: NIL

2 teaspoons grated lemon rind
⅓ cup lemon juice
½ cup sugar
½ cup dry white wine
8 medium passionfruit
2 cups heavy cream
3¼ cups medium blueberries
4 cups medium raspberries
2 tablespoons confectioners' sugar
3⅓ cups halved medium strawberries
confectioners' sugar, extra, to dust

Stir the rind, juice, sugar and white wine together in a bowl and set aside for 10 minutes. Cut the passionfruit in half and push the pulp through a sieve to remove the seeds. Add half the passionfruit pulp to the lemon, sugar and wine mixture.

Beat the cream with electric beaters until soft peaks form. Gradually beat in the lemon and passionfruit syrup until all the syrup is added (the mixture will have the consistency of softly whipped cream). Stir in the remaining passionfruit, cover and refrigerate for 1 hour.

Combine the blueberries, raspberries and confectioners' sugar and place in a 10–12-cup serving bowl. Spoon the cream mixture over the top, decorate with strawberries, dust with confectioners' sugar and serve immediately.

NOTE: This thick, custardy dessert was originally made by beating milk or cream with wine, sugar, lemon juice and possibly spices, the acid curdling and thickening the mixture. Some versions were based on hard cider while others were further fortified with brandy. Syllabub was sometimes used in place of cream on desserts such as trifle, and instead of meringue for floating islands. A thinner version was made as a drink and served at festive occasions in special syllabub glasses.

Peach Charlottes with Melba Sauce

❋ SERVES 4

❋ PREPARATION TIME: 30 MINUTES
   + 20 MINUTES STANDING

❋ COOKING TIME: 40 MINUTES

1 cup sugar
4 cups water
6 medium peaches
1/3 cup peach liqueur
2 loaves brioche
1/3 cup melted butter
1/2 cup apricot jam, warmed and sieved

MELBA SAUCE
2 1/2 cups fresh or thawed frozen
   raspberries
2 tablespoons confectioners' sugar

Preheat the oven to 350°F. Brush four 1-cup ovenproof ramekins with melted butter. Combine the sugar and water in large, heavy-based pan. Stir over medium heat until the sugar completely dissolves. Bring to a boil, reduce heat slightly and add the whole peaches. Simmer, covered for 20 minutes. Drain and cool. Peel the skins and slice the flesh thickly. Place in a bowl, sprinkle with liqueur and set aside for 20 minutes.

Cut the brioche into 1/2 inch thick slices; remove the crusts. With a scone-cutter, cut rounds to fit the tops and bases of each mold. Cut the remaining slices into 3/4 inch wide fingers and trim to fit the height of the mold. Dip the first round into melted butter and place in the base of the mold. Dip brioche fingers into melted butter and press around the side of the mold, overlapping slightly. Line all the molds in this manner.

Fill the lined mold evenly with peach slices and top with the last round of brioche dipped in melted butter. Press to seal. Place the mold on a baking sheet and bake for 20 minutes.

To make the sauce, process the berries in a food processor and add confectioners' sugar, to taste. Push through a fine sieve.

Turn the molds onto serving plates, brush with jam and pour Melba Sauce alongside. Serve with fresh berries, if desired.

NOTE: The peaches can be cooked, the molds lined with brioche and the sauce made, up to 6 hours ahead. Refrigerate the charlottes, then fill and bake them close to serving time.

Sticky Date Pudding

❈ SERVES 6–8
❈ PREPARATION TIME: 35 MINUTES
❈ COOKING TIME: 55 MINUTES

1¼ cups chopped dates
1 teaspoon baking soda
½ cup unsalted butter
¾ cup sugar
2 eggs, at room temperature, lightly beaten
1 teaspoon natural vanilla essence
1½ cups self-rising flour
whipped cream and raspberries, to serve,
    optional

SAUCE
1 cup unpacked brown sugar
½ cup cream
½ cup unsalted butter

Preheat the oven to 350°F. Lightly grease an 8 inch square cake tin. Line the base with baking paper. Combine the dates with 1 cup water in a small saucepan. Bring to a boil and remove from the heat. Stir in the baking soda and set aside to cool to room temperature.

Using electric beaters, beat the butter and sugar in a small bowl until light and creamy. Add the eggs gradually, beating thoroughly after each addition. Add the vanilla essence and beat until combined. Transfer to a large bowl.

Using a metal spoon, fold in the flour and dates with the liquid and stir until just combined — do not overbeat. Pour into the prepared tin and bake for 50 minutes, until a skewer comes out clean when inserted into the center of the pudding. Leave in the tin for 10 minutes before turning out.

To make the sauce, combine the sugar, cream and butter in a small saucepan. Stir until the butter melts and the sugar dissolves. Bring to a boil, reduce the heat and simmer for 2 minutes. Pour over slices of pudding and serve immediately, with extra cream and raspberries (if desired).

Panna Cotta with Ruby Sauce

🌼 SERVES 6
🌼 PREPARATION TIME: 20 MINUTES
🌼 COOKING TIME: 20 MINUTES

3 cups whipping cream
3 teaspoons gelatin
1 vanilla bean
1/3 cup sugar

RUBY SAUCE
1 cup sugar
1 cinnamon stick
1 cup fresh or frozen raspberries,
    plus extra, to serve
1/2 cup red wine

Lightly grease six 2/3-cup ramekins with flavorless oil. Place 1/4 cup of the cream in a small bowl, sprinkle the gelatin in an even layer over the surface and leave to go spongy.

Put the remaining cream in a saucepan with the vanilla bean and sugar and heat gently while stirring. Remove from the heat. Whisk the gelatin into the cream mixture. Pour into the molds and chill for 2 hours, or until set. Unmold by wiping a cloth dipped in hot water over the mold and upending it onto a plate.

While the panna cotta is chilling, make the ruby sauce. Stir the sugar with 1 cup water in a saucepan over medium heat until the sugar has dissolved. Add the cinnamon stick and simmer for 5 minutes. Add the raspberries and wine and boil rapidly for 5 minutes. Remove the cinnamon stick and push the sauce through a sieve. Discard the seeds. Cool, then chill before serving with the panna cotta. Serve with raspberries.

Bellini Sorbet

🌼 SERVES 6
🌼 PREPARATION TIME: 20 MINUTES
🌼 COOKING TIME: 25 MINUTES

2 cups sugar
5 large peaches
3/4 cup Champagne
2 egg whites, at room temperature,
    lightly beaten

Combine the sugar with 4 cups water in a large saucepan and stir over low heat until the sugar has dissolved. Bring to a boil, add the peaches and simmer for 20 minutes. Remove the peaches and cool. Reserve 1 cup of the poaching liquid.

Peel the peaches, remove the stones and cut the flesh into chunks. Chop in a food processor until smooth, add the reserved liquid and the Champagne and process briefly until combined. Pour into a shallow metal tray and freeze for about 6 hours, until just firm. Transfer to a large bowl and beat until smooth using electric beaters. Refreeze and repeat this step twice more, adding the egg white on the final beating. Place in a storage container, cover the surface with baking paper and freeze until firm. Serve the sorbet in scoops.

Panna Cotta with Ruby Sauce

Feuilleté with Cherries Jubilee

❋ SERVES 4
❋ PREPARATION TIME: 15 MINUTES
❋ COOKING TIME: 25 MINUTES

2 sheets frozen puff pastry, thawed
1 egg, at room temperature, lightly beaten
1 1/3 tablespoons unsalted butter
1 1/3 tablespoons sugar
2 1/4 cups pitted cherries
1 1/3 cups heavy cream
1/2 cup brandy or kirsch
confectioners' sugar, to dust

To make the feuilletés, roll the pastry out on a floured work surface and cut out four rectangles of 4 x 4 1/2 inches each. Put them on a baking sheet and brush with the beaten egg, being careful not to let any egg drip down the sides of the pastry. Refrigerate for 30 minutes. Preheat the oven to 425°F.

Melt the butter and sugar together in a saucepan and add the cherries. Cook over high heat for about 1 minute, then reduce the heat and simmer for about 3 minutes, or until the cherries are tender. Reduce the heat to low and keep the cherries warm.

Bake the feuilletés on the top shelf of the oven for 15 minutes until golden and puffed, then cut them in half horizontally and gently pull any doughy bits out of the center. Turn the oven off and put the feuilletés back in the oven and allow to dry out for a couple of minutes.

When you are ready to serve, whisk the cream until it reaches stiff peaks. Place a warm feuilleté base on each serving plate. Heat the brandy or kirsch in a small saucepan and set it alight, then pour it over the cherries (keep a saucepan lid nearby in case the flames get too high). Spoon some cherries into each feuilleté base and top with a little cream. Put the lids on the feuilletés and dust with confectioners' sugar before serving.

Banana and Coconut Pancakes

🌼 SERVES 4–6

🌼 PREPARATION TIME: 10 MINUTES

🌼 COOKING TIME: 30 MINUTES

1 tablespoon fresh shredded coconut
   (unsweetened)

⅓ cup all-purpose flour

2 tablespoons rice flour

¼ cup sugar

¼ cup desiccated coconut

1 cup coconut milk

1 egg, at room temperature, lightly beaten

butter, for frying

¼ cup butter, extra

4 large bananas, cut diagonally into
   thick slices

⅓ cup unpacked brown sugar

⅓ cup lime juice

shredded lime zest, to serve

Spread the shredded coconut on a baking sheet and toast it in a 300°F oven for 10 minutes, or until it is dark golden, shaking the tray occasionally. Remove from the tray and set aside. Sift the flours into a bowl. Add the sugar and shredded coconut and mix. Make a well in the center, pour in the combined coconut milk and egg, and beat until smooth.

Melt a little butter in a non-stick frying pan. Pour ¼ cup of the pancake mixture into the pan and cook over medium heat until the underside is golden. Turn the pancake over and cook the other side. Transfer to a plate and cover with a dish towel to keep warm. Repeat with the remaining pancake batter, buttering the pan when necessary.

Heat the extra butter in the pan, add the banana, toss until coated, and cook over medium heat until the banana starts to soften and brown. Sprinkle with the brown sugar and shake the pan gently until the sugar has melted. Stir in the lime juice. Divide the banana among the pancakes and fold over to enclose. Sprinkle with the toasted coconut and shredded lime zest.

Sweet Couscous

❋ SERVES 4–6

❋ PREPARATION TIME: 10 MINUTES
   + 10 MINUTES STANDING

❋ COOKING TIME: 5 MINUTES STANDING

1 cup combined pistachio nuts,
   pine nuts and blanched almonds
1/4 cup dried apricots
1/2 cup pitted dried dates
1 1/3 cups instant couscous
1/4 cup sugar
1 cup boiling water
1/3 cup softened unsalted butter
2 tablespoons sugar, to serve
1/2 teaspoon ground cinnamon, to serve
1 1/2 cups hot whole milk, to serve

Preheat the oven to 325°F. Spread the nuts on a baking sheet and bake for about 5 minutes, until light golden. Allow to cool, then roughly chop and place in a bowl. Slice the apricots into matchstick-sized pieces and quarter the dates lengthways. Add both to the bowl and toss to combine.

Put the couscous and sugar in a large bowl and cover with the boiling water. Stir well, then add the butter and a pinch of salt. Stir until the butter melts. Cover with a dish towel and set aside for 10 minutes. Fluff with a fork, then toss half the fruit and nut mixture through.

To serve, pile the warm couscous in the center of a platter. Arrange the remaining nut mixture around the base. Combine the sugar and cinnamon in a small bowl and serve separately for sprinkling. Pass around the hot milk in a pitcher for guests to help themselves.

NOTE: This can be made up to 4 days ahead. Spoon it into an ovenproof dish, cover with foil and refrigerate. To reheat, bring to room temperature, then place in a 350°F oven for 20 minutes.

White Chocolate Fondue with Fruit

※ SERVES 6–8
※ PREPARATION TIME: 30 MINUTES
※ COOKING TIME: 20 MINUTES

½ cup light corn syrup
⅔ cup heavy cream
¼ cup orange-flavored liqueur
1¾ cups chopped white chocolate
marshmallows and chopped fresh fruit,
    (for example, strawberries, pears,
    cherries and bananas), to serve

Combine the corn syrup and cream in a small pan or fondue pot. Bring to a boil, then remove from the heat.

Add the orange-flavored liqueur and white chocolate and stir until melted. Serve with marshmallows and fresh fruit.

Dark Chocolate Fondue with Fruit

※ SERVES 6–8
※ PREPARATION TIME: 30 MINUTES
※ COOKING TIME: 20 MINUTES

1⅔ cups chopped good-quality dark
    chocolate
½ cup heavy cream
marshmallows and chopped fresh fruit
    (for example, strawberries, pears,
    cherries and bananas), to serve

Put the chocolate and cream in a fondue pot or heatproof bowl. If using a fondue pot, heat gently, stirring until smooth. If using a heatproof bowl, place the bowl over a saucepan of water which has been brought to a boil and then taken off the heat — make sure the base of the bowl is not touching the water.

Serve from the bowl or fondue pot with some marshmallows and fresh fruit for dipping.

White Chocolate Fondue with Fruit

Stuffed Figs (Higos Rellenos)

❈ MAKES 18
❈ PREPARATION TIME: 30 MINUTES
   + 3 HOURS SOAKING
❈ COOKING TIME: 30 MINUTES

1/2 cup honey
1/2 cup sweet dark sherry
1/4 teaspoon ground cinnamon
18 large dried figs
18 blanched almonds
2/3 cup shards dark chocolate
butter, for greasing
heavy cream, to serve, optional

Combine the honey, sherry, cinnamon and figs with 1 1/2 cups water in a large saucepan over high heat. Bring to a boil then reduce the heat and simmer for 10 minutes. Remove the pan from the heat and set aside for 3 hours. Remove the figs with a slotted spoon, reserving the liquid.

Preheat the oven to 350°F. Return the pan of liquid to the stove and boil over high heat for 5 minutes, or until syrupy, then set aside. Snip the stems from the figs with scissors then cut a slit in the top of each fig with small sharp knife. Push an almond and a few shards of chocolate into each slit. Place the figs in a lightly buttered dish and bake for 15 minutes or until the chocolate has melted.

Serve three figs per person with a little of the syrup and a dollop of cream.

Tapioca Plum Pudding with Rum Butter

❋ SERVES 6–8
❋ PREPARATION TIME: 35 MINUTES
❋ COOKING TIME: 4 HOURS

¹/₃ cup tapioca
1 cup whole milk
1 teaspoon baking soda
³/₄ cup dark brown sugar
2 cups fresh white breadcrumbs
¹/₂ cup golden raisins
¹/₂ cup currants
¹/₂ cup chopped dried dates
2 eggs, at room temperature, lightly beaten
¹/₄ cup melted and cooled unsalted butter
raspberries, to decorate
blueberries, to decorate
confectioners' sugar, to decorate

RUM BUTTER
¹/₂ cup softened butter
³/₄ cup dark brown sugar
¹/₃ cup rum

Combine the tapioca and milk in a bowl, cover and refrigerate overnight.

Lightly grease a 6-cup steamed pudding mold with butter and line the base with baking paper. Place the empty basin in a large saucepan on a trivet or upturned saucer and pour in enough cold water to come halfway up the side of the basin. Remove the basin and put the water on to boil.

Transfer the soaked tapioca and milk to a large bowl and stir in the baking soda until dissolved. Stir in the sugar, breadcrumbs, dried fruit, beaten eggs and melted butter and mix well. Spoon into the basin and smooth the surface with wet hands, then cover the pudding.

Cover the basin with the lid and make a string handle. Gently lower the basin into the boiling water, reduce to a fast simmer and cover the saucepan with a tight-fitting lid. Cook for 3¹/₂–4 hours, or until a skewer inserted into the center of the pudding comes out clean. Check the water level every hour and top up with boiling water as necessary.

To make the rum butter, beat together the butter and sugar with electric beaters for about 3–4 minutes, or until light and creamy. Gradually beat in the rum, 1 tablespoon at a time. You can add more rum, to taste. Transfer to a serving dish, cover and refrigerate until required.

Carefully remove the steamed pudding mold from the saucepan, remove the coverings and leave for 5 minutes before turning out the pudding onto a large serving plate. Loosen the edges with a palette knife, if necessary. Serve decorated with raspberries and blueberries and lightly dusted with confectioners' sugar. Serve hot with the cold rum butter.

Kheer Rice Pudding

※ SERVES 4
※ PREPARATION TIME: 15 MINUTES
※ COOKING TIME: 1 HOUR 50 MINUTES

⅓ cup basmati rice
6 cups whole milk
6 cardamom pods, lightly crushed
½ cup sugar
¼ cup chopped raisins
¼ cup slivered almonds
pinch of saffron threads
1 tablespoon rosewater, optional
ground cinnamon, optional

Soak the rice in water for 30 minutes, then drain.

Pour the milk into a saucepan, add the cardamom pods and bring to a boil. Add the rice, reduce the heat and simmer for 1 hour, stirring often or until the rice is cooked. Add the sugar, raisins and slivered almonds, bring to a low boil and cook for 50 minutes, or until it is the consistency of porridge. Stir frequently to avoid the mixture sticking to the base of the pan. Remove the cardamom pods.

Mix the saffron threads with a little water and add to the mixture — just enough to give a pale yellow color to the pudding. Stir in the rosewater, if using, when cooled. Serve warm or cold, with a sprinkling of cinnamon on top, if desired.

NOTE: Served at banquets, weddings and religious ceremonies, kheer is the "Queen of desserts" or "Queen of creams" in India, and is particularly popular in northern India. It is exotically delicious, rich and creamy, with the cardamom and almonds giving it a distinctive texture and flavor.

Almond Semi Freddo

- SERVES 8–10
- PREPARATION TIME: 30 MINUTES
- COOKING TIME: NIL

1 1/4 cups whipping cream
4 eggs, at room temperature, separated
2/3 cup confectioners' sugar
1/4 cup amaretto
1/2 cup chopped toasted almonds
8 amaretti cookies, crushed
fresh fruit or extra amaretto, to serve

Whip the cream until firm peaks form, then cover and refrigerate. Line a 4 x 8 1/2 inch bar tin with plastic wrap so that it overhangs the two long sides.

Beat the egg yolks and confectioners' sugar in a large bowl until pale and creamy. Whisk the egg whites in a separate bowl until firm peaks form. Stir the amaretto, almonds and amaretti cookies into the egg yolk mixture, then carefully fold in the chilled cream and egg whites until well combined. Carefully pour or spoon into the lined bar tin and cover with the overhanging plastic. Freeze for 4 hours, or until frozen but not rock hard. Serve slices with fresh fruit or a sprinkling of amaretto.

NOTES: Semi freddo means semi frozen, so if you leave it in the freezer overnight, put it in the refrigerator for 30 minutes before serving. The semi freddo can also be frozen in individual molds or serving dishes.

Figs in Honey Syrup

- SERVES 4
- PREPARATION TIME: 20 MINUTES
- COOKING TIME: 1 HOUR

2/3 cup blanched whole almonds
12 whole medium fresh figs
(about 1 lb 10 oz)
1/2 cup sugar
1/3 cup honey
2 tablespoons lemon juice
2 1/2 inch piece lemon peel
1 cinnamon stick
1 cup Greek-style yogurt

Preheat the oven to 350°F. Place the almonds on a baking sheet and bake for 5 minutes, or until golden. Cut the stems off the figs and make a small crossways incision 1/4 inch deep on top of each fig. Push a blanched almond into the base of each fig. Roughly chop the remaining almonds.

Put 3 cups water in a large saucepan, add the sugar and stir over medium heat until the sugar dissolves. Bring to a boil. Stir in the honey, lemon juice, lemon peel and cinnamon stick. Reduce the heat to medium, add the figs and simmer gently for 30 minutes. Remove with a slotted spoon and place on a large serving dish.

Boil the liquid over high heat for about 15–20 minutes, or until thick and syrupy. Remove the cinnamon and lemon peel. Cool the syrup slightly and pour over the figs. Sprinkle with the chopped almonds. Serve warm or cold with the yogurt.

Almond Semi Freddo

Banana Fritters in Coconut Batter

❋ SERVES 6
❋ PREPARATION TIME: 15 MINUTES
❋ COOKING TIME: 20 MINUTES

$^1/_2$ cup glutinous rice flour
$1^2/_3$ cups freshly grated coconut
   or $^2/_3$ cup desiccated coconut
$^1/_4$ cup sugar
1 tablespoon sesame seeds
$^1/_4$ cup coconut milk
6 medium sugar bananas
oil, for deep-frying
vanilla ice cream, to serve
sesame seeds, toasted, extra, to garnish

Combine the flour, coconut, sugar, sesame seeds, coconut milk and $^1/_4$ cup water in a large bowl. Whisk to a smooth batter, adding more water if the batter is too thick. Set aside to rest for 1 hour.

Peel the bananas and cut in half lengthways.

Fill a wok or large heavy-based saucepan one-third full of oil and heat to 350°F, or until a cube of bread dropped into the oil browns in 15 seconds. Dip each piece of banana into the batter then drop gently into the hot oil. Cook in batches for 4–6 minutes, or until golden brown all over. Remove with a slotted spoon and drain on crumpled paper towel. Serve hot with vanilla ice cream and a sprinkling of extra toasted sesame seeds.

Charlotte Malakoff

※ SERVES 8–12
※ PREPARATION TIME: 1 HOUR + CHILLING
※ COOKING TIME: NIL

8 oz ladyfingers
1/2 cup Grand Marnier
3 1/3 cups hulled and halved medium
    strawberries
whipped cream and strawberries, to serve

ALMOND CREAM
1/2 cup unsalted butter
1/3 cup sugar
1/4 cup Grand Marnier
1/4 teaspoon almond essence
3/4 cup whipping cream, whipped
1 1/3 cups ground almonds

Brush a deep 4–6-cup soufflé dish with melted butter or oil. Line the base with baking paper and grease the paper. Trim the ladyfingers to fit the sides of the dish. Quickly dip the ladyfingers into the liqueur that has been mixed with 1/2 cup water. Arrange upright around the side of the dish, rounded-side-down.

To make the almond cream, using electric beaters, beat the butter and sugar until light and creamy. Add the liqueur and almond essence. Continue beating until the mixture is smooth and the sugar has dissolved. Using a metal spoon, fold in the cream and almonds.

Spoon one-third of the almond cream into the base of the dish and cover with strawberry halves. Top with a layer of dipped ladyfingers. Continue layering, finishing with a layer of ladyfingers, then press down.

Cover with foil and place a small plate and weight on top. Refrigerate for 8 hours, or overnight. Remove the plate and foil and turn onto a chilled serving plate. Remove the baking paper. Decorate with whipped cream and strawberries.

NOTE: This dessert is very rich and should be served after a light main course. It is also splendid to serve when you have guests for coffee and cake, rather than a meal, and is lovely for a party.

Custard Pie

SERVES 6–8

PREPARATION TIME: 30 MINUTES

COOKING TIME: 1 HOUR

1 vanilla bean, sliced in half lengthways
3 cups whole milk
1/2 cup sugar
3 3/4 oz semolina
1 tablespoon finely grated lemon zest
1 cinnamon stick
2 2/3 tablespoons cubed unsalted butter
4 large eggs, at room temperature, lightly
    beaten
12 sheets filo pastry
1/4 cup melted unsalted butter, extra

SYRUP
1/3 cup sugar
1/2 teaspoon ground cinnamon
1 tablespoon lemon juice
2 inch strip lemon zest

Scrape the vanilla bean seeds into a saucepan. Add the bean, milk, sugar, semolina, lemon zest and cinnamon stick and gently bring to a boil, stirring constantly. Reduce the heat to low and simmer for 2 minutes so the mixture thickens. Remove from the heat. Mix in the butter. Cool for 10 minutes, then remove the cinnamon stick and vanilla bean and gradually mix in the egg. Preheat the oven to 350°F.

Cover the filo with a damp dish towel. Remove a sheet, brush one side with melted butter and place, buttered side down, in a 1 1/4 x 8 x 12 inch baking tin. The filo will overlap the edges. Repeat with five more sheets, buttering one side of each as you go.

Pour the custard over the filo and cover the top with the remaining pastry, brushing each sheet with butter as you go. Brush the top with butter. Using a small sharp knife, trim the pastry to the edges of the tin. Bake for 40–45 minutes, or until the custard has puffed up and set and the pastry is golden brown. Leave to cool.

Mix all the syrup ingredients with 1/3 cup water in a saucepan. Slowly bring to a boil, then reduce the heat to low and simmer for 10 minutes. The syrup will thicken. Remove from the heat and cool for 10 minutes. Remove the lemon zest.

If the filo has risen above the edges of the tin, flatten the top layer with your hand then pour the syrup over the pie. This will prevent the syrup running over the sides. Allow to cool again before serving.

Strawberries Romanoff

🌸 SERVES 4
🌸 PREPARATION TIME: 20 MINUTES
🌸 COOKING TIME: NIL

5 cups quartered medium strawberries
2 tablespoons orange-flavored liqueur
¼ teaspoon finely grated orange zest
1 tablespoon sugar
½ cup whipping cream
2 tablespoons confectioners' sugar

Combine the strawberries, orange-flavored liqueur, orange zest and sugar in a large bowl, cover and refrigerate for 1 hour. Drain the strawberries, reserving any juices. Purée about one-quarter of the strawberries with the reserved juices.

Divide the remaining strawberries among four glasses. Beat the cream and confectioners' sugar until soft peaks form, then fold the strawberry purée through the whipped cream. Spoon the mixture over the top of the strawberries, cover and refrigerate until required.

Fruit Kebabs with Honey Cardamom Syrup

🌸 MAKES 8
🌸 PREPARATION TIME: 20 MINUTES
🌸 COOKING TIME: 5 MINUTES

¼ small pineapple or 2 rings canned
    pineapple
1 medium peach
1 medium banana
16 medium strawberries
whipping cream or yogurt, to serve,
    optional

HONEY CARDAMOM SYRUP
2 tablespoons honey
1⅓ tablespoons melted unsalted butter
½ teaspoon ground cardamom
1 tablespoon rum or brandy, optional
1 tablespoon unpacked brown sugar

Soak eight wooden skewers in cold water for 30 minutes to prevent them burning during cooking. Cut the pineapple into eight bite-sized pieces. Cut the peach into eight wedges and slice the banana. Thread the fruit alternately on skewers and place in a shallow dish.

To make the honey cardamom syrup, combine all the ingredients in a bowl. Pour the mixture over the kebabs and brush to coat. Cover and leave to stand at room temperature for 1 hour. Prepare and heat a barbecue or broiler.

Cook the kebabs on the hot, lightly greased barbecue or under the broiler for 5 minutes. Brush with the syrup occasionally during cooking. Serve drizzled with the remaining syrup, and cream or yogurt (if desired).

Strawberries Romanoff

Butterscotch Tart

❈ SERVES 6–8
❈ PREPARATION TIME: 30 MINUTES
❈ COOKING TIME: 1 HOUR

SHORTCRUST PASTRY
2 cups all-purpose flour
$1/2$ cup chopped chilled unsalted butter
2 tablespoons sugar
1 egg yolk, at room temperature
1 tablespoon iced water

BUTTERSCOTCH FILLING
1 cup unpacked brown sugar
$1/3$ cup all-purpose flour
1 cup whole milk
$1/4$ cup unsalted butter
1 teaspoon natural vanilla essence
1 egg yolk, at room temperature

MERINGUE
2 egg whites, at room temperature
2 tablespoons sugar

Preheat the oven to 350°F. Grease a deep $8^1/2$ inch tart tin. Sift the flour into a large bowl. Using your fingertips, rub in the butter until the mixture resembles fine breadcrumbs. Stir in the sugar, egg yolk and iced water. Mix to a soft dough with a flat-bladed knife, using a cutting action, then gather into a ball. Wrap and refrigerate for 20 minutes.

Roll the pastry between two sheets of baking paper, large enough to cover the base and side of the tin. Trim the edge and prick the pastry evenly with a fork. Refrigerate for 20 minutes. Line the pastry with baking paper and spread baking beads or uncooked rice over the paper. Bake for 35 minutes, then remove the paper and beads.

To make the filling, place the sugar and flour in a small saucepan. Make a well in the center and gradually whisk in the milk to form a smooth paste. Add the butter and stir with a whisk over low heat for 8 minutes, or until the mixture boils and thickens. Remove from the heat, add the vanilla essence and egg yolk and whisk until smooth. Spread into the pastry case and smooth the surface.

To make the meringue, beat the egg whites until firm peaks form. Add the sugar gradually, beating until thick and glossy and all the sugar has dissolved. Spoon over the filling and swirl into peaks with a fork or flat-bladed knife. Bake for 5–10 minutes, or until the meringue is golden. Serve warm or cold.

Millefeuille with Passionfruit Curd

❋ SERVES 4
❋ PREPARATION TIME: 30 MINUTES
❋ COOKING TIME: 45 MINUTES

6 sheets frozen puff pastry, thawed
1¼ cups whipping cream
2 tablespoons confectioners' sugar
1 teaspoon natural vanilla essence
1 large mango, thinly sliced
sifted confectioners' sugar, extra
    to sprinkle

PASSIONFRUIT CURD
3 eggs, at room temperature
¼ cup unsalted butter
½ cup passionfruit pulp
½ cup sugar

To make the passionfruit curd, beat the eggs well, then strain into a heatproof bowl and add the remaining ingredients. Place the bowl over a saucepan of simmering water and stir with a wooden spoon for 15–20 minutes, or until the butter has melted and the mixture has thickened slightly and coats the back of the wooden spoon. Cool, then transfer to a bowl, cover with plastic wrap and chill until required.

To make the millefeuille, preheat the oven to 400°F. Line a large baking sheet with baking paper. Roll the pastry to a 12 x 14 inch rectangle and transfer to the tray. Cover and refrigerate for 20 minutes. Sprinkle lightly with water and prick all over with a fork. Cook for 25 minutes, or until puffed and golden. Allow to cool completely on a wire rack.

Whisk the cream with the confectioners' sugar and vanilla essence until firm peaks form. Carefully trim the pastry sheet and cut into three even-sized strips, lengthways. Spread one layer of pastry with half the passionfruit curd, spreading evenly to the edges. Top this with half of the whipped cream and then top with half of the mango flesh. Place a second sheet of pastry on top and repeat the process. Top with the remaining pastry sheet and sprinkle liberally with confectioners' sugar. Carefully transfer to a serving plate. Use a serrated knife to cut into slices.

NOTE: Instead of making one long millefeuille, you might prefer to make four individual ones.

Lemon Meringue Pie

❋ SERVES 6

❋ PREPARATION TIME: 1 HOUR

❋ COOKING TIME: 45 MINUTES

1½ cups all-purpose flour

2 tablespoons confectioners' sugar

½ cup chopped chilled unsalted butter

¼ cup iced water

FILLING AND TOPPING

¼ cup cornstarch

¼ cup all-purpose flour

1 cup sugar

¾ cup lemon juice

3 teaspoons grated lemon zest

2⅔ tablespoons chopped unsalted butter

6 eggs, at room temperature, separated

1½ cups sugar, extra

½ teaspoon cornstarch, extra

Sift the flour and confectioners' sugar into a large bowl. Using your fingertips, rub in the butter until the mixture resembles fine breadcrumbs. Add almost all the water and mix with a flat-bladed knife, using a cutting action, until the mixture forms a firm dough. Add more liquid if the dough is too dry. Turn onto a lightly floured surface and gather together into a ball. Roll between two sheets of baking paper until large enough to fit a 9 inch pie dish. Line the pie dish with the pastry, trim the edge and refrigerate for 20 minutes. Preheat the oven to 350°F.

Line the pastry with a sheet of baking paper and spread a layer of baking beads or uncooked rice evenly over the paper. Bake for 10 minutes, then remove the paper and beads. Bake for a further 10 minutes, or until the pastry is lightly golden. Leave to cool.

To make the filling, put the flours and sugar in a saucepan. Whisk in the lemon juice, zest and 1½ cups water. Whisk continually over medium heat until the mixture boils and thickens. Reduce the heat and cook for 1 minute, then whisk in the butter and egg yolks, one yolk at a time. Transfer to a bowl, cover the surface with plastic wrap and allow to cool completely.

To make the topping, preheat the oven to 425°F. Beat the egg whites in a small dry bowl using electric beaters, until soft peaks form. Add the extra sugar gradually, beating constantly until the meringue is thick and glossy. Beat in the extra cornstarch. Pour the cold filling into the cold pastry shell. Spread with meringue to cover, forming peaks. Bake for 5–10 minutes, or until lightly browned. Serve hot or cold.

Sicilian Cannoli

* MAKES 12
* PREPARATION TIME: 30 MINUTES
* COOKING TIME: 5 MINUTES

$2^1/_2$ cups all-purpose flour
1 tablespoon sugar
1 teaspoon ground cinnamon
$2^2/_3$ tablespoons unsalted butter
$^1/_4$ cup Marsala
vegetable oil, for deep-frying
confectioners' sugar, to dust

FILLING
2 cups ricotta cheese
1 teaspoon orange flower water
$^1/_2$ cup diced cedro or candied lemon peel
    (see Notes)
$^1/_2$ cup coarsely grated or chopped
    bittersweet chocolate
1 tablespoon grated orange zest
$^1/_2$ cup confectioners' sugar

To make the filling, combine all the ingredients in a bowl and mix. Add 2 tablespoons water and mix well to form a dough. Cover with plastic wrap and refrigerate.

Combine the flour, sugar and cinnamon in a bowl, rub in the butter and add the Marsala. Mix until the dough comes together in a loose clump, then knead on a lightly floured surface for 4–5 minutes, or until smooth. Wrap in plastic wrap and refrigerate for at least 30 minutes.

Cut the dough in half and roll each portion on a lightly floured surface into a thin sheet about $^1/_4$ inch thick. Cut each dough half into six $3^1/_2$ inch squares. Place a metal tube (see Note) diagonally across the middle of each square. Fold the sides over the tube, moistening the overlap with water, then press together.

Heat the oil in a large deep frying pan to 350°F, or until a cube of bread dropped into the oil browns in 15 seconds. Drop one or two tubes at a time into the hot oil. Fry gently until golden brown and crisp. Remove from the oil, gently remove the molds and drain on crumpled paper towels. When they are cool, fill an icing bag with the ricotta mixture and fill the shells. Dust with confectioners' sugar and serve.

NOTES: Cannoli tubes are available at kitchenware shops. You can also use ¾ inch diameter wooden dowels cut into 4½ inch lengths. Cedro, also known as citron, is a citrus fruit with a very thick, knobbly skin. The skin is used to make candied peel. You can also use candied lemon peel if cedro is unavailabe.

Pumpkin Pie

FILLING
3 1/4 cups small chunks pumpkin
2 eggs, at room temperature, lightly beaten
3/4 cup unpacked brown sugar
1/3 cup whipping cream
1 tablespoon sweet sherry
1 teaspoon ground cinnamon
1/2 teaspoon freshly grated nutmeg
1/2 teaspoon ground ginger

PASTRY
1 1/4 cups all-purpose flour
1/2 cup cubed unsalted butter
2 teaspoons sugar
1/3 cup iced water
1 egg yolk, at room temperature, lightly
    beaten, to glaze
1 tablespoon whole milk, to glaze

Lightly grease a 9 inch round pie dish. Steam or boil the winter squash for 10 minutes, or until just tender. Drain the winter squash thoroughly, then mash and set aside to cool.

To make the pastry, sift the flour into a large bowl. Using your fingertips, rub in the butter until the mixture resembles fine breadcrumbs. Stir in the sugar. Make a well in the center, add almost all the water and mix with a flat-bladed knife, using a cutting action, until the mixture comes together in beads. Add the remaining water if the dough is too dry.

Gather the dough together and roll out between two sheets of baking paper until large enough to cover the base and side of the pie dish. Line the dish with pastry, trim away the excess pastry and crimp the edges. Roll out the pastry trimmings to 1/16 inch thick. Using a sharp knife, cut out leaf shapes of different sizes and score vein markings onto the leaves. Refrigerate the pastry-lined dish and the leaf shapes for about 20 minutes.

Preheat the oven to 350°F. Cut baking paper to cover the pastry-lined dish. Spread baking beads or uncooked rice over the paper. Bake for 10 minutes, remove the paper and beads and bake for another 10 minutes, or until lightly golden. Meanwhile, place the leaves on a baking sheet lined with baking paper, brush with the combined egg yolk and milk and bake for 10–15 minutes, or until lightly golden. Set aside to cool.

To make the filling, whisk the eggs and brown sugar in a large bowl. Add the cooled mashed winter squash, cream, sherry, cinnamon, nutmeg and ginger and stir to combine thoroughly. Pour the filling into the pastry shell, smooth the surface with the back of a spoon, then bake for 40 minutes, or until set. If the pastry edges begin to brown too much during cooking, cover the edges with foil. Allow the pie to cool to room temperature and then decorate the top with the leaves. Winter squash pie can be served with ice cream or whipped cream.

Apple Strudel

❋ MAKES 2 STRUDELS
❋ PREPARATION TIME: 20 MINUTES
❋ COOKING TIME: 30 MINUTES

2 tablespoons unsalted butter

4 medium granny smith apples, peeled, cored and thinly sliced

2 tablespoons orange juice

1 tablespoon honey

1/4 cup sugar

1/2 cup golden raisins

2 sheets frozen puff pastry, thawed

1/4 cup ground almonds

1 egg, at room temperature, lightly beaten

2 tablespoons unpacked brown sugar

1 teaspoon ground cinnamon

Preheat the oven to 425°F. Brush two baking sheets lightly with melted butter or oil. Heat the butter in a saucepan. Add the apple slices and cook for 2 minutes until lightly golden. Add the orange juice, honey, sugar and golden raisins. Stir over medium heat until the sugar dissolves and the apple is just tender. Transfer the mixture to a bowl and leave until completely cooled.

Place one sheet of pastry on a flat work surface. Fold it in half and make small cuts in the folded edge of the pastry at 3/4 inch intervals. Open out the pastry and sprinkle with half the ground almonds. Drain away the liquid from the apple and place half of the mixture in the center of the pastry. Brush the edges with some of the lightly beaten egg, and fold together, pressing firmly to seal.

Place the strudel on a prepared tray, seam side down. Brush the top with egg and sprinkle with half of the combined brown sugar and cinnamon. Repeat the process with the other sheet of pastry, remaining filling and the rest of the brown sugar and cinnamon. Bake for 20–25 minutes, or until the pastry is golden and crisp. Serve hot with cream or ice cream, or at room temperature.

NOTE: Many types of fresh or canned fruit, such as pears, cherries or apricots, can be used to make strudel. Just make sure that the fruit is well drained before using, or the pastry base will become soggy.

Paris Brest

* SERVES 6–8
* PREPARATION TIME: 50 MINUTES
* COOKING TIME: 1 HOUR 15 MINUTES

CHOUX PASTRY
3 1/3 tablespoons unsalted butter
3/4 cup all-purpose flour, sifted
3 eggs, at room temperature, lightly beaten

FILLING
3 egg yolks, at room temperature
1/4 cup sugar
2 tablespoons all-purpose flour
1 cup whole milk
1 teaspoon natural vanilla essence
1 cup whipping cream, whipped
1 2/3 cups medium raspberries or 1 2/3 cups
    medium strawberries, halved,
    or a mixture of both

TOPPING
3/4 cup chopped dark chocolate
2 tablespoons unsalted butter
1 tablespoon whipping cream

Preheat the oven to 425°F. Brush a large tray with melted butter or oil and line the tray with baking paper. Mark a 9 inch circle on the paper.

To make the pastry, stir the butter with 3/4 cup water in a saucepan over low heat until the butter has melted and the mixture boils. Remove from the heat, add the flour all at once and, using a wooden spoon, beat until smooth. Return to the heat and beat until the mixture thickens and comes away from the side of the pan. Remove from the heat and cool slightly. Transfer to a large bowl. Using electric beaters, add the eggs gradually, beating until stiff and glossy. Place heaped tablespoons of mixture touching each other, using the marked circle as a guide. Bake for 25–30 minutes, or until browned and hollow sounding when the base is tapped. Turn off the oven and leave the pastry to dry in the oven.

To make the filling, whisk the egg yolks, sugar and flour in a bowl until pale. Heat the milk in a saucepan until almost boiling. Gradually add to the egg mixture, stirring constantly. Return to the pan and stir constantly over medium heat until the mixture boils and thickens. Cook for another 2 minutes, stirring constantly. Remove from the heat and stir in the vanilla essence. Transfer to a bowl, cover the surface with plastic wrap to prevent a skin forming and set aside to cool.

To make the topping, combine all the ingredients in a heatproof bowl. Stand the bowl over a saucepan of simmering water and stir until the chocolate has melted and the mixture is smooth. Cool slightly.

To assemble, cut the pastry ring in half horizontally using a serrated knife. Remove any excess dough that remains in the center. Fold the whipped cream through the custard and spoon into the base of the pastry. Top with the fruit. Replace the remaining pastry half on top. Using a flat-bladed knife, spread the chocolate mixture over the top of the pastry. Leave to set.

Banana Tart

❀ SERVES 6
❀ PREPARATION TIME: 40 MINUTES
❀ COOKING TIME: 35 MINUTES

zest and juice of 2 oranges
1/3 cup unpacked brown sugar
1/4 teaspoon cardamom seeds
1 tablespoon rum
3–4 ripe medium bananas

FLAKY PASTRY
1 3/4 cups all-purpose flour
1/4 cup unsalted butter
2/3 cup iced water
1/2 cup chilled unsalted butter, extra

To make the pastry, sift the flour into a bowl with a pinch of salt. Using your fingertips, rub in the butter until the mixture resembles fine breadcrumbs. Add enough of the iced water, mixing with a flat-bladed knife and using a cutting action, to make a dough-like consistency. Turn onto a lightly floured work surface and knead until just smooth.

Roll into a rectangle 4 x 12 inches, cut one-third of the extra chilled butter into cubes and dot all over the top two-thirds of the pastry, leaving a little room around the edge. Fold the bottom third of the pastry up and the top third down and press the edges down to seal. Now turn the pastry to your left, so the hinge is on your right, and roll and fold as before. Refrigerate for 20 minutes, then with the hinge to your right, roll it out again, cover the top two-thirds of the pastry with another third of the butter and roll and fold. Repeat, using the rest of the butter and then roll and fold once more without adding any butter.

Roll the pastry out on a lightly floured work surface into a rectangle 10 x 12 inches, cut a 3/4 inch strip off each side and use this to make a frame on the pastry by brushing the edges of the pastry with water and sticking the strips onto it. Trim off any excess and put the tart base on a baking sheet lined with baking paper, cover with plastic wrap and refrigerate until required.

Combine the orange zest, juice, brown sugar and cardamom seeds in a small saucepan, bring to a boil, simmer for 5 minutes, then remove from the heat and add the rum. Set aside to cool. Preheat the oven to 425°F.

Slice the bananas in half lengthways, arrange on the tart in an even layer, cut side up, and brush with a little syrup. Bake on the top shelf of the oven for 20–30 minutes, making sure the pastry does not overbrown. Brush with syrup and serve.

Apple Tarte Tatin

* SERVES 6
* PREPARATION TIME: 30 MINUTES
* COOKING TIME: 35 MINUTES

1²/₃ cups all-purpose flour
¹/₂ cup cubed chilled unsalted butter
2 tablespoons sugar
1 egg, at room temperature, lightly beaten
2 drops natural vanilla essence
8 medium granny smith apples
¹/₂ cup sugar
2²/₃ tablespoons chopped unsalted butter, extra

Sift the flour into a bowl. Using your fingertips, rub in the butter until the mixture resembles fine breadcrumbs. Stir in the sugar, then make a well in the center. Add the egg and vanilla essence and mix with a flat-bladed knife, using a cutting action, until the mixture comes together in beads. Gather the dough together, then turn out onto a lightly floured work surface and shape into a disc. Wrap in plastic wrap and refrigerate for at least 30 minutes, to firm.

Peel and core the apples and cut each into eight slices. Put the sugar and 1 tablespoon water in a heavy-based 10 inch frying pan that has a metal or removable handle, so that it can safely be placed in the oven. Stir over low heat for 1 minute, or until the sugar has dissolved. Increase the heat to medium and cook for 4–5 minutes, or until the caramel turns golden. Add the extra butter and stir to incorporate. Remove from the heat.

Place the apple slices in neat circles to cover the base of the frying pan. Return the pan to low heat and cook for 10–12 minutes, or until the apples are tender and caramelized. Remove the pan from the heat and leave to cool for 10 minutes.

Preheat the oven to 425°F. Roll the pastry out on a lightly floured surface to a circle ¹/₂ inch larger than the frying pan. Place the pastry over the apples to cover them completely, tucking it down firmly at the edges. Bake for 30–35 minutes, or until the pastry is cooked. Leave for 15 minutes before turning out onto a plate. Serve warm or cold with cream or ice cream.

NOTE: Special high-sided tatin tins are available from specialty kitchenware shops.

Cherry Pie

* SERVES 6–8
* PREPARATION TIME: 25 MINUTES
* COOKING TIME: 40 MINUTES

1¼ cups all-purpose flour
¼ cup confectioners' sugar
½ cup chopped chilled unsalted butter
½ cup ground almonds
¼ cup iced water
4½ cup pitted morello cherries, drained
1 egg, at room temperature, lightly beaten, to glaze
sugar, to sprinkle
whipping cream or ice cream, to serve, optional

To make the pastry, sift the flour and confectioners' sugar into a bowl. Using your fingertips, rub in the butter until the mixture resembles fine breadcrumbs. Stir in the ground almonds, then add almost all the water. Mix with a flat-bladed knife, using a cutting action, until the mixture forms a dough. Add the remaining water if the dough is too dry. Turn the dough onto a lightly floured work surface and gather together into a ball. Roll out on a sheet of baking paper into a circle about 10½ inches in diameter. Flatten slightly, cover with plastic wrap and refrigerate for 20 minutes. Spread the cherries into a 9 inch round pie dish.

Preheat the oven to 400°F. Cover the pie dish with the pastry and trim the overhanging edge. Roll out the remaining scraps of pastry and use a small sharp knife to cut out decorations. Brush the pastry top all over with beaten egg and arrange the decorations on top. Brush these with beaten egg as well, and then sprinkle lightly with sugar. Place the pie dish on a baking sheet (the cherry juice may overflow a little) and cook for 35–40 minutes, or until golden brown.

Pear and Almond Tart

* SERVES 8
* PREPARATION TIME: 15 MINUTES
* COOKING TIME: 1 HOUR 10 MINUTES

PASTRY

1¼ cups all-purpose flour
⅓ cup cubed chilled unsalted butter
¼ cup sugar
2 egg yolks, at room temperature, lightly
  beaten

FILLING

⅔ cup softened unsalted butter
⅔ cup sugar
3 eggs, at room temperature
1¼ cups ground almonds
1½ tablespoons all-purpose flour
2 very ripe medium pears

Lightly grease a shallow 9½ inch round, loose-based, fluted tart tin.

To make the pastry, sift the flour into a bowl. Using your fingertips, rub in the butter until the mixture resembles fine breadcrumbs. Stir in the sugar and mix together. Make a well in the center, add the egg yolks and mix with a flat-bladed knife, using a cutting action, until the mixture comes together in beads. Turn out onto a lightly floured work surface and gather into a ball. Wrap in plastic wrap and refrigerate for 30 minutes.

Preheat the oven to 350°F. Roll out the pastry between two sheets of baking paper until large enough to line the base and side of the tin. Line the tin with the pastry and trim the edge. Sparsely prick the base with a fork. Line the base with baking paper, pour in some baking beads or uncooked rice and bake for 10 minutes. Remove the paper and beads and bake for another 10 minutes. Cool.

To make the filling, beat the butter and sugar in a bowl using electric beaters for 30 seconds (don't cream the mixture). Add the eggs one at a time, beating after each addition. Fold in the ground almonds and flour and spread the filling smoothly over the cooled pastry base.

Peel the pears, halve lengthways and remove the cores. Cut crossways into ⅛ inch slices. Separate the slices slightly, then place the slices on top of the tart to form a cross. Bake for about 50 minutes, or until the filling has set (the middle may still be a little soft). Cool in the tin, then refrigerate for at least 2 hours before serving. Can be dusted with confectioners' sugar.

Exotic Fruit Platter

❋ SERVES 4–6
❋ PREPARATION TIME: 15 MINUTES
❋ COOKING TIME: 5 MINUTES

1 lemongrass stem, white part only,
    chopped
3/4 inch piece ginger, roughly chopped
1 teaspoon unpacked brown sugar
1/2 cup coconut milk
2 medium mangoes
1 medium nashi pear, quartered
6 medium lychees or rambutans, halved
    and stones removed
1/2 medium pawpaw, seeded and cut into
    wedges
1/2 medium red papaya, seeded and cut
    into wedges
2 medium star fruit, thickly sliced
1 medium lime, quartered

Simmer the lemongrass, ginger, sugar and coconut milk in a small saucepan over low heat for 5 minutes. Strain and set aside.

Cut down both sides of the mangoes close to the stones. Score a crisscross pattern into each half, without cutting through the skin. Fold the outer edges under, pushing the center up from underneath. Arrange with the rest of the fruit on a platter. Add the lime, for squeezing on the fruit.

Serve the coconut dressing on the side as a dipping sauce or drizzle over just before serving.

NOTE: Some of these fruits may not be readily available, but a selection of those that are will be just as delicious.

Summer Fruit Compote

❋ SERVES 8
❋ PREPARATION TIME: 40 MINUTES
❋ COOKING TIME: 30 MINUTES

5 medium apricots, halved
4 medium nectarines, halved
4 medium blood plums or other plums,
    pitted
4 medium peaches, quartered
1 cup canned pitted cherries
1 cup claret
1/3 cup dry sherry
3/4 cup sugar
whipped cream, to serve, optional

Gently plunge the fruit in small batches into boiling water for 30 seconds. Remove with a slotted spoon and put in a bowl of iced water. Peel all the fruit except the cherries.

Combine the claret, sherry, sugar and 1 cup water in a large heavy-based saucepan. Stir over low heat without boiling until the sugar has dissolved. Bring to a boil, reduce the heat and simmer for 5 minutes.

Add the drained fruit to the syrup in small batches and simmer each batch for 5 minutes. Remove with a slotted spoon. Pile the fruit into a bowl. Bring the syrup to a boil, reduce the heat and simmer for a further 5 minutes. Remove from the heat and allow to cool slightly — it should be the consistency of a syrup. Pour over the fruit. Serve with a dollop of freshly whipped cream.

Eastern Fruit Platter

Jalousie

❋ SERVES 4–6
❋ PREPARATION TIME: 40 MINUTES
❋ COOKING TIME: 45 MINUTES

2 tablespoons unsalted butter
$\frac{1}{4}$ cup soft brown sugar
3 cups peeled, cored and cubed medium
    apples
1 teaspoon grated lemon zest
1 tablespoon lemon juice
$\frac{1}{4}$ teaspoon freshly grated nutmeg
$\frac{1}{4}$ teaspoon cinnamon
$\frac{1}{4}$ cup golden raisins
2 sheets frozen puff pastry, thawed
1 egg, at room temperature, lightly beaten,
    to glaze

Preheat the oven to 425°F. Lightly grease a baking sheet and line with baking paper.

Melt the butter and sugar in a frying pan. Add the apple, lemon zest and lemon juice. Cook over medium heat for 10 minutes, stirring occasionally, until the apples are cooked and the mixture is thick and syrupy. Stir in the nutmeg, cinnamon and golden raisins. Cool completely.

Cut the block of puff pastry in half. On a lightly floured surface roll out one half of the pastry to a 7 x 9$\frac{1}{2}$ inch rectangle. Spread the fruit mixture onto the pastry, leaving a 1 inch border. Brush the edges lightly with the beaten egg.

Roll the second half of the pastry on a lightly floured surface to a 7 x 10 inch rectangle. Using a sharp knife, cut slashes in the pastry across its width, leaving a $\frac{3}{4}$ inch border around the edge. The slashes should open slightly and look like a venetian blind (*jalousie* in French). Place over the fruit and press the edges together. Trim away any extra pastry. Knock up the puff pastry (brush the sides upwards) with a knife to ensure rising during cooking. Glaze the top with egg. Bake for 25–30 minutes, or until puffed and golden.

Profiteroles with Dark Chocolate Sauce

❋ SERVES 4–6

❋ PREPARATION TIME: 40 MINUTES
  + COOLING

❋ COOKING TIME: 50 MINUTES

1/4 cup chopped butter

3/4 cup all-purpose flour

3 eggs, at room temperature, lightly beaten

WHITE CHOCOLATE FILLING

1/4 cup custard powder or instant vanilla
   pudding mix

1 tablespoon sugar

1 1/2 cups whole milk

1 cup chopped white chocolate buttons

1 tablespoon Grand Marnier

DARK CHOCOLATE SAUCE

1 cup chopped dark chocolate

1/2 cup whipping cream

Preheat the oven to 425°F. Line a baking sheet with baking paper. Put the butter and 3/4 cup water in a saucepan. Bring to the boil, then remove from the heat. Add the flour all at once. Return to the heat and stir until the mixture forms a smooth ball. Set aside to cool slightly. Transfer to a bowl and, while beating with electric beaters, gradually add the eggs a little at a time, beating well after each addition, to form a thick, smooth, glossy paste.

Spoon 2 heaped teaspoons of the mixture onto the tray at 2 inch intervals. Sprinkle lightly with water and bake for 12–15 minutes, or until the dough is puffed. Turn off the oven. Pierce a small hole in the base of each profiterole with the point of a knife and return the profiteroles to the oven. Leave them to dry in the oven for 5 minutes.

To make the filling, combine the instant vanilla pudding mix and sugar in a saucepan. Gradually add the milk, stirring until smooth, then continue to stir over low heat until the mixture boils and thickens. Remove from the heat and add the white chocolate and Grand Marnier. Stir until the chocolate is melted. Cover the surface with plastic wrap and allow to cool. Stir the custard until smooth, then spoon into an icing bag fitted with a 1/2 inch plain nozzle. Pipe the filling into each profiterole.

For the dark chocolate sauce, combine the chocolate and cream in a small saucepan. Stir over low heat until the chocolate is melted and the mixture is smooth. Serve warm, drizzled over the profiteroles.

NOTE: The profiteroles can be made a day ahead. Fill just before serving. You can also make miniature profiteroles, using 1 teaspoon of the mixture. Dip the tops of the cooked profiteroles in melted chocolate. When set, fill them with whipped cream.

Free-Form Blueberry Pie

※ SERVES 4
※ PREPARATION TIME: 20 MINUTES
※ COOKING TIME: 35 MINUTES

1½ cups all-purpose flour
½ cup confectioners' sugar
½ cup cubed chilled unsalted butter
¼ cup lemon juice
3¼ cups blueberries
¼ cup confectioners' sugar, extra
1 teaspoon finely grated lemon zest
½ teaspoon ground cinnamon
1 egg white, at room temperature,
    lightly beaten
confectioners' sugar, extra, to dust
whipped cream or ice cream, to serve

Preheat the oven to 350°F. Sift the flour and confectioners' sugar into a bowl. Using your fingertips, rub in the butter until the mixture resembles fine breadcrumbs. Make a well in the center and add almost all the lemon juice. Mix together with a flat-bladed knife, using a cutting action, until the mixture comes together in beads. Add the remaining juice if the dough is too dry.

Gently gather the dough together and lift onto a sheet of baking paper. Roll out to a circle 12 inches in diameter. Cover with plastic wrap and refrigerate for 10 minutes. Put the blueberries in a bowl and sprinkle them with the confectioners' sugar, lemon zest and cinnamon.

Place the pastry (still on the baking paper) on a baking sheet. Brush the center of the pastry lightly with egg white. Pile the blueberry mixture onto the pastry in an 8 inch diameter circle, then fold the edges of the pastry over the filling, leaving the center uncovered. Bake for 30–35 minutes. Dust with confectioners' sugar and serve warm with whipped cream or ice cream.

Plum Tart

※ SERVES 6
※ PREPARATION TIME: 20 MINUTES
※ COOKING TIME: 35 MINUTES

6 sheets frozen puff pastry, thawed

TOPPING
1 tablespoon plum jam
5 large plums, very thinly sliced
1 tablespoon brandy
1 tablespoon sugar

Preheat the oven to 400°F. Roll out the pastry on a lightly floured work surface to make an irregular rectangular shape, about 8 x 12 inches and ¼ inch thick. Place the pastry on a greased baking sheet.

Heat the plum jam with 2 teaspoons water in a small saucepan over low heat until the jam is softened and spreadable. Brush the jam over the pastry base, leaving a ¾ inch border. Lay the plum slices along the pastry, leaving a ¾ inch border all around. Lightly brush the fruit with the brandy and sprinkle with the sugar. Bake for 30 minutes, or until the pastry is puffed and golden. Cut into slices and serve warm with cream or ice cream.

Free-Form Blueberry Pie

Lime Chiffon Pie

❋ SERVES 12
❋ PREPARATION TIME: 30 MINUTES
❋ COOKING TIME: 1 HOUR

ALMOND PASTRY
1¼ cups all-purpose flour
1 cup ground almonds
⅓ cup chopped chilled unsalted butter
1–2 tablespoons iced water

FILLING
6 egg yolks, at room temperature
½ cup sugar
½ cup melted unsalted butter
⅓ cup lime juice
2 teaspoons finely grated lime zest
2 teaspoons powdered gelatin
½ cup whipping cream, whipped

LIME ZEST
½ cup sugar
zest of 4 limes, finely shredded

Sift the flour into a large bowl and add the almonds. Using your fingertips, rub in the butter until the mixture resembles fine breadcrumbs. Add almost all the iced water and mix with a flat-bladed knife, using a cutting action, until the mixture forms a firm dough. Add more water if necessary. Turn onto a lightly floured surface and gather together into a ball. Roll the pastry out to fit a 9 inch fluted tart tin. Line the tin, trim the edges and refrigerate for 20 minutes.

Preheat the oven to 350°F. Line the pastry-lined tin with a sheet of baking paper and spread a layer of baking beads or uncooked rice evenly over the paper. Bake for 20 minutes, then remove the paper and beads and bake for another 20 minutes, or until lightly golden. Allow to cool completely.

To make the filling, put the egg yolks, sugar, butter, lime juice and zest in a heatproof bowl. Whisk to combine thoroughly and dissolve the sugar. Stand the bowl over a saucepan of simmering water, making sure the base of the bowl does not touch the water, and stir constantly for 15 minutes, or until the mixture thickens. Remove from the heat and cool slightly. Put 1 tablespoon water in a small heatproof bowl, sprinkle the gelatin in an even layer over the surface and leave to go spongy. Do not stir. Bring a small saucepan filled with about 1½ inches water to a boil, remove from the heat and place the bowl into the pan. The water should come halfway up the side of the bowl. Stir the gelatin until clear and dissolved. Cool slightly, add to the lime curd and stir to combine. Cool to room temperature, stirring occasionally.

Fold the cream through the lime curd and pour into the pastry case. Refrigerate for 2–3 hours, until set. Leave the pie for 15 minutes at room temperature before serving.

To prepare the lime zest, combine the sugar with 1 tablespoon water in a saucepan. Stir over low heat until the sugar has dissolved. Bring to a boil, add the zest and simmer for 3 minutes. Drain the zest on a wire rack, then decorate the lime chiffon pie before serving.

Lemon Brûlée Tarts

❋ SERVES 4
❋ PREPARATION TIME: 40 MINUTES
❋ COOKING TIME: 35 MINUTES

1 1/4 cups whipping cream
2 teaspoons grated lemon zest
4 egg yolks, at room temperature
2 tablespoons sugar
2 teaspoons cornstarch
2 tablespoons lemon juice
2 sheets frozen puff pastry, thawed
1/3 cup sugar

Heat the cream in a saucepan with the lemon zest until almost boiling. Allow to cool slightly. Whisk the egg yolks, sugar, cornstarch and lemon juice in a bowl until thick and pale.

Add the cream gradually, whisking constantly. Strain into a clean saucepan and stir over low heat until thickened slightly — the mixture should coat the back of a wooden spoon. Pour into a heatproof bowl, cover with plastic wrap and refrigerate for several hours or overnight.

Preheat the oven to 425°F. Lightly grease four 4 1/2 inch shallow loose-based tart tins. If using block pastry roll it to 10 x 19 inches, then cut four rounds, large enough to fit the base and side of the tins. If using sheets, cut two rounds of pastry from each sheet to line the tins. Line each tin with pastry, trim the edges and prick the bases lightly with a fork. Line with baking paper and spread a layer of baking beads or uncooked rice evenly over the paper. Bake for 15 minutes, remove the paper and beads and bake for another 5 minutes, or until lightly golden. Leave to cool.

Spoon the lemon custard into each pastry shell, smooth the top, leaving a little room for the sugar layer. Cover the edges of the pastry with foil and sprinkle sugar generously over the surface of the custard in an even layer. Cook under a preheated broiler until the sugar just begins to color. Put the tarts close to the broiler so they brown quickly, but watch carefully that they do not burn. Serve immediately.

New York Cheesecake

❋ SERVES 10–12
❋ PREPARATION TIME: 1 HOUR
❋ COOKING TIME: 1 HOUR 50 MINUTES

½ cup self-rising flour
1 cup all-purpose flour
¼ cup sugar
1 teaspoon grated lemon zest
⅓ cup chopped unsalted butter
1 egg, at room temperature
1½ cups whipping cream, to serve

FILLING
3 cups softened cream cheese
1 cup sugar
¼ cup all-purpose flour
2 teaspoons grated orange zest
2 teaspoons grated lemon zest
4 eggs, at room temperature
⅔ cup whipping cream

CANDIED ZEST
finely shredded zest of 3 medium limes,
    3 medium lemons and 3 medium
    oranges
1 cup sugar

Preheat the oven to 425°F. Lightly grease a 9 inch spring-form cake tin.

To make the pastry, combine the flours, sugar, lemon zest and butter for about 30 seconds in a food processor, until crumbly. Add the egg and process briefly until the mixture just comes together. Turn out onto a lightly floured surface and gather together into a ball. Refrigerate in plastic wrap for about 20 minutes, or until the mixture is firm.

Roll the dough between two sheets of baking paper until large enough to fit the base and side of the tin. Ease into the tin and trim the edges. Cover the pastry with baking paper, then baking beads or uncooked rice. Bake for 10 minutes, then remove the baking paper and beads. Flatten the pastry lightly with the back of a spoon and bake for another 5 minutes. Set aside to cool.

To make the filling, reduce the oven to 300°F. Beat the cream cheese, sugar, flour and orange and lemon zest until smooth. Add the eggs, one at a time, beating after each addition. Beat in the cream, pour over the pastry and bake for 1½ hours, or until almost set. Turn off the oven and leave to cool with the door ajar. When cool, refrigerate.

To make the candied zest, place a little water in a saucepan with the lime, lemon and orange zest, bring to a boil and simmer for 1 minute. Drain the zest and repeat with fresh water. This will get rid of any bitterness in the zest and syrup. Put the sugar in a saucepan with ¼ cup water and stir over low heat until dissolved. Add the zest, bring to a boil, reduce the heat and simmer for 5–6 minutes, or until the zest looks translucent. Allow to cool, drain the zest and place on baking paper to dry (you can save the syrup to serve with the cheesecake). Whip the cream, spoon over the cold cheesecake and top with candied zest.

NOTE: To make the cheesecake easier to cut, heap the zest in mounds, then cut between the mounds of zest.

Rhubarb Lattice Pie

※ SERVES 4–6

※ PREPARATION TIME: 35 MINUTES

※ COOKING TIME: 1 HOUR

1 1/4 cups all-purpose flour
1/4 teaspoon baking powder
1/3 cup cubed chilled unsalted butter
1 tablespoon sugar
2 1/2–3 1/2 fl oz iced water
whole milk, to glaze
demerara sugar, to decorate

RHUBARB FILLING
1 lb 2 oz rhubarb, trimmed,
    leaves discarded
1/2 cup sugar
2 inch piece orange zest, pith removed
1 tablespoon orange juice
14 1/2 oz canned apple pie filling
sugar, extra, to taste

To make the rhubarb filling, preheat the oven to 350°F. Cut the rhubarb into 1 1/4 inch lengths and combine in a large casserole dish with the sugar, orange zest and juice. Cover the dish with a lid or foil and bake for 30 minutes, or until the rhubarb is just tender. Drain away any excess juice and discard the zest. Cool, then stir in the apple. Add more sugar to taste.

While the rhubarb is cooking, sift the flour and baking powder into a bowl. Using your fingertips, rub in the butter until the mixture resembles fine breadcrumbs. Stir in the sugar. Make a well in the center and add almost all the water. Mix with a flat-bladed knife, using a cutting action, until the mixture comes together in beads. Add more water if the dough is too dry. Gather together, wrap in plastic wrap and chill for 20 minutes.

Roll the pastry out between two sheets of baking paper to a 11 1/4 inch circle. Cut the pastry into 5/8 inch strips, using a sharp knife or a fluted cutter. Lay half the strips on a sheet of baking paper, leaving a 1/2 inch gap between each strip. Interweave the remaining strips to form a lattice. Cover with plastic wrap and refrigerate, flat, for 20 minutes.

Increase the oven to 425°F. Pour the filling into an 8 inch pie dish and smooth the surface. Invert the pastry lattice on the pie, remove the paper and trim the pastry edge. Bake for 10 minutes. Remove from the oven, brush with milk and sprinkle with demerara sugar. Reduce the oven to 350°F and bake the pie for 20 minutes, or until the pastry is golden and the filling is bubbling.

Lemon Tart (Tarte au Citron)

❋ SERVES 6–8
❋ PREPARATION TIME: 1 HOUR
❋ COOKING TIME: 1 HOUR 40 MINUTES

3 eggs, at room temperature
2 egg yolks, at room temperature
3/4 cup sugar
1/2 cup whipping cream
3/4 cup lemon juice
1 1/2 tablespoons finely grated lemon zest
2 small lemons
2/3 cup sugar

PASTRY
1 cup all-purpose flour
1/3 cup unsalted butter
1 egg yolk, at room temperature
2 tablespoons confectioners' sugar, sifted

To make the pastry, sift the flour and a pinch of salt into a large bowl. Make a well in the center and add the butter, egg yolk and confectioners' sugar. Work together the butter, yolk and sugar with your fingertips, then slowly incorporate the flour. Bring together into a ball — you may need to add a few drops of cold water. Flatten the ball slightly, cover with plastic wrap and refrigerate for 20 minutes.

Preheat the oven to 400°F. Lightly grease a shallow loose-based tart tin, about 3/4 inch deep and 8 1/4 inches across the base.

Roll out the pastry between two sheets of baking paper until it is 1/8 inch thick, to fit the base and side of the tin. Trim the edge. Refrigerate for 10 minutes. Line the pastry with baking paper, fill with baking beads or uncooked rice and bake for 10 minutes. Remove the paper and beads and bake for another 6–8 minutes, or until the pastry looks dry all over. Cool the pastry and reduce the oven to 300°F.

Whisk the eggs, egg yolks and sugar together, add the cream and lemon juice and mix well. Strain and then add the lemon zest. Place the tart tin on a baking sheet on the middle shelf of the oven and carefully pour in the filling right up to the top. Bake for 40 minutes, or until it is just set — it should wobble in the middle when the tin is firmly tapped. Cool the tart before removing from its tin.

Meanwhile, wash and scrub the lemons well. Slice very thinly (1/16 inch thick). Combine the sugar and 7 fl oz water in a small frying pan and stir over low heat until the sugar has dissolved. Add the lemon slices and simmer over low heat for 40 minutes, or until the peel is very tender and the pith looks transparent. Lift out of the syrup and drain on baking paper. If serving the tart immediately, cover the surface with the lemon slices. If not, keep the slices covered and decorate the tart when ready to serve. Serve warm or chilled, with a little cream.

Chocolate Collar Cheesecake

❋ SERVES 8–10
❋ PREPARATION TIME: 1 HOUR 30 MINUTES
❋ COOKING TIME: 50 MINUTES

$^1/_2$ cups crushed plain chocolate cookies
$4^1/_2$ tablespoons melted unsalted butter
2 cups softened cream cheese
$^1/_3$ cup sugar
2 eggs, at room temperature
1 tablespoon unsweetened cocoa powder
$1^1/_4$ cups sour cream
$1^2/_3$ cups melted dark chocolate
$^1/_3$ cup Bailey's Irish Cream
$^1/_3$ cup melted white chocolate
1 cup melted dark chocolate
$1^1/_4$ cups whipping cream, whipped
unsweetened cocoa powder and
    confectioners' sugar, to dust

Brush a 9 inch round spring-form cake tin with melted butter and line the base and side with baking paper. Mix together the cookie crumbs and butter, press firmly into the base of the tin and refrigerate for 10 minutes. Preheat the oven to 350°F.

Beat the cream cheese and sugar using electric beaters until smooth and creamy. Add the eggs, one at a time, beating thoroughly after each addition. Beat in the cocoa and sour cream until smooth. Beat in the cooled melted dark chocolate. Beat in the liqueur and pour over the base. Smooth the surface and bake for 45 minutes. The cheesecake may not be fully set, but will firm up. Refrigerate, until cold.

Remove the cheesecake from the tin and put it on a board. Measure the height and add $^1/_4$ inch. Cut a strip of baking paper this wide and $29^1/_2$ inches long. Pipe or drizzle the melted white chocolate in a figure eight pattern along the paper. When just set, spread the dark chocolate over the entire strip of paper. Allow the chocolate to set a little, but you need to be able to bend the paper without it cracking. Wrap the paper around the cheesecake with the chocolate inside. Seal the ends and hold the paper in place until the chocolate is completely set. Peel away the paper. Spread the top with cream, then dust with cocoa and confectioners' sugar.

Banoffee Pie

❋ SERVES 8
❋ PREPARATION TIME: 35 MINUTES
❋ COOKING TIME: 30 MINUTES

WALNUT PASTRY
1¼ cups all-purpose flour
2 tablespoons confectioners' sugar
¾ cup ground walnuts
⅓ cup chopped chilled unsalted butter
2–3 tablespoons iced water

FILLING
1¼ cups canned condensed milk
2 tablespoons unsalted butter
1 tablespoon dark corn syrup
4 medium bananas, sliced
1½ cups whipping cream, whipped
⅓ cup melted dark chocolate

To make the walnut pastry, sift the flour and confectioners' sugar into a large bowl and add the walnuts. Using your fingertips, rub in the butter until the mixture resembles fine breadcrumbs. Mix in the iced water with a flat-bladed knife, using a cutting action, until the mixture forms a firm dough. Add more water if the dough is too dry. Turn onto a lightly floured work surface and gather together into a ball. Wrap and refrigerate for 15 minutes. Roll out to fit a 9 inch tart tin. Refrigerate for 20 minutes.

Preheat the oven to 350°F. Line the pastry base with baking paper and spread baking beads or uncooked rice over the paper. Bake for 15 minutes, remove the paper and beads and bake for another 10 minutes, or until lightly golden. Set aside to cool completely.

To make the filling, put the condensed milk, butter and dark corn syrup in a small saucepan. Stir over medium heat for 5 minutes, until it boils and thickens and turns a light caramel color. Cool slightly, then arrange half the bananas over the pastry and pour the caramel over the top. Smooth the surface and refrigerate for 30 minutes.

Drop spoonfuls of cream over the caramel and arrange the remaining banana on top. Drizzle with melted chocolate.

Apple Fritters (Beignets de Fruits)

❋ SERVES 4

❋ PREPARATION TIME: 25 MINUTES

❋ COOKING TIME: 10 MINUTES

3 medium granny smith or golden
   delicious apples
4½ tablespoons raisins
¼ cup calvados or rum
1½ tablespoons sugar
oil, for frying
2 tablespoons all-purpose flour,
   for coating
confectioners' sugar, for dusting

BATTER
1 egg, at room temperature, separated
2¼ fl oz warm beer
½ cup all-purpose flour
1 teaspoon oil

Peel and core the apples and cut into ½ inch cubes. Place in a bowl with the raisins, calvados and sugar and marinate for 3 hours.

To make the batter, beat the egg yolk and beer together in a large bowl. Blend in the flour, oil and a pinch of salt. Stir until smooth. The batter will be very thick at this stage. Cover and leave in a warm place for 1 hour.

Pour the oil into a large saucepan to a depth of 4 inches and heat to 325°F, or until a cube of bread dropped into the oil browns in 20 seconds. Add 1½ tablespoons of the calvados marinade to the batter and stir until smooth. Whisk the egg white until stiff and gently fold into the batter. Drain the apples and raisins, toss with the flour to coat, then lightly fold them through the batter. Carefully lower heaped tablespoons of batter into the oil in batches and fry for 1–2 minutes, until the fritters are golden on both sides. Remove with a slotted spoon and drain on paper towels. Keep them warm. Dust with confectioners' sugar and serve.

Indian Ice Cream (Kulfi)

❋ SERVES 6
❋ PREPARATION TIME: 20 MINUTES
❋ COOKING TIME: 50 MINUTES

6 cups whole milk
8 cardamom pods
4 tablespoons sugar
1/4 cup finely chopped blanched almonds
1/4 cup chopped pistachio nuts plus extra,
    to garnish
vegetable oil, for greasing

Put the milk and cardamom pods in a large heavy-based saucepan, bring to a boil then reduce the heat and simmer, stirring often until it has reduced by about one-third, to 4 cups — this will take some time. Keep stirring or it will stick.

Add the sugar and cook for 2–3 minutes. Strain out the cardamom pods and add the nuts. Pour the kulfi into a shallow metal or plastic container, cover the surface with a sheet of baking paper and freeze for 1 hour. Remove from the freezer and beat to break up any ice crystals, freeze again and repeat twice more.

Lightly brush six 1-cup steamed pudding molds with the oil and divide the kulfi among them, then freeze overnight. To serve, unmold each kulfi and cut a cross 1/4 inch deep in the top. Serve with extra pistachio nuts sprinkled over the top.

Spicy Coconut Custard

❋ SERVES 8
❋ PREPARATION TIME: 20 MINUTES
❋ COOKING TIME: 1 HOUR

2 cinnamon sticks
1 teaspoon freshly grated nutmeg
2 teaspoons whole cloves
1 1/4 cups whipping cream
1/2 cup chopped jaggery or unpacked
    brown sugar
9 1/2 fl oz coconut milk
3 eggs, at room temperature, lightly beaten
2 egg yolks, at room temperature,
    lightly beaten
whipped cream, to serve
toasted flaked coconut, to serve

Preheat the oven to 300°F. Combine the cinnamon, nutmeg, cloves, cream and 1 cup water in a saucepan. Bring to simmering point, reduce the heat to very low and leave for 5 minutes to allow the spices to infuse the liquid. Add the sugar and coconut milk, return to low heat and stir until the sugar has dissolved.

Whisk the eggs and egg yolks in a bowl until combined. Stir in the spiced mixture, then strain, discarding the whole spices. Pour into eight 1/4-cup ramekins. Place in an ovenproof dish and pour in enough hot water to come halfway up the sides of the ramekins. Bake for 40–45 minutes until set. The custards should wobble slightly when the dish is shaken lightly. Remove the custards from the ovenproof dish. Serve hot or chilled with whipped cream and toasted flaked coconut sprinkled over the top.

Kulfi

Pecan Pie

✳ SERVES 6
✳ PREPARATION TIME: 30 MINUTES
✳ COOKING TIME: 1 HOUR 15 MINUTES

SHORTCRUST PASTRY
1 1/2 cups all-purpose flour
1/2 cup chopped chilled unsalted butter
2–3 tablespoons chilled water

FILLING
2 cups pecans
3 eggs, at room temperature, lightly beaten
3 1/3 tablespoons melted and cooled
   unsalted butter
3/4 cup unpacked brown sugar
2/3 cup light corn syrup
1 teaspoon natural vanilla essence

Preheat the oven to 350°F. Sift the flour into a large bowl. Using your fingertips, rub in the butter until the mixture resembles fine breadcrumbs. Add almost all the water and mix with a flat-bladed knife, using a cutting action, until the mixture comes together in beads. Add more water if the dough is too dry. Turn out onto a lightly floured work surface and gather together into a ball.

Roll out the pastry to a 14 inch round. Line a 9 inch tart tin with pastry, trim the edges and refrigerate for 20 minutes. Pile the pastry trimmings together, roll out on baking paper to a rectangle about 1/16 inch thick, then refrigerate.

Line the pastry-lined tin with a sheet of baking paper and spread a layer of baking beads or uncooked rice evenly over the paper. Bake for 15 minutes, remove the paper and beads and bake for another 15 minutes, or until lightly golden. Cool completely.

Spread the pecans over the pastry base. Whisk together the eggs, butter, sugar, corn syrup, vanilla essence and a pinch of salt until well combined, then pour over the nuts.

Using a fluted pastry wheel or small sharp knife, cut narrow strips from half of the pastry trimmings. Cut out small stars with a cookie cutter from the remaining trimmings. Arrange decoratively over the filling. Bake the pie for 45 minutes, or until firm. Allow to cool completely and serve at room temperature.

Raspberry Shortcake

❋ SERVES 6–8

❋ PREPARATION TIME: 30 MINUTES

❋ COOKING TIME: 35 MINUTES

PASTRY

1 cup all-purpose flour

$^{1}/_{3}$ cup confectioners' sugar

$^{1}/_{3}$ cup chopped chilled unsalted butter

1 egg yolk, at room temperature

$^{1}/_{2}$ teaspoon natural vanilla essence

$^{1}/_{2}$–1 tablespoon iced water

TOPPING

6 cups fresh medium raspberries

$^{1}/_{4}$ cup confectioners' sugar

$^{1}/_{3}$ cup redcurrant jelly

whipping cream, to serve

To make the pastry, sift the flour and confectioners' sugar into a large bowl. Using your fingertips, rub in the butter until the mixture resembles fine breadcrumbs. Add the egg yolk, vanilla essence and enough of the iced water to make the ingredients come together, then mix to a dough with a flat-bladed knife, using a cutting action. Turn out onto a lightly floured work surface and gather together into a ball. Flatten slightly, wrap in plastic wrap and refrigerate for 30 minutes.

Preheat the oven to 350°F. Roll out the pastry to fit a fluted 4 x 13$^{1}/_{2}$ inch loose-based tart tin and trim the edge. Prick all over with a fork and refrigerate for 20 minutes. Line the pastry with baking paper and spread a layer of baking beads or uncooked rice evenly over the paper. Bake for 15–20 minutes, or until golden. Remove the paper and beads and bake for another 15 minutes. Cool on a wire rack.

To make the topping, set aside 4 cups of the best raspberries and mash the rest with the confectioners' sugar. Spread the mashed raspberries over the shortcake just before serving.

Cover with the whole raspberries. Heat the redcurrant jelly in a small saucepan until melted and smooth. Use a soft pastry brush to coat the raspberries heavily with warm glaze. Cut into slices and serve with cream.

Poached Pears with Ginger Zabaglione

※ MAKES 6
※ PREPARATION TIME: 30 MINUTES
※ COOKING TIME: 1 HOUR

2 cups red wine
4 pieces crystallized ginger
½ cup sugar
6 medium pears, peeled

GINGER ZABAGLIONE
8 egg yolks, at room temperature
⅓ cup sugar
1 teaspoon ground ginger
1¼ cups Marsala

Put the wine, ginger and sugar in a large saucepan with 4 cups water and stir over medium heat until the sugar has dissolved. Add the pears, cover and simmer for 45 minutes, or until tender.

To make the zabaglione, put a large saucepan half-filled with water on to boil. When boiling, remove from the heat. Beat the egg yolks, sugar and ginger in a metal or heatproof bowl, using electric beaters, until pale yellow. Set the bowl over the saucepan of steaming water, making sure the base of the bowl does not touch the water, and beat continuously, adding the Marsala gradually. Beat for 5 minutes, or until very thick and foamy and like a mousse.

Remove the pears from the pan with a slotted spoon. Arrange on plates and pour ginger zabaglione over each. Serve immediately.

Cherry Cheese Strudel

✢ SERVES 8–10
✢ PREPARATION TIME: 25 MINUTES
✢ COOKING TIME: 45 MINUTES

2 cups ricotta cheese
2 teaspoons grated lemon or orange zest
¼ cup sugar
½ cup fresh white breadcrumbs
2 tablespoons ground almonds
2 eggs, at room temperature
2 cups 2 tablespoons canned pitted black
    cherries
2 teaspoons cornstarch
8 sheets filo pastry
¼ cup melted unsalted butter
2 tablespoons dry white breadcrumbs
confectioners' sugar, for dusting

Preheat the oven to 350°F. Grease a baking sheet.

Combine the ricotta, zest, sugar, fresh breadcrumbs and almonds in a bowl. Add the eggs and mix well. Drain the cherries, reserving half the juice. Blend the cornstarch with the reserved cherry juice in a saucepan. Stir over medium heat until the mixture boils and thickens, then cool slightly.

Layer the pastry sheets, brushing between each sheet with melted butter and sprinkling with a few dry breadcrumbs. Form a large square by placing the second sheet halfway down the first sheet. Alternate layers, brushing with melted butter and sprinkling with breadcrumbs.

Put the ricotta mixture along one long edge of the pastry. Shape into a log and top with cherries and cooled syrup. Roll the pastry around the ricotta filling, folding in the edges as you roll. Finish with a pastry edge underneath. Place on the prepared tray and bake for 35–40 minutes, or until the pastry is golden. Dust with confectioners' sugar. Serve cold, cut into slices.

Apple Pie

❋ SERVES 6
❋ PREPARATION TIME: 45 MINUTES
❋ COOKING TIME: 50 MINUTES

2 tablespoons marmalade
1 egg, lightly beaten
1 tablespoon sugar

FILLING
6 large granny smith apples, peeled,
   cored and cut into wedges
2 tablespoons sugar
1 teaspoon finely grated lemon zest
pinch of ground cloves

PASTRY
2 cups all-purpose flour
1/4 cup self-rising flour
3/4 cup cubed chilled unsalted butter,
   cubed
2 tablespoons sugar
2 1/2–3 1/2 fl oz iced water

Lightly grease a 9 inch pie dish.

To make the filling, put the apple in a saucepan with the sugar, lemon zest, cloves and 2 tablespoons water. Cover and cook over low heat for 8 minutes, or until the apples are just tender, shaking the pan occasionally. Drain and cool completely.

To make the pastry, sift the flours into a bowl. Using your fingertips, rub in the butter until the mixture resembles fine breadcrumbs. Stir in the sugar, then make a well in the center. Add almost all the iced water and mix with a flat-bladed knife, using a cutting action, until the mixture comes together in beads. Add more water if the dough is too dry. Gather together and lift out onto a lightly floured work surface. Press into a ball and divide into two, making one half a little bigger. Cover with plastic wrap and refrigerate for 20 minutes.

Preheat the oven to 400°F. Roll out the larger piece of pastry between two sheets of baking paper to line the base and side of the pie dish. Line the pie dish with the pastry. Use a small sharp knife to trim away any excess pastry. Brush the marmalade over the base and spoon the apple mixture into the shell. Roll out the other pastry between the baking paper until large enough to cover the pie. Brush water around the rim then lay the pastry top over the pie. Trim off any excess pastry, pinch the edges and cut a few slits in the top to allow steam to escape.

Re-roll the pastry scraps and cut into leaves for decoration. Lightly brush the top with egg, then sprinkle with sugar. Bake for 20 minutes, then reduce the oven temperature to 350°F and bake for another 15–20 minutes, or until golden.

index

A

aïoli 23
ajo blanco 21
almonds
    almond cream 333
    almond semi freddo 329
    chicken and almond pilaff 189
    kulfi 385
    pear and almond flan 359
apples
    apple fritters (beignets de fruits) 383
    apple pie 395
    apple strudel 349
    apple tarte tatin 355
    jalousie 363
artichokes, stuffed 35
Asian oysters 77
asparagus with citrus hollandaise 39

B

baharat 189
Balinese seafood curry 149
bananas
    banana and coconut pancakes 317
    banana fritters in coconut batter 331
    banana tart 353
    Banoffee pie 381
basil
    chicken, Thai basil and cashew
        stir-fry 187
    fettucine with zucchini and crisp fried
        basil 105
    linguine pesto 109
    pesto 27
    shrimp and basil soup 25
beans
    braised lamb shanks with haricot
        beans 197
    Mexican beef chili with beans and
        rice 239
    pasta and bean soup 17
    pork sausages with white beans 217
    see also black beans
béarnaise sauce 215
beef
    beef Provençale 221
    beef Wellington 209
    carpaccio 81
    Chinese beef and black bean
        sauce 225
    Mexican beef chili with beans and
        rice 239

peppered beef fillet with béarnaise
    sauce 215
roast beef with Yorkshire puddings 233
roast sirloin with mustard sauce 237
steak and kidney pie 241
surf 'n' turf 229
Thai beef salad 41
Thai beef curry 231
beets, fresh, and goat's cheese salad 45
beignets de fruits 383
bellini sorbet 313
berries
    charlotte Malakoff 333
    free-form blueberry pie 367
    lemon passionfruit syllabub with
        berries 307
    panna cotta with ruby sauce 313
    Paris Brest 351
    raspberry cranachan 301
    raspberry shortcake 389
    strawberries Romanoff 337
    summer berry tart 289
black beans
    Chinese beef and black bean sauce 225
    mussels with black beans and cilantro 75
Black Forest gateau 285
blue cheese tagliatelle 105
blueberry pie, free-form 367
bourride 23
brandade de morue 57
bream with tomato cheese crust 155
buckwheat noodles, chilled 59
butter chicken 191
butterscotch tart 339

C

Caesar salad 43
cakes
    Black Forest gateau 285
    devil's food cake 271
    orange and lemon syrup cake 299
California rolls 69
candied zest 373
cannoli, Sicilian 345
carpaccio 81
cedro 345
charlotte Malakoff 333
cheese
    baked eggplant with tomato and
        mozzarella 261
    blue cheese tagliatelle 105
    bream with tomato cheese crust 155
    cheese and mushroom pies 117
    cheese tortellini with nutty herb
        sauce 93
    fennel risotto balls with cheesy
        filling 95
    fettucine alfredo 101
    prosciutto, camembert and fig salad 41

tomato and small mozzarella cheese balls
    salad 37
    see also feta; goat's cheese
cheese sauce 251
chocolate collar cheesecake 379
New York 373
cherries
    cherry cheese strudel 393
    cherry pie 357
    chocolate cherry trifle 269
    feuilleté with cherries jubilee 315
chicken
    barbecued chicken with Thai sticky
        rice 181
    butter chicken 191
    chicken with 40 cloves of garlic 179
    chicken and almond pilaff 189
    chicken braised with ginger and
        star anise 187
    chicken caccitore 169
    chicken and chorizo paella 199
    chicken laksa 173
    chicken mulligatawny 167
    chicken with peppers and olives 179
    chicken pie with feta 165
    chicken, Thai basil and cashew
        stir-fry 187
    Chinese chicken and corn soup 33
    clay pot chicken and vegetables 177
    General Tso's chicken 195
    Hainanese chicken rice 183
    Indonesian spicy chicken soup 201
    kung pao chicken 175
    Moroccan chicken pie 115
    tandoori chicken with cardamom rice 159
    Thai green chicken curry 185
chickpea and vegetable casserole, spicy 259
chickpeas, soaking 259
chili
    chili satay noodles 261
    Mexican beef chili with beans and
        rice 239
    seared scallops with chili bean
        paste 151
    spaghettini with garlic and chili 93
    steamed fish cutlets with ginger
        and chili 139
Chinese beef and black bean sauce 225
Chinese chicken and corn soup 33
chocolate
    Black Forest gateau 285
    chocolate bavarois 293
    chocolate cherry trifle 269
    chocolate collar cheesecake 379
    chocolate hazelnut torte 287
    chocolate pots 273
    dark chocolate fondue with fruit 321
    hazelnut torte 279
    profiteroles with dark chocolate
        sauce 365
    white chocolate fondue with fruit 321

citrus
    asparagus with citrus hollandaise 39
    orange and lemon syrup cake 299
    tarte au citron 377
    see also lemons; limes
clams
    clams in white wine 53
    New England clam chowder 15
    spaghetti vongole 109
clay pot chicken and vegetable 177
coconut
    banana and coconut pancakes 317
    banana fritters in coconut batter 331
    crab and mango salad 47
    spicy coconut custard 385
    coconut vinegar 153
corn
    Chinese chicken and corn soup 33
    corn chowder 29
couscous, sweet 319
crab
    crab cakes with avocado salsa 63
    crab and corn eggflower noodle
        broth 21
    crab and mango salad 47
    crispy fried crab 71
cream 301
crème brûlée 291
croutons 43
    garlic 45
    frisée and garlic crouton salad 45
curry
    Balinese seafood curry 149
    pea, egg and ricotta curry 255
    Sri Lankan fish fillets in tomato
        curry 153
    Thai duck and pineapple curry 171
    Thai green chicken curry 185
    Thai beef curry 231
custard
    custard pie 335
    savory egg custard 87
    spicy coconut custard 385

D

date pudding, sticky 311
devil's food cake 271
dip, brandade de morue 57
dressings
    aïoli 23
    pesto 27
    vinaigrette 45
    see also sauces
duck
    braised duck with mushrooms 203
    duck breast with walnut and pomegranate
        sauce 171
    duck breast with wild rice 91
    Thai duck and pineapple curry 171

E

egg noodles
    chili satay noodles 261
    crab and corn eggflower noodle broth 21
    seared scallops with chili bean paste 151
    tofu, peanut and noodle stir-fry 253
eggplant
    baked, with tomato and mozzarella 261
    chili satay noodle 261
eggs
    pea, egg and ricotta curry 255
    salad Niçoise 51
    savory egg custard 87
    stuffed shrimp omelets 83
English trifle (zuppa Inglese) 303
espresso granita 273
exotic fruit platter 361

F

fennel
    fennel risotto balls with cheesy filling 95
    grilled fish with fennel and lemon 139
    salmon and fennel salad 49
feta
    baked shrimp with feta 65
    chicken pie with feta 165
    sweet potato, feta and pine nut
        strudel 125
fettucine alfredo 101
fettucine with zucchini and crisp fried
    basil 105
feuilleté with cherries jubilee 315
figs
    figs in honey syrup 329
    prosciutto, camembert and fig salad 41
    stuffed figs 323
filo risotto pie 247
fish
    baked fish with tomato and onion 147
    brandade de morue 57
    bream with tomato cheese crust 155
    fish fillets with harissa and olives 147
    fish Wellington 127
    garlic fish stew (bourride) 23
    grilled fish with fennel and lemon 139
    lemony herb and fish risotto 103
    Sri Lankan fish fillets in tomato curry 153
    steamed fish cutlets with ginger and
        chili 139
fruit
    apple fritters (beignets de fruits) 383
    exotic fruit platter 361
    fresh fruit pavlova 295
    fruit kebabs with honey cardamom
        syrup 337
    macerated oranges 283
    mango fool 297
    melon medley 305

    summer fruit compote 361
    white chocolate fondue with fruit 321
    see also berries; figs; peaches; pears

G

garlic
    chicken with 40 cloves of garlic 179
    garlic bucatini 89
    garlic croutons 45
    garlic shrimp 65
    snails with garlic and herb butter 81
    spaghettini with garlic and chili 93
gazpacho, red 11
General Tso's chicken 195
ginger
    chicken braised with ginger and
        star anise 187
    poached pears with ginger
        zabaglione 391
    steamed fish cutlets with ginger and
        chili 139
gnocchi
    gnocchi Romana 121
    spinach and ricotta gnocchi 113
goat's cheese
    fresh beets and goat's cheese
        salad 45
    goat's cheese galette 129
granita, espresso 273
gravlax with mustard sauce 61
gravy
    gravy with wine 223
    red wine gravy 233
    green chicken curry Thai 185
green pea soup 29
green tea ice cream 297
gremolata 243
gumbo, shrimp and okra 157

H

Hainanese chicken rice 183
hazelnut torte 279
herb-filled ravioli with sage
    butter 99
higos rellenos 323
honey cardamom syrup 337

I

ice cream
    green tea ice cream 297
    ice cream cassata 267
    Indian ice cream 385
    praline ice cream with caramel bark 275
icing, chocolate 271
Indonesian sambal squid 137
Indonesian spicy chicken soup 201

J

jalousie 363

K

kebabs
  fruit kebabs with honey cardamom
    syrup 337
  shish kebabs with peppers and herbs 207
kecap manis 151
kheer rice pudding 327
kulfi 385
kung pao chicken 175

L

laksa
  chicken laksa 173
  shrimp laksa 145
lamb
  braised lamb shanks with haricot
    beans 197
  lamb crown roast with sage stuffing 237
  lamb tagine with quince 213
  rack of lamb with herb crust 219
  shish kebabs with peppers and herbs 207
  slow-roasted lamb with cumin and
    paprika 245
  stuffed leg of lamb 211
lasagne, seafood 141
lemon
  lemon brûlée tarts 371
  lemon and herb risotto with fried
    mushrooms 257
  lemon meringue pie 343
  lemon mustard sauce 229
  lemon passionfruit syllabub with
    berries 307
  lemony herb and fish risotto 103
  salmon and lemon cannelloni 163
lettuce
  Caesar salad 43
  salad Niçoise 51
  san choy bau with noodles 55
lime chiffon pie 369
lime soufflé, chilled 277
linguine pesto 109
linguine with roasted vegetable
    sauce 253
liver, sweet and sour 85
lobster bisque 19

M

mangoes
  crab and mango salad 47
  mango fool 297

Melba sauce 309
melon medley 305
meringue
  butterscotch tart 339
  fresh fruit pavlova 295
  lemon meringue pie 343
Mexican beef chili with beans
    and rice 239
millefeuille with passionfruit curd 341
Moroccan chicken pie 115
mushrooms
  braised duck with mushrooms 203
  cheese and mushroom pies 117
  lemon and herb risotto with fried
    mushrooms 257
  mushroom nut roast with tomato
    sauce 263
  pie-crust mushroom soup 31
  risoni and mushroom broth 25
  salmon stew 143
  stuffed mushrooms 49
mussels with black beans and
    cilantro 75
mustard sauce 61

N

New England clam chowder 15
New York cheesecake 373
noodles
  chilled buckwheat noodles 59
  san choy bau with noodles 55
  scallops with buckwheat noodles and dashi
    broth 13
  see also egg noodles
nuts
  cheese tortellini with nutty herb sauce 93
  chicken, Thai basil and cashew
    stir-fry 187
  duck breast with walnut and pomegranate
    sauce 171
  mushroom nut roast with tomato
    sauce 263
  pecan pie 387
  sweet couscous 319

O

octopus, barbecued 73
olives
  chicken with peppers and olives 179
  fish fillets with harissa and olives 147
  salad Niçoise 51
omelets, stuffed shrimp 83
onions
  baked fish with tomato and onion 147
  pissaladière 119
  potato and onion pizza 123
orange and lemon syrup cake 299

orange sorbet 305
oranges, macerated 283
osso bucco alla Milanese 243
oysters, Asian 77
oysters with bloody Mary sauce 61

P

paella
  chicken and chorizo 199
  seafood 133
pancakes, banana and coconut 317
panna cotta with ruby sauce 313
Paris Brest 351
parmesan and rosemary crusted veal
    chops 205
passionfruit
  lemon passionfruit syllabub with
    berries 307
  millefeuille with passionfruit curd 341
pasta
  blue cheese tagliatelle 105
  cheese tortellini with nutty herb
    sauce 93
  fettucine alfredo 101
  fettucine with zucchini and crisp fried
    basil 105
  garlic bucatini 89
  giant shell pasta with ricotta and
    rocket 251
  linguine pesto 109
  linguine with roasted vegetable
    sauce 253
  pasta and bean soup 17
  pasta and spinach timbales 113
  penne alla Napolitana 97
  rigatoni with Italian-style oxtail
    sauce 227
  risoni and mushroom broth 25
  salmon and lemon cannelloni 163
  spaghettini with garlic and chili 93
  spinach and ricotta cannelloni 249
  tagliatelle with chicken livers and
    cream 107
  tagliatelle with veal, wine and
    cream 245
  see also spaghetti
pavlova, fresh fruit 295
peaches
  bellini sorbet 313
  peach charlottes with Melba sauce 309
peanuts
  chili satay noodles 261
  kung pao chicken 175
  tofu, peanut and noodle stir-fry 253
pears
  pear and almond flan 359
  pears poached in wine 281
  poached pears with ginger
    zabaglione 391

peas
    green pea soup 29
    pea, egg and ricotta curry 255
    rice and peas (risi e bisi) 89
pecan pie 387
penne alla Napolitana 97
peppered beef fillet with béarnaise sauce 215
peppers
    chicken with peppers and olives 179
    filo risotto pie 247
    linguine with roasted vegetable
      sauce 253
    shish kebabs with peppers and herbs 207
pesto 27
pheasant, roast 193
picada sauce 135
pie-crust mushroom soup 31
pies
    apple pie 395
    Banoffee pie 381
    cheese and mushroom pies 117
    cherry pie 357
    chicken pie with feta 165
    custard pie 335
    filo risotto pie 247
    free-form blueberry pie 367
    lemon meringue pie 343
    lime chiffon pie 369
    Moroccan chicken pie 115
    pecan pie 387
    pumpkin pie 347
    rhubarb lattice pie 375
    seafood pie 163
    steak and kidney pie 241
pine nuts, toasting 125
pissaladière 119
pizza, potato and onion 123
plum tart 367
pork
    pork with apple and prune stuffing 223
    pork sausages with white beans 217
    san choy bau with noodles 55
potatoes
    brandade de morue 57
    potato and onion pizza 123
praline ice cream with caramel bark 275
profiteroles with dark chocolate
    sauce 365
prosciutto, camembert and fig salad 41
puddings
    kheer rice pudding 327
    sticky date pudding 311
    tapioca plum pudding with rum
      butter 325
    tapioca pudding 281
pumpkin pie 347

Q

quail in grape leaves 85

R

rabbit with rosemary and white wine 235
raspberry cranachan 301
raspberry shortcake 389
ravioli, herb-filled, with sage butter 99
red gazpacho 11
red wine gravy 233
rhubarb lattice pie 375
rice
    barbecued chicken with Thai
      sticky rice 181
    California rolls 69
    Hainanese chicken rice 183
    kheer rice pudding 327
    rice and chestnut stuffing 161
    rice and peas (risi e bisi) 89
    tandoori chicken with cardamom rice 159
    see also risotto
rice and peas (risi e bisi) 89
ricotta
    cherry cheese strudel 393
    giant shell pasta with ricotta and
      rocket 251
    pea, egg and ricotta curry 255
    Sicilian cannoli 345
    spinach and ricotta cannelloni 249
    spinach and ricotta gnocchi 113
ricotta cheese, baked 255
rigatoni with Italian-style oxtail sauce 227
risotto
    fennel risotto balls with cheesy
      filling 95
    filo risotto pie 247
    lemon and herb risotto with fried
      mushrooms 257
    lemony herb and fish risotto 103
risoni and mushroom broth 25
ruby sauce 313
rum butter 325

S

sage butter 99
salads
    Caesar salad 43
    crab and mango 47
    frisée and garlic crouton 45
    fresh beets and goat's cheese salad 45
    prosciutto, camembert and fig 41
    salad Niçoise 51
    salmon and fennel salad 49
    Thai beef salad 41
    tomato and small mozzarella cheese
      balls 37
salmon
    gravlax with mustard sauce 61
    salmon and fennel salad 49
    salmon and lemon cannelloni 163
    salmon stew 143

salsa
    avocado salsa 63
    salsa verde 73
saltimbocca 197
san choy bau with noodles 55
sauces
    béarnaise sauce 215
    cheese sauce 251
    gravy with wine 223
    lemon mustard sauce 229
    Melba sauce 309
    mustard sauce 61
    picada sauce 135
    red wine gravy 233
    ruby sauce 313
    rum butter 325
    sage butter 99
    sesame seed sauce 143
    sofrito sauce 135
    tomato sauce 249
scallops
    creamy baked scallops 79
    scallop ceviche 77
    scallops Provençale 67
    scallops with buckwheat noodles and
      dashi broth 13
    seared scallops with chili bean paste 151
seafood
    Asian oysters 77
    baked shrimp with feta 65
    Balinese seafood curry 149
    barbecued octopus 73
    clams in white wine 53
    crab cakes with avocado salsa 63
    crab and corn eggflower noodle broth 21
    creamy baked scallops 79
    crispy fried crab 71
    garlic shrimp 65
    grilled squid with salsa verde 73
    Indonesian sambal squid 137
    lobster bisque 19
    mussels with black beans and
      cilantro 75
    New England clam chowder 15
    oysters with bloody Mary sauce 61
    salmon and fennel salad 49
    scallop ceviche 77
    scallops Provençale 67
    scallops with buckwheat noodles and
      dashi broth 13
    seafood lasagne 141
    seafood paella 133
    seafood pie 163
    seafood stew (zarzuela) 135
    seared scallops with chili bean paste 151
    shrimp and basil soup 25
    shrimp cocktail 57
    shrimp and cucumber salad 37
    shrimp laksa 145
    shrimp and okra gumbo 157
    spaghetti vongole 109

stuffed shrimp omelets 83
surf 'n' turf 229
see also fish
sesame seed sauce 143
shish kebabs with peppers and herbs 207
shrimp
  baked shrimp with feta 65
  garlic shrimp 65
  san choy bau with noodles 55
  shrimp and basil soup 25
  shrimp cocktail 57
  shrimp and cucumber salad 37
  shrimp laksa 145
  shrimp and okra gumbo 157
  stuffed shrimp omelets 83
  shrimp paste, roasting 173
  shrimp stock 157
Sicilian cannoli 345
snails with garlic and herb butter 81
sofrito sauce 135
sorbet
  bellini sorbet 313
  orange 305
soufflé, chilled lime 277
soup
  chicken laksa 173
  chicken mulligatawny 167
  Chinese chicken and corn soup 33
  corn chowder 29
  crab and corn eggflower noodle
    broth 21
  garlic fish stew (bourride) 23
  green pea soup 29
  Indonesian spicy chicken soup 201
  New England clam chowder 15
  pasta and bean soup 17
  pie-crust mushroom soup 31
  risoni and mushroom broth 25
  shrimp and basil soup 25
  shrimp laksa 145
  soup with pesto 27
  tofu miso soup 33
  tomato bread soup (pappa al
    pommodoro) 17
  see also soup, cold
soup, cold
  red gazpacho 11
  white gazpacho (ajo blanco) 21
spaghetti
  spaghetti carbonara 101
  spaghetti puttanesca 97
  spaghetti vongole 109
  spaghettini with garlic and chili 93
spinach
  filo risotto pie 247
  pasta and spinach timbales 113
  spinach and ricotta cannelloni 249
  spinach and ricotta gnocchi 113
squid
  grilled squid with salsa verde 73
  Indonesian sambal squid 137

Sri Lankan fish fillets in tomato
    curry 153
steak and kidney pie 241
sticky date pudding 311
stir-fries
  chicken, Thai basil and cashew 187
  tofu, peanut and noodle 253
strawberries Romanoff 337
strudel
  apple 349
  cherry cheese 393
  sweet potato, feta and pine nut 125
surf 'n' turf 229
sweet couscous 319
sweet potato, feta and pine nut
    strudel 125
sweet and sour liver (fegato garbo e dolce) 85

T

tagliatelle
  blue cheese tagliatelle 105
  tagliatelle with chicken livers and
    cream 107
  tagliatelle with veal, wine and
    cream 245
tandoori chicken with cardamom rice 159
tandoori paste 159
tapioca plum pudding with rum
    butter 325
tapioca pudding 281
tarts
  apple tarte tatin 355
  banana tart 353
  butterscotch tart 339
  lemon brûlée tarts 371
  lemon tart (tarte au citron) 377
  pear and almond tart 359
  plum tart 367
  summer berry tart 289
Thai beef salad 41
Thai duck and pineapple curry 171
Thai green chicken curry 185
Thai beef curry 231
timbales, pasta and spinach 113
tofu
  tofu miso soup 33
  tofu, peanut and noodle stir-fry 253
tomato bread soup (pappa al
    pommodoro) 17
tomato sauce 249
tomatoes
  baked eggplant with tomato and
    mozzarella 261
  baked fish with tomato and onion 147
  linguine with roasted vegetable
    sauce 253
  pappa al pommodoro 17
  penne alla Napolitana 97
  pissaladière 119

Sri Lankan fish fillets in tomato
    curry 153
  tomato and small mozzarella cheese
    balls salad 37
trifle
  chocolate cherry trifle 269
  English trifle (zuppa Inglese) 303
turkey, roast, with rice and chestnut
    stuffing 161

V

veal
  osso bucco alla Milanese 243
  parmesan and rosemary crusted veal
    chops 205
  saltimbocca 197
  tagliatelle with veal, wine and
    cream 245
vinaigrette 45
vol-au-vents 111

W

walnut pastry 381
wild rice, duck breast with 91

Y

Yorkshire puddings 233

Z

zarzuela 135
zuppa Inglese 303